Sun in Winter

Sun in Winter

~ A Toronto Wartime Journal ~

1942
to
1945

Gunda Lambton

McGill-Queen's University Press
Montreal & Kingston · London · Ithaca

© McGill-Queen's University Press 2003
ISBN 0-7735-2582-3

Legal deposit third quarter 2003
Bibliothèque nationale du Québec

Printed in Canada on acid-free paper that is 100% ancient forest free (100% post-consumer recycled), processed chlorine free.

McGill-Queen's University Press acknowledges the support of the Canada Council for the Arts for our publishing program. We also acknowledge the financial support of the Government of Canada through the Book Publishing Industry Development Program (BPIDP) for our publishing activities.

National Library of Canada Cataloguing in Publication

Lambton, Gunda, 1914–
Sun in winter: a Toronto wartime journal, 1942 to 1945 / Gunda Lambton.
Includes index.
ISBN 0-7735-2582-3

1. Lambton, Gunda, 1914– – Diaries. 2. German Canadians – Diaries. 3. World War, 1939–1945 – Personal narratives, German. 4. World War, 1939–1945 – Personal narratives, British. 5. World War 1939–1945 – Ontario – Toronto. 6. Toronto (Ont.) – Social conditions. I. Title.

FC3097.26 L33 A3 2003   971.3'54193'092   C2003-902089-4
F1059.5.T6853L33 2003

This book was designed by Mantz/Eiser graphic design and typeset in 11/14 Sabon

This journal is dedicated to
Jean McAdam

and all those who helped us during the
war years but are not mentioned in its pages;
and, of course, to all those who are;

and to a younger, quieter city of Toronto
only a few of us now remember.

1942

How many people in this wartorn world, I wonder, are at this moment able to sit peacefully in a room that holds two sleeping children, able to write uninterruptedly by a shaded lamp? In many countries this room, this space, however alien, however crowded, would be a luxury. At this time of day, the sirens would begin to howl in England, in Germany, in Russia, in countless small countries drawn into this endless battle.

Living in one room is not too bad. I've become used to it, and to using the evening hours, by a shaded lamp, to take stock of our situation. Such confinement in the midst of so much space and so much peace may seem incongruous, but confinement is relative. Crouching in a damp air-raid shelter, waiting for the all-clear – sometimes all night – is much worse. After that, the large room beside the kitchen of Ovenden School's Junior House in Barrie, on Lake Simcoe, seemed a calm, ordered paradise. So why did we ever leave it for this alien one in downtown Toronto?

We arrived in November 1940 on the last government-sponsored boat carrying evacuees out of Britain. We'd not been told that it was more dangerous to cross the Atlantic than to stay in England; we found out about that much later. On the voyage over, I was more worried about Fiona's bronchitis than about torpedoes. Just over a year old, she'd developed this sickness during the many nights in air-raid shelters. But this country's clear, dry air cured it in a few weeks.

At Ovenden we were "war guests." I tried to compensate for our board by teaching art and Italian and working as matron of the Junior House. But there were few hours when I could leave the children. Once Bettina was born, in March 1941, finding time became a major problem, except in the evenings, when I could leave my door open, could listen to every sound from our room, while I roamed the upstairs halls.

In this impersonal boarding house I dare not leave the children for more than two minutes – just enough time to go down the hall to the depressing washroom or the slightly more cheerful kitchen. A big, blousy blonde occupies this kitchen, smoking nervously, listening to the radio for war news. Her husband is overseas. She has allowed us to stay here, defying the landlady's rules (no children), which are those of most other Toronto rooming houses.

Strange that times of the most bitter hostilities produce unexpected acts of kindness. The Londùger, and suffering brought out the best in people when you
least expected it. People whom you hadn't known at all, who'd lived next door all the time, suddenly shared with you the small space of a shelter. You automatically saved their property – some-times their lives – when, in a rain of incendary bombs, you dragged the stirrup pump from the bathroom to the attic to put out a fire on their roof.

In comparison, this vast country is tranquil. I expected to find the competitive, acquisitive society described by Upton Sinclair or, earlier, Charles Dickens. However, the school was still a part of England, run along the lines of some of the English boarding schools for girls that had been started by early feminists.

I had to thank my mother-in-law for this refuge. Dé, Garth's mother and, like him, an artist, helped to start Ovenden School during the First World War. She left her husband, an illustrator in New York, to join two friends from suffragette days, Mary Elgood and Jean Ingram, who were starting a small school in Barrie, Ontario. Remarkably, early in the century these two had obtained master's degrees at Oxford. In 1934, as a student teacher at St George's School, Ascot, I'd admired such women graduates from Oxford. They knew far more about German politics than I, who came from that country.

In many ways I'm now re-enacting my mother's life story, but in reverse. She too had been a student teacher when, in 1903, aged seventeen, she left the Wirral Peninsula in Lancashire for

Germany and its music. The Darmstadt school to which she came was run by descendants of Scottish immigrants, named Davidson. She married their cousin, Eduard von Davidson, and I, her first child, was born a month after the outbreak of World War I – a terrible shock to both of us (if you believe in the trauma of the not-yet-born).

My English relations originally welcomed me when I married an English artist. But once the war broke out, they began to see me as an embarrassment. My grandmother's life was far from

My mother,
Maud Lee Williams,
before her marriage
in 1912

easy: her eldest daughter, my godmother, was dying of breast cancer. Living so close to Liverpool, the constant bombing of that harbour affected them as well.

At Ovenden the wonderful peace, the clear atmosphere, the merry girls' voices singing in the auditorium close to our room, gave me a feeling of security. Then, when my second daughter was born at the Barrie hospital, I discovered that in Canada there's no health insurance. I never knew who paid my doctor's and hospital bills. While Garth still lived in London, he earned three pounds a week working on air-raid patrols (ARP). He had dual nationality, and when he chose America (he was born in New Jersey) and eventually got to New York, that in-come ceased (slight as it was for such grim and hazardous labour). He arrived a week before Pearl Harbor and found

3

himself eligibile for American military service. The fact that he had renounced British for American citizenship did not go down well among Barrie's patriotic citizens, who had until then supported us in every way.

During my second year at Ovenden I'd overhear remarks like:

"The other war guests pay their way."

Or "Hospitals and doctors over here cost money, you know."

Or "Are you too busy with the children to take prep duty this afternoon?"

Or "That baby of yours will grow up to be an opera singer. She's got such a strong voice, it kept me awake most of the night."

These remarks never came from Mary Elgood. She was the one who'd invited us, as during the First World War she'd invited Dé, who found shelter in Ovenden from a wrecked marriage (and now mine is going the same way). These remarks were made by senior teachers or adult war guests who had children at Ovenden. Nine girls from an evacuated Yorkshire college stretched the school's resources to the limit.

The difference was that Dé had independent means. She'd lived in her own house, a bungalow between the school and Lake Simcoe. She taught art at Ovenden, as I did while there. But I had no money to pay anyone to look after the children. I could only teach during the hours the children were sleeping: evenings and sometimes early afternoons.

That didn't work out well. One afternoon I left the baby in her pram, outside in the sun. She kicked off her covers, and as often happens, a cold wind blew up from Lake Simcoe. She developed pneumonia and had to go to hospital.

So my reasons for coming to Toronto are complex. The school was responsible for us until Garth came to New York. Now I think it's his turn. He's a graduate of the British Royal Academy and received the Prix de Rome for sculpture in 1936. But in London, where we shared an artists' co-op, even such highly trained artists could not find jobs in the late thirties. I could, though. I worked as secretary-translator (French, Spanish, German, Italian) until a couple of weeks before Fiona was born. I made four pounds a week, good money in 1939. One pound went into the kitty that paid for the co-op's food. We shared the cooking.

I should be able to do the same here, but the part-time job I have for the time being is badly paid. Factory work pays better. There are supposed to be nursery schools now for those who do war work. What I hadn't realized was how terribly hard it is to find a place to live if you have children. To find an apartment is next to impossible. Florence Morris, a friend I made last summer, the one who helped me to find this room, believes that one can only find a room if one pays the landlady for board and daycare. That way people make a little more money than they would renting off a single room. But nursery schools are surely better.

We were lucky to find this room, not too far from the Morrises's apartment house, where no one will take children. She's a teacher, married to a teacher. Because of a rule dating back to the Depression, only one member of a couple may work. So at present she's taking up shorthand. She's offered to spend early afternoons practising shorthand while sitting with my children during their nap time, so I can go to my part-time job. I am taking the place of a secretary on holiday and earn eight dollars a week. This room costs seven dollars a week. It's scary.

There'll be some solution. Every solution I've found in life so far has been escape. Flight. Long before the flight from the Blitz, which at least was for the sake of my children, there was the flight from a country I had started to hate. If you turn against the country of your childhood, you turn against a significant part of yourself. It's very destructive. Most of the happiness of our childhood had come from our English mother. England remained a distant paradise. Marrying an English artist was another form of escape.

Never marry an artist if you want to be an artist yourself. The one with the less-developed ego will lose. So flight from my marriage too. And now flight from the hints and asides, the wretched feeling of dependence. I should have developed a tough hide. Ignored everything except my children's comfort. But what comfort?

When there is death all around you and you survive, a curious feeling of predestination takes hold of you. Why were we spared when the boat crossing the Atlantic before ours was sunk? When our own convoy was torpedoed? And earlier, when houses all around our square turned into rubble overnight, their curtains and scraps of paper hanging in the trees the next morning? The injured had been carefully removed by the ARP. Why did our house still stand?

I've unpacked my sketchbook. There is just enough space for it on this unfamiliar desk – a sideboard, really, cluttered with china and dusty photographs in elaborate frames. My paints are not unpacked yet. I am using the sketchbook as a writing pad. I have put a towel over the old-fashioned brass lamp beside me, so it does not shine directly into Fiona's eyes. She's sleeping on a little sofa with a curved back, not really meant for a bed. She is not four yet, short enough to fit its length. I'm worried about its width – she may fall off – so I've pushed it close to the pull-out couch I'm sharing with the baby, Bettina. Pulled out, the couch occupies almost the entire room, still crammed with all the furniture of a former parlour, doing duty as bedroom in this boarding house, one of many that have sprung up because of the housing shortage in Toronto.

The wallpaper may have been beautiful at one time, or at least expensive. It's a beige and brown fantasy of ferns, trees, and strange birds. The pattern of the carpet can't be seen; it's entirely covered by my belongings: a duffle bag, rucksack, and battered suitcase – everything that came with me from the school in Barrie, where, two years ago, Fiona and I arrived after a harrowing ocean voyage.

But then, ocean voyages of most immigrants have been gruelling. In the last century children were lost to typhoid, cholera, ship's fever. Their parents had to battle immigration authorities and were quarantined on an island in the St. Lawrence, where many of them died. We, on the other hand, were welcomed at the Montreal harbour by ladies from the Red Cross, looking somewhat puzzled because we'd been given up for lost. They'd received the wrong message when our convoy was torpedoed and thought that we'd shared the fate of the *City of Benares*, sunk with all passengers on board, mostly women and children, six weeks earlier. But there we were, pale, sick, overdressed against the famous Canadian winter, but alive, having miraculously escaped the fate that overtook the freighter in our convoy. One especially stormy night the stewardess, more tight-lipped than usual, took extra care, checking the blackout on our portholes. Then our boat veered north into iceberg territory, leaving seventeen sailors to drown in the freezing North Atlantic – something I was horrified to find out months later.

Most of us were seasick. The boat was one of the "rolling Duchesses." Its name had been carefully covered with black paint, but we knew it was the *Duchess of Richmond*, one of the worst of the Cunard liners. Somewhere in its hold was part of the British treasury. In its first-class cabins were high executive military staff whom we never met. Every day we had emergency lifeboat practice. Fiona, not quite two then, was totally obscured by her huge lifebelt except for a small blond head and tiny feet. I was soon too sick to go on deck. We shared a cabin with another war guest going to Canada for what is described as "the duration." Her child was sick, so she took Fiona on deck while her six-year-old girl and I shared the cabin and our misery. I got no sympathy from the ship's doctor; according to him, I had no business even attempting the journey while pregnant.

Mary Elgood, Ovenden's headmistress, had been on the *Athenia*, the first liner to be torpedoed when war broke out three years ago. She survived even more miraculously than we did. For us, the numb terror an immigrant experiences on arrival was somehow mitigated by the serene order of the school, the sun and snow of our first winter. Now it's catching up with me.

But it's easier here to escape the terrible duality I felt in Britain. My cousin Paul, in the British army, is reported missing. In 1941 my English grandmother wrote that the Swiss Red

Cross had taken a year to get through to her the information that another grandson of hers, my brother, is also missing, presumably somewhere over the North Sea.

In Canada your ethnic origin doesn't seem to matter as much as it does in Europe. The early German immigrants who really impress me are the Mennonites. I'd never heard of them in Europe, of these people who emigrated when their principles were threatened. I tried to find out all I could about these so-called Pennsylvania Dutch, who left their prosperous farms if they were forced into military service. They'd done so in Prussia, in Russia, in America. I feel a deep affection for these peace-loving people, the opposite of German militarism.

At Ovenden, I represented my husband's family. No one held it against me that I was brought up in Germany. My husband's name gave me a cloak of invisibility, as my father's name had for my mother during World War I. My new friends assume correctly that I've rejected my country of origin. Others opposed to its politics have not been as lucky as I've been. No one knows what's happening to them now.

The ironies of war: new antibiotic drugs developed under pressure of the war's terrible casualties saved me a year ago from a deadly kidney infection developed after Bettina's birth. In the London hospital where Fiona was born three months before the war broke out, women died of such infections. But miraculously I was given a new life. I vaguely remember the darkness of that high fever. Even in that darkness I felt my children pulling at me.

Rebirth is a very powerful feeling I now associate with this new world. Here there never were those bitter border quarrels that fill European history books. The country has its inner divisions. But then, what country hasn't? However, its long undefended border is not for me to cross. In the USA I am regarded as an enemy alien. Not that I have the least desire to go there. For me, Canada has the potentials of a magnificent future. I can't imagine that territorial hostilities could develop here to destroy this golden peace.

For almost two years the feeling of stability, of space and calm, made our room in the Barrie school a secure haven. The only thing that brought back nightmares was the hooting of trains. Their sound is exactly that of air-raid sirens. Northbound trains roar past at night very close, between the lake and the school buildings. Their hooting would shake me out of my sleep night after night. Then, before I grabbed my clothes and the baby to make for the shelter, I knew we were safe.

Every morning around eight-thirty the narrow passage leading to the gym, divided from our room by a thin partition, resounded with a thundering gallop (a herd of buffaloes?). The stampede was followed by a respectful silence (school assembly: the gym was also the auditorium). A creeking of chairs (all stand up), then, before the hymns and the announcements, the reassuring sound of young voices, high and clear, singing "O Canada." Every morning the voices assured me, once again, that we were safe.

Some of the daytime was spent in the large school kitchen adjoining our room (the maid's room, when the two large buildings housing the school were still private residences). In the evenings I roamed the halls upstairs, put out lights, and tucked up homesick little girls, some of them war guests like ourselves.

Little chance for me to go anywhere, unless I took my children with me. There was one house, though, a short walk from the school, where we were always welcome. This house had been constructed by a group of friends from a small barn, on a side road leading up hill from the main highway. Miss Elgood, herself an old-time liberal, described The Barn's inhabitants as "socialists and psychologists." This was only partly correct, since they had graduated in English and philosophy and were now engaged in an adult education project for the University of Toronto. It took me some time to discover that the socialist party in Canada, the CCF, had grown out of largely Christian ethics, unlike the anticlerical socialists I had known in Spain and Germany. These ethics in some ways determined David and Edith Smith's community project, though not overtly.

They had started a rural credit union. I learned from them that credit unions had originated in Germany. Local people, some of them teachers, spent evenings at The Barn, reading plays by American authors like Maxwell Anderson or John Steinbeck, quite new to me. The Smiths had an impressive library, but my greatest solace was their record collection. Some-how, during the late thirties, records improved so much that now Bach's Brandenburg concertos and Mozart's sym-

~~

*Unfinished
oil sketch of Ovenden
schoolgirl, 1941*

phonies sounded as I had not heard their music since leaving Germany. (Our London artists were jazz musicians.)

At Ovenden Miss Elgood had given me her old box of oil paints. I began using them to paint portraits of some of the girls at school. I had started doing pastel portraits, but for oils I could charge more. I built up a tiny fund at the Kempenfelt credit union, ten dollars in all. I was allowed to borrow three times that amount from this co-operative when we left for Toronto.

Some of the thirty dollars went on the train fare. Here I can't expect anything like the help I was given in Barrie, where we became a regular project for the Red Cross and the IODE. Everyone in town seemed to knit something for the new baby. Mrs Lay, the sister of the Canadian prime minister, Mackenzie King, sent a large crib from her house across the road from the school. At the time I was ill, I gladly accepted all this, but now I feel we must make our own way.

Garth's work for the ARP during the Blitz was as horrendous as that of any front-line stretcher bearer. But when he came to New York (where he tried his best not to join up yet had no job), the kindness that had surrounded us in Barrie began to cool. Those who remained the same were Mary Elgood and the

Smiths; they looked after Fiona while Bettina was born, and after both children when I was in hospital last year.

My first impression of Toronto, arriving by train from Montreal, had been one of blinding lights. After months of blacked-out rooms, dimmed car lights, sidewalks barely illuminated by timid flashlight, the garish neon lights for mere ads and the harsh brilliance of station and streets were overwhelming.

On the train from Montreal that November, we had crossed a flat autumnal landscape with barns like strange castles. A middle-aged lady sitting beside us (the first I'd ever seen with a blue hair rinse) offered us a meal in the dining car. Thinking that Fiona and I had recovered (her bronchitis seemed better, my motion sickness was gone), I gladly accepted. I chose fried oysters from the menu, something I'd never eaten before, and

Edith Smith
holding baby Bettina,
born March 1941

after some deliberation, added pumpkin pie, another complete novelty for us. To my great embarrassment, neither Fiona nor I could eat any of this, though Fiona's meal was a child's portion. And we'd been so hungry only a month earlier.

I then had a flashback memory of all this happening before, when my mother took me to England for the first time, after World War I. I was to be presented to my English relations as a terrible example of a starved child, with stick legs, a scar left on my neck where a tubercular gland had been removed, and suffering from after-effects of diphtheria. My mother never forgave

England for the blockade, the malnutrition on which doctors blamed all her children's diseases.

In the splendid English train, with soft, upholstered seats instead of the wooden ones in German trains, a similar kind lady had offered me a piece of chocolate. I wondered what it was; I had never seen chocolate. I was sick when I ate it. Or drank milk. Butter I found impossible to eat, ever. I was introduced to the rich English food by a mixture of white bread crumbs in hot milk, in a pink and white cup I'll never forget. For me, the tea parties in my grandmother's Victorian drawing room, its fireplace ornaments of polished brass, its heavy silverware and delicate china, remained memories of a paradise to which, all through my childhood, I hoped to return.

Grannie Williams with her great-granddaughter Fiona just before we left Liverpool for Canada, November 1940

I stayed with Grannie Williams, perhaps for the last time, before we boarded our liner, to the tune of air-raid sirens hooting all around Liverpool harbour. While we were crossing the Atlantic, Coventry was destroyed almost completely by the bombers we escaped that morning.

From the Montreal train that brought back these memories, we'd changed in brilliantly lit Toronto to a slower train that would take us to Barrie. We'd travelled all day and arrived towards evening. At the small Barrie station we were met by the two school heads, Miss Elgood and Miss Ingram, two intrepid spinsters dressed in English tweeds. I'd made a little coat and leggings for Fiona from just such tweed. With faltering steps, my tiny child walked between the two similarly clad Englishwomen, her leggings dragging on the station paving – planning for the future, I'd made them much too long.

Miss Elgood drove us to the school. There are many more cars on the road here than in England, though gas is supposed to be rationed. The school is surrounded by majestic trees, mostly evergreens. It consists of two large Victorian brick houses in grounds separated from Lake Simcoe by a railway track and a road.

Mary Elgood had expected a mother and child, but no future baby. The last telegram Garth sent had not arrived (but had he really sent it?). It dawned on me that here I'd be entirely responsible for medical bills. I only gradually, with great embarrassment, realized that either Miss Elgood had paid my medical bills or they had simply not been sent. I never found out. When I tried to broach the subject, it was firmly changed. But my embarrassment grew. Because of the difficulties taking money out of England, these two Englishwomen might well be strapped financially, had perhaps been too generous taking so many war guests. Now, a year later, with Garth arrived in New York, I could not ignore this problem any longer.

Leaving Barrie was very hard. Those winter mornings when we saw the first snow after our arrival, fresh and brilliant, weighing down the branches of the great trees with their heavy load. The lake, not yet frozen over, steaming in the cold air; the loud blue sky. Later, the schoolchildren would skate on the lake until it was covered by snow. Then they would try to ski on the Barrie common, just up the hill, where they were driven in an enormous sleigh pulled by two of the horses the school keeps for riding. Sometimes Fiona and I were allowed to sit at the back of that sleigh, watching Miss Elgood's two dogs, Leo and Spring, wildly excited, racing behind us.

Miss Elgood's box of oil paints, most of the tubes still fresh and whole, is in my rucksack. But I cannot hope to survive by painting portraits in Toronto. I have no teaching certificate either. I had tried plain housekeeping for an elderly lady during the summer, when the school was closed. I tied Bettina to an apple tree while I did the cleaning, but she howled. She felt less confined, eventually, in a former dog kennel, turned into a super playpen. I'm finding out that neither as housekeeper nor as secretary would I make enough to support us and have the children cared for during my working time.

The housekeeping job came to an abrupt end when the nurse where I'd boarded Fiona fell ill. But I'd made enough to survive the summer with what I'd earned and my portrait money. For the rest of the summer, I shared a cabin at a Y camp on Lake Couchiching with a young couple who became my friends, Florence and Bruce Morris. When I thought of going to Toron-

Gunda and Fiona
at Y camp,
Lake Couchiching,
1942

to, I contacted them and came on a day-return to arrange for the part-time job that was to tide us over until I could find something better.

Even here in Toronto, the Smiths' influence continues through their friends. One of the people I met at The Barn was Frank Hines, who, with a good university degree, had not found work during the Depression except at the Barrie post office. Now that medically fit men have joined the army, he is with the Canadian Press in Toronto. Frank has weak eyes and asthma; he is small and looks younger than his age. But his sense of humour and his intelligence just shone on those winter evenings, reading plays at The Barn. When he heard we were coming to Toronto, he suggested meeting for breakfast (his free time: his working hours are afternoons and evenings). We'll meet at a little corner café on Bay Street, just around the corner.

I have no way of preparing food here. To tide us over meals, I bought some fruit and milk and a packet of cereal. I'll have to

14

learn all over again about the cost of food, for in Barrie we had school meals. They were not exciting, but we were never hungry. And that might very well happen to us now.

I sit at this desk going over and over my priorities for to-morrow. First, I should see the government department that organizes wartime nursery schools. There might even be a job for me there. The great drawback is that Bettina will not be two years old until March. Most nursery schools will not accept children under two.

Frank Hines
(crayon sketch made
at The Barn,
1942)

My next step must be for more permanent shelter. Who knows? I might find a landlady willing to look after the children, increasing her income that way. To save on transportation, it's important to find a place near my future job. And that job is the most important of all. It has to be factory work, because that would be the only kind paying enough to support us.

These calculations go round and round my head. It is getting late. I'll have to go along the dark hall to the khaki-coloured toilet to rinse out Bettina's diapers. The wash basin there is small, with a rusty rim. I borrowed a pail for diapers from Mrs Wallace, the good-natured blonde who smuggled us into these lodgings. The owner of the house, the real landlady, is at her son's farm near Oshawa. I'll have to find another place before she comes back.

"Can't let you be without a room," Mrs Wallace said."Two kiddies. Wish they were mine." She wears her hair in curlers, and so far I've only seen her in a housecoat. The radio is play-ing "Saturday night is the loneliest night of the week."

The landlady will only take single people, men who do war work and are out most of the time. That's what the lodgers are, upstairs. But I could have the parlour for a few days. Mrs Wallace knows how hard it is, especially with kids. Though she would not mind that, if only she had some. Landlords, they're the devil.

"Is your hubby in the army too?" she asked, wiping a tear from her large puffy face.

I shook my head.

"Don't tell me ... you lost him?" Her voice trembled, and the hand that held her cigarette.

"I did, in a way. We're separated. We'll get a divorce when we can afford it."

"Oh, this bloody war. It does things to people ..."

In a subtle way our status has been reversed. I, in my respectable linen suit, with my hard-heeled shoes, am now less respectable than she is in housecoat and slippers, who has an entire husband.

I can't listen to the radio for long, and reading a paper is even harder. War news is all there is. I still can't take it.

It is a warm night and the children are restless. Fiona lies on her stomach on the sofa bed, a wistful expression on her small, heart-shaped face, as if she, not I, were carrying our burden. Her light brown hair is soft and wild, damp with perspiration. She will be the one to remind me that Bettina's diapers need changing. She'll ask where we should wash them. In the school we did these chores together. In her enthusiasm, she often threw things that already were washed back into the hand basin.

I slip under the covers beside Bettina, who snores a little because she's had a cold. She is a heavy child, large for her age. Perhaps she'll be taken for two at the places I have to see in the morning.

~ September 26th, evening ~

This morning I discovered that the milk – kept on the windowsill of our room – had turned sour. The cereal I'd bought for breakfast was not much good without it. I'd have to spend a dollar or more getting something at the small restaurant where we were to meet Frank. For the time being, the children were each given an apple, while I dressed Bettina. Fiona manages dressing herself. Bettina still can't walk long distances, so I harness her into a stroller that folds up and can be carried (a hand-me-down from Barrie friends). Fiona looked very proud in her blue summer dress, pushing the stroller along like a mother.

Frank was sitting at one of the restaurant tables partitioned off from others, so we had a little privacy. Bettina saw him at once and was overjoyed: she loves him. The children have often seen Frank in Barrie. He thinks that Bettina, with her blond bangs, short nose, and full lips, looks like the models of his favourite painter, Renoir.

We had toast with jam. It spread all over Bettina's face, so we had to do a clean-up job before we moved on. Frank suggested Queen's Park, the Ontario legislature, because its Department of Welfare organizes the daycare centres for war workers. Frank is about half my height (well, he comes up to my shoulder), but he heroically walked along besde me and the two children, though he did not go so far as to push the stroller.

These September days can get very warm. At Queen's Park there were people sitting on the grass enjoying the sun, and many of the benches were occupied. We found one where Frank could wait while I made inquiries at the legislature. Fiona chased after some pretty red and golden leaves rustling on the ground while I slipped away into the formidable building. Wide stairs, endless corridors, rows and rows of closed doors. I smelled bureaucracy, my old enemy. The smell of unaired waiting rooms, passport offices, classrooms. Places where you sit for hours, waiting for a visa or some other document. In Germany it had been my certificate of fitness for marriage. It had taken more than a year to get that.

The person you are told to see is never in. I asked at the first open door that seemed to lead to the right department. It was the right place but the

Fiona, Bettina, and Gunda with stroller from Barrie friends

wrong time. The administrator was at a meeting. The secretary who handed me an application form over the counter said she was going on her tea break; someone else would take my application, once filled in. The form told me that to work in a wartime nursery school, I would first have to take a six weeks' course. (What to do with the children for six weeks?) Second point: mothers who have children in these centres will be the last to be considered for jobs there.

The application is for a place in the only nursery school for mothers doing war work that exists so far. There is a long waiting list – no vacancies right now. All centres open at eight-thirty in the morning and close at five p.m. Acceptable age: two to five years.

"What about shift work? Most war plants have night shifts?" The girl who took my application shrugged.

"Factories open at seven or seven-thirty. How do women manage when the nursery schools don't open until eight-thirty?"

"I guess they get someone, a relation or a landlady, to take the children to the centre."

I have no relations. I couldn't possibly impose on friends like Frank or Florence (whose husband finds our multiple presence disturbing even now). I can see that those who'll profit from government nursery schools will be middle-class women who live in their own homes, can take time to find a job, have a mother – or other close relation – living nearby. Those who have husbands in the army get an allowance, a "mother's allowance" if they're Canadian citizens. All that is out of my reach.

Frank was not surprised that I had no luck. He's a Catholic; he knows of a crèche run by nuns on St Patrick Street. You don't have to be a Catholic to take your children there, he maintains. We set off on the long walk from Queen's Park to St Patrick Street, Fiona and I slowly pushing the stroller along College, then Spadina, towards Dundas.

"See, Fiona, there are swings and slides in this yard," I said to my daughter, for whom slides or swings anywhere are still a novelty. Inside the building, the atmosphere was hushed. The nun who came to speak to us wore thick glasses. They made her eyes look remote, but her voice was gentle if a little rusty. Yes, they might be able to take the older girl, but what about the baby? When would she be two? Not till March? Well, that was not such a long way off. Perhaps I could find a landlady who ...

March, for me, seems as far off as the moon, or the end of the war. But, I told myself, we'll get over this; we're a hundred times better off than most people in the world. The huge destruc-

~~

Toronto skyline from
St Patrick Street
in 1945

tive force of the war does produce tiny positive areas. They may spread. I feel so certain about this that our discomforts seem minor to me. Frank, who loves comfort, sees them as more threatening than I do.

His journalist's working hours start at one p.m., so he took his leave. I found my way back on the College streetcar, folded stroller, two children, and all. At a corner grocery I bought some rolls and bananas to take to our room, where Florence arrived a few minutes after us. We drew down the blinds to make the room still darker, so that the children would sleep.

Florence is as tall as I am, and she has long, dark hair. She braids this abundant hair and coils it around her small head. She wears glasses. This restrained appearance is deceptive. When

I first saw her on Lake Couchiching, her hair hung down all around her. She was wearing a white bathing suit – two-piece, if you please – and she was very tanned. Dripping wet, she rose from those blue-green waters like a northern-lake Venus. She was born in China, the daughter of missionaries. Her voice and accent are what I think of as Midwestern though she has never lived in the Midwest.

I hoped she had enough light to get her shorthand done, that the children wouldn't pester her. They know that, whether they sleep or not, they have to go to bed for a couple of hours in the afternoon, a practice established at the school to enable me to teach.

This precarious arrangement can't continue for long, I know. I galloped down Bay Street to my temporary office and arrived out of breath. This office organizes music teaching in Toronto; the letters I have to type are repetitive but undemanding.

Florence and Bruce have no children. Bruce, though he is much older than Florence, has somehow become a demanding child-substitute. When we shared a cottage, I took the children out to the beach as often as I could. For him it will be a sacrifice to have us all at their small apartment tomorrow night, so we can use the telephone for house-hunting. In some ways, though, Bruce is thoughtful, and he is always methodical: he sent a newspaper with Florence, so that we can look up ads ahead of time. Florence and Frank have offered to repeat today's routine for another day.

Florence especially likes Fiona. In the summer she used to play with her while I did the chores for the baby. And Fiona is attached to Florence. She is a little too old to sleep every afternoon. Today she quietly crayoned a colouring book and talked with Florence in whispers, so that Bettina could sleep. She has accepted the whole

~~

Florence Morris

business of makeshift meals, pushing the stroller along endless streets, waiting outside buildings, with near-adult understanding. She does not whine, as other four-year-olds often do. It frightens me a little to see her so composed. Everyone loves her because she is so "good." Pretty, too, with her light-brown, slightly curly hair, her lovely dimpled smile. I saw that the nun liked her at once. But all this uncertainty is much harder on her than on Bettina. Wildly and unrealistically, I hope for a really good nursery school, where children will do art and music and read stories. That would be a hundred times better than a landlady adding to her rent by minding children.

For supper we managed with some raisin bread and baloney, an incongruous mixture that we ate on pieces of Kleenex so as not to spoil the surface of the desk. I got the children washed in the small lavatory basin and left more diapers in the pail, which is beginning to smell. I'll have to wash them in the sink there, with its brown rim around a stopper than never stays in properly. I can't afford to buy soap flakes right now. The piece of soap we use to wash ourselves will have to do.

After I've read to the children from books that are old friends, I sit by the shaded lamp to look at ads. The National Selective Service advertises jobs at John Inglis and de Havilland's. I'd love to work on aircraft. All those months before Pearl Harbor, when Britain was alone, isolated, without help from any other country, it seemed to me that what was most needed were aircraft to fight those insuperable dark forces. But the de Havilland factory is way outside town, while John Inglis is on the downtown lakeshore. John Inglis normally made the kind of appliance that to me remained a dream out of reach: washing machines. But now it has become a munitions factory.

The children are soon asleep. A subdued light, a mother's presence – what more could they want? Bettina is again snoring a little. It is suddenly very quiet. The radio, which has accompanied all my excursions along the hall, getting louder as I approach the kitchen, has suddenly stopped. Then I hear voices back there. I hold my breath, for it could be the landlady, coming home unexpectedly to find us here as stowaways.

I open the door a little, not much. If the children wake up, they'll make a noise. I'd have to take them along the hall to the toilet again, and that's too close to the kitchen. With a sinking, feeling I remember the pail there with the unwashed diapers.

I can distinguish some words now, a high scratchy voice: "... told you, no kids. For Pete's sake, diapers. Not even house-trained. Wors'n cats and dogs. Mess up the place, break the dishes, scratch the wallpaper. No. Not even for a short time." My hand tightens around the paper bag with diapers that, sooner or later, have to be added to the rest of the wash.

Then I hear those beautiful words, words that should have been spoken hundreds of times in Germany, in any place where Jews were hidden (not enough ever were). It's the sodden voice of the soldier's wife booming fearlessly. It has a ringing quality and, for me, a nobility no curlers, no messy housecoat, can disguise. The voice towers over the small, scratchy voice as I imagine the big blonde woman to tower over a tiny, mouse-like landlady.

"If you turn them out," the voice booms, "I'll go too. See if anyone else in this place will mind the house for you while you run yer son's business. People can pick'n choose, these days. Like te be indipendent. Those men upstairs, see if they'll do any cleaning. I'm telling you, if you turn them out, I go too."

Silence. No sharp reply. No one speaks. No one comes to turn us out of the house. The paper bag in my hands is wet through as I wait, clutching it. Back there, the lights go out. Heavy, slurred steps move upstairs, followed by a staccato of sharp heels. Then all is quiet.

Now I know why that woman's housecoat bulges the way it does. It hides a huge pair of wings.

~ September 28th ~

Selective Service, the government's wartime employment agency, is located on Spadina Avenue, a wide road that reminds me of Barcelona. Not that the buildings have that classical Barcelona design; no, it's the atmosphere. The buildings vary. Some are nondescript; none have the more English character of houses on Yorkville, the street where we room at present. I was prepared for bureaucracy, but the interview was short and had immediate results. I can still hardly believe that I found work at the blueprint office of John Inglis. They pay twenty-five dollars a week, more than I made in London as secretary with language extras. The interviewer, a sympathetic middle-aged woman, even took the time to explain that once you learn to read blueprints, you have the chance to move up into inspection, with better pay.

I am my own woman again. But there's much I still have to find out about living in this city. If I rent just one room with a hot plate, say, will I be able to feed the children well enough? That's what we had in London before we started the artists' co-op. Florence suggests that I find a landlady who has children and doesn't mind commotion, who can add to the rent by charging for board and care of the children.

We had a good meal at Florence's apartment on Avenue Road. It's just south of St Clair, which, Bruce says, is the borderline. North of that is Forest Hill and it's too expensive. Even in their modest four-storey building I couldn't afford an apartment; not that there are any available. Climbing the stairs to the third floor, we were met by the smell of cooking in the long halls with numbered doors. The sort of meal Florence produced is rare now in England, though once it was a favourite: roast beef, two vegetables, apple pie.

Bruce is quite good-looking and probably an excellent teacher. In his methodical way, he maintained that no more than a quarter of one's income should go for rent. In my case that would be less than seven dollars a week. Once the dining table was cleared, we spread out the daily papers and a map of Toronto. Then we singled out ads for areas close to John Inglis. Those in expensive districts, those that asked for "adults only," "single applicants," "no children," we crossed out at once. No luck. Everyone wants to live close to work, and factories – other than those outside town – concentrate along the lakeshore.

Florence knows of some charity-funded so-called crèches downtown, but none that will accept children under two. They are in the poorest districts. There are also private nursery schools, but they're expensive.

In the warm, slightly stuffy apartment, my eyes began to drop shut. Bettina fell asleep on the couch while we were talking. We covered her with an afghan.

"There *is* a nursery school north of St Clair a few blocks," Florence suddenly remembered. "It would be ideal … if they'd consider taking Bettina. I know the person who runs it. She's the daughter of one of my old professors, Barker Fairley. She's married to the artist John Hall. Her name is Joan. She's a weaver."

"But it's in Forest Hill. Impossible to find rooms there," Bruce reminded us.

"Let's look east of Yonge. That's less expensive. Merton Street is a bit rundown, with the railway shunting close by," Florence suggested. "A streetcar ticket to take you to work costs the same, whether you come from nearby or have to take a longer ride with several changes. It's more tiring, of course."

Once again we searched through the papers.

"Look, here's a room advertised on Merton Street. We just didn't look in places that far from John Inglis." I was proud to have found it on the map.

But Bruce shook his head. "An hour by streetcar and two changes," he mumbled.

"But walking distance from Joan's nursery school," Florence said, looking smug.

I'd begun to dread phoning. Every time I mentioned two – well-behaved – little girls, there was a silence, a grunt "no kids," or short, gruff explanations why kids were not wanted. Some people simply hung up. By now I was so nervous that I could barely speak. When some one on Merton Street answered the phone, I cleared my throat and croaked, "Will the room be large enough for me and two … very good … children?" I rushed to add what was a fantasy so far: "They'll be at nursery school all day."

A friendly, unhurried voice at the other end of the line assured me that it would be.

"Is there some kind of cooking facility? Or are meals possible – if we pay board, of course. I'll be on shift work, so I could eat at the cafeteria." I became aware that I was saying too much. All was over. But at the other end of the line there was a leisurely consultation.

"Yes, why not? We could talk about it, if you want to see the room."

My hand was shaking as I replaced the receiver. But it was not anxiety alone; it was a stream of energy that ran through me. I'd try and do everything in this one evening. It was not likely that Bruce would want his orderly household disturbed again by the three of us. Right now, Bettina was safely asleep. Fiona was invited to help in the kitchen, something she likes to do.

"You go," Florence urged. "Do everything while the girls are here. Fiona can sleep on our bed if she wants to. But first, phone Joan Hall, the one with the nursery school."

"How much is the room rent?" Bruce wanted to know.

In my excitement I'd forgotten to ask. I was crestfallen. And I still had to phone Joan Hall. If, by a miracle, both places worked out, the cost might be staggering. My future salary began to look much less impressive.

The voice that replied to my next telephone call, a beautiful, low voice, gave me clear directions on how to find the house. At present the school has mostly children from nearby homes, not the children of war workers, the voice continued. They would like to make room for people who work in factories. I did not dare express my wild hope: that there might be two places at the school.

Out in the mild autumn night I started running. I ran all the way to Yonge Street. I would have run up Yonge Street too, but a streetcar came rattling up the hill just then and I wanted to save time. I rode a block past Merton Street and ran back past a large park-like area that I'd been told was a cemetery. Still, it was green; there were trees outlined against the sky that here in the city is never dark. I'd become used to absolute blackness in London and great, starry skies in Barrie.

At the corner of Yonge and Merton a second-hand furniture store gave me a moment of bliss. Among the furniture placed

Yonge Street
looking south towards
Merton in 1944
∽

out on the pavement stood a small, light-blue desk, exactly the right size for Fiona. I had to harden my heart to pass it.

Auction sales and used furniture stores are my weakness. At our London co-op almost all the furniture had come from the Gloucester Road auction rooms. During the Czech crisis, wealthy Londoners moved to the country and some of their magnificent furniture was auctioned off. In 1938 it was possible to buy a Sheraton table for ten shillings. We did, and bought a Victorian mahogany wardrobe for the same price. To transport these items, we borrowed a gigantic wheelbarrow from the South Kensingon Museum, a barrow the size of a horse-drawn cart. It was at the disposal of artists submitting work to the Royal Academy, as two of our sculptors did from time to time.

Later, during the Blitz, those pieces of furniture were shifted to the top floor of the house, while everyone moved to the basement. Most of that beautiful furniture was ruined by pieces of shrapnel and by our pumping water on to the neighbours' roof to put out incendiary bombs.

I took the scrap of newspaper out of my pocket to check the street numbers. Houses on Merton Street have once seen better days. They are of a type common in Barrie and probably in Toronto too: they look like brick structures, but the bricks are really a veneer added to a wooden building. Most of them have a porch, its roof supported by wide (probably hollow) columns. At the one where I stopped, the porch had a ramshackle railing. There was a bell, but it didn't work. So I knocked. A light went on, illuminating a pane of cracked stained glass in the front door.

When the door opened, all I could see, all that mattered, was the face of a large, plump woman, a face like a sound, rosy apple framed by chestnut brown hair. Large brown eyes smiled as she said, "Come on in." I hadn't noticed the Scottish burr on the telephone.

The shabbiness of the hall linoleum didn't matter to me. I cared only about the people in this house. I followed the woman, Mrs McNair, through the hall to the kitchen at the back, which was very warm. At the kitchen table sat Mr McNair, his top clad in a sleeveless vest tucked into his trousers. His face looked lined and weary, his eyes kind; his dark hair was streaked with grey. With an indescribable gesture of tenderness, he held on his knees a baby younger than Bettina. The McNairs have five children. No wonder they cannot easily find single war workers, who have to sleep after night shift. With my two, that would be seven. All but the baby are at school during the day, though. That should help.

Mrs McNair walked ahead of me to show me the room on the second floor. Like the front room directly below, it has a bay window. The wallpaper is a loud blue, decorated with red roses and tulips. There is a large bed, small rocker, built-in cupboards, table and chair. I'd have to buy or borrow a crib for Bettina. What there is in this room is clean, though, and like the landlords, friendly.

When we came back to the kitchen, Mrs McNair took a teapot from the stove and poured me a cup of strong black tea. I drank it from the thick-rimmed cup set out on the oilcloth of the table. The heat, the tea, the rush to get here made me glow like an oven.

My greatest problem, I explained, was shift work. Most war work has alternate shifts, changing from days to nights every two weeks. Day shift might be more of a problem because I'd have to go to work long before the children could get to the nursery school.

Taking them there, though, Mrs McNair remarked, would be easier for her than looking after them all day.

"Then, when I'm on night shift, I'd worry if there weren't someone at home all night."

"There always is. I'm always home. Even if Fred is out late driving. He drives a taxi, and that's often at night."

They knew what it was like, they said, when their children had to sleep alone. They never did. They all shared beds.

"I could do some washing on weekends," I ventured. "But if you have a machine, could I put some things in for the kids, if and when you do your main wash?" There's so much washing to do here, Mrs McNair uses the machine every day. She doesn't think my added washing will be too much trouble. We'd see soon enough.

This had been a nagging problem. Another, bigger one was the price for the room. "The room is six dollars a week," Mrs McNair said. "Will the kids have meals here?"

"They'll have a good meal at school, at noon, I'm told," I was trying to convince myself that all that was settled. I was not even sure whether I could afford the school or whether they'd take a child as young as Bettina.

"What about nine dollars a week, then," she asked, hesitating, as if asking for an enormous sum. I knew I could not possibly do better anywhere.

"If you want a bite of breakfast or supper, we could make it ten."

I calculated quickly. Ten dollars for rent and food. Ten (perhaps twelve) for the nursery school. That left less than five dollars, perhaps only three, for fares. I'd have to do without meals at the cafeteria. Unless I got portrait commissions. Less than ten dollars are left of my credit union loan.

I made a down payment for the room. I thought of large towns where I'd lived. There seemed to be, in Toronto, some of the innocence I'd found in Barcelona before the Civil War. In large towns people can be hard; they were in London until the raids started. Having read Upton Sinclair's harrowing description of Chicago immigrant life, I had not expected people like Mrs McNair or Mrs Wallace. (Chicago is said to resemble Toronto in size, situation, even in architecture.)

Then I thought of the sleeping places in the London Underground, patiently chalked off so that each family had a little
area to lie down. You stepped over and around them to get
your train. Most of the night the trains continued roaring by
the sleeping people on the platforms. All over the world, I
thought, there are these people who own next to nothing and
share it. I began to feel an affection for this town.

Out on the street the air was now cool and fresh. I crossed
Yonge Street to find my way to the nursery school. A fairly long
walk even without pushing a stroller.

On the west side of Yonge the houses are far apart and have
gardens. At the Halls' address the garden space has been made
into a play area. Florence told me that Barker Fairley is a professor of German, a Goethe expert. He's also an art critic. Then
I remembered seeing his articles in the *Canadian Forum*, at The
Barn in Barrie. His daughter, Joan, has eyes as clear as the voice
I'd heard over the phone – clear and luminous. Her skin too is
luminous, her features distinct.

In the hall of their house there's a portrait of Joan, painted by
her husband. It catches some of this luminosity. There's a lot of
green in the eyes and skin, the soft green of that wonderful painting *Vera* by Frederick Varley. John Hall, too, loves that painting. He is a tall, thin redhead. His paintings and graphics are all
over the house, as well as Joan's weaving. Everything in this
house is made of good, genuine materials, the kind you find in
an artist's house. What a long time it's been since I stood in one.

Here in Toronto, as well as in Barrie, there's an absence of
those sharp class distinctions you sense in Britain, even now in
wartime (though they've blurred a little lately). Distinctions
here are by wealth. The Merton Street household from which
I'd just come would be called "working-class" in Europe, but
perhaps not here. In Britain the McNairs would probably belong to a labour party. I know from Barker Fairley's writing

that, politically, he is as far left as one can be in Canada, where the law-abiding CCF is still considered communist. A strange contrast: this moderately prosperous household of left-wing intellectuals and the McNairs (examples of what Marx would call "the true proletariat," yet here perhaps politically conservative). I don't know whether taxi drivers here even have unions.

When we talked about my job and where I intended to live, I found that Joan, too, was aware of the discrepancy between poverty east of Yonge and comparative wealth in Forest Hill. Her husband teaches at Upper Canada College. It makes sense living nearby.

Their nursery school is what I've dreamed of for Fiona. She'd get all the art and music and stories she needs. About Bettina – well, we'd have to find out. Joan Hall doesn't normally accept children under two, but she decided to take her on. She even reduced the fee for the second child. She said she always did this, but I'm aware that in our case the second child means extra work.

Here everything is arranged to create well-being in children and to stimulate creativity. I need have no worries during the times my children will spend in this school. There is a menu for each day, for which vitamins and calories are carefully calculated. The meals look better, in fact, than the school meals we had for the last two years. There will be orange juice mid-mornings. There are enough helpers to create a ratio of one staff member to five children. For play there are many ingenious devices, some taken from everyday surplus: wooden bowls that once contained shaving soap, cardboard rolls, paper bags, string, wood shavings. Eleven dollars a week will buy my children first-class care in the daytime. And they'll still be part of the working world at night. And there they'd have me, too.

I walked south towards St Clair with a light step. My friend Florence's apartment did not seem far now. If I had to pay six dollars for one child, five for the other, ten for rent and some board, that would still leave me four dollars for fares. However long the streetcar ride down to John Inglis, it would be the same fare as if I lived close to my work.

Florence and Bruce were impressed: I couldn't possibly have accomplished more in so short a time. Now, finally, Florence said, one can see that the Depression is over. People can find employment in one day. Too bad that it took a war to get rid of unemployment.

I detected a note of sadness in her voice as she said this: as if she herself would have liked to work in a blueprint office, with the possibility of "moving up to inspection." Florence is a qualified teacher, but because of rules dating back to Depression years, they cannot both hold teaching jobs. She takes courses in shorthand at Toronto's Central Technical School. Also in painting – her instructor is Carl Schaefer.

Bruce thinks I should just pay my landlady to mind the children. The nursery, he says, costs too much. But he has simply no idea what it means, adding two more children when you already have five. I am the eldest of five. I know how my mother felt.

Rationing here is very tame, practically non-existent compared to Britain. Except for sugar, and having less of that can do no harm, according to Bruce. He agrees that a landlady would probably appreciate a few extra ration cards in her household.

I hardly remember how I got back to the Yorkville boarding house with my sleepy children. Today I've packed most of my things; we're leaving in the morning.

My new energies make me resent the heat in these buildings. What a waste! I remember how, for the first few weeks in Canada, the heat indoors overwhelmed me. In the Montreal hotel where the Red Cross had put us up the first night, I tried in vain to turn off radiators, open windows. At the school I finally found a way to cool off our room, a room I'm longing for now, with its chaste blue cotton covers, its whitewashed walls. But I was always warned by the teacher in charge of the Junior House that opening the window would send the furnace into compensating activity. What is it about countries with severe winters – Russia too, I'm told – that makes them so frantically overheat their buildings?

Night shift at John Inglis starts at seven-thirty, so I have to be on the Yonge streetcar by six-thirty at the latest. There are two changes, one at King, the other close to the factory. If one had time, one could walk down Dovercourt instead of taking the last streetcar, but there never is time. For much of this trip one has to stand up, because there are other people going to night shift in factories along the lakeshore.

King Street and Strachan Avenue, near the John Inglis plant, in 1943

~~

We work a ten-hour shift, so we don't get out till six a.m. There's a half-hour break for a meal at midnight, and it's just as well that I'm never hungry then, for I can't afford cafeteria meals. Mrs McNair, in the goodness of her heart, sometimes slips me a baloney sandwich, and all I have to do is buy a cup of coffee to keep awake. The graveyard hours are hardest, between twelve-thirty and six a.m. Luckily, we're allowed a short break around three-thirty a.m. Between three and four a.m. seems to be the hardest time to keep awake.

The blueprint office is a glassed-in cubicle at the centre of the department where inspectors check gauges, using delicate tools for measuring, microscopes, and blueprints. Each gauge has a special number, and sometimes we have to get additional prints from a central blueprint office. The interesting part of the job is trying to visualize from the drawings what parts they represent.

Since we don't work on machines, we are the envy of the girls "out on the floor" because in our cubicle we don't have to cover our hair with bandanas. But like them, we are issued cotton coveralls that cover our clothes. They're charged against the second month of pay. The first few weeks, before a paycheque comes in, are known to be hard.

I don't know what I'd do if it were not for these coveralls. They're cheap; they cover old and mended clothes. One does-n't even have to wear stockings, though it's cold without. Some girls wear men's woollen socks because of the cold cement floors. No one cares what shoes you wear; loafers or running shoes are best, especially if you have to climb around on ma-chines. We won't need overshoes yet. By the time we do, I hope I can afford a pair. These overshoes are sometimes covered with velvety material and edged with fur fabric, the sort of thing you never see in Europe. Like English wellingtons, they're made of rubber, good for Toronto slush. We have lockers where we put coats, purses, fancy shoes, before we punch the time clock.

There is a hum of machines. The whole factory is brilliantly lit. Loudspeakers near the ceiling trumpet popular music, usu-ally in march time, to keep us awake. Many songs have nothing to do with our work or with the war:

Take a dozen roses
Put my heart in beside them
And send them to the one I love

That's a favourite because of its pounding rhythm.

The girls who work in the blueprint office with me are coun-try girls who've come to Toronto for jobs. Jean wants to be a teacher. Carol, dark-eyed, rosy, very quiet, harbours a silent grief. Her husband left her "for her best friend," as the saying goes, while she had a bout of pneumonia. Her small children are with her parents in Simcoe County. She's a heavy smoker with a smoker's cough. She goes out at break mainly to smoke, in company with a young woman who has made it as inspec-tor. This girl, whom everybody calls Sweeney, has to wear a bandana because she's "out on the floor" checking gauges. In coffee break, when she takes off her bandana, I see that her hair is prematurely white, though she cannot be more than thirty.

Marguerite Sweeney is not only an inspector; she's a union organizer. During the Depression she helped to support a family of nine brothers and sisters as cashier in a beer parlour. She's tolerant of coarseness in others without being coarse herself. She seems quite unaware of her own charm. Her large blue eyes, mobile features, ready wit, make her the most attractive person around. She's considered to be a very good inspector and should really be made lead hand. But that won't

Girl at John Inglis blueprint office (crayon sketch)

happen while there are still men around to do the job. Dennis, the inspection foreman, cannot be much above military age. From him and Sweeney I'm learning to read blueprints.

Over-awake, over-tired, I am near hallucinating on those dark mornings when we leave the factory before sunrise. There is a ghostly blue light high above the gate. It is harsh on the features of the tired people streaming out to cars and streetcars, making them look like hollow-cheeked peasants, revolutionaries in a Daumier painting. But they're unlike European workers. They may wear cloth caps, kerchiefs, coveralls, but few have the stunted growth of Cockney factory workers. They don't think of themselves as "working-class." From what I hear around me, most of them think they're "as good as the boss." This self-confidence in some ways makes Sweeney's job of organizing a union more difficult.

In the streetcar there's standing room only; we're packed like sardines. I accomplish the change to King, then to Yonge, in a kind of trance that helps me to overcome the sickly hollowness I feel these mornings. The used smell of people who've been up all night, of their sweat (and mine), is nauseating. But at least I can't fall: there's not room enough around me.

When I reach Merton Street, it's not worth while going to bed for half an hour, then wake the children and take them to nursery school. So I have a bite of breakfast in the kitchen. At seven-thirty I go upstairs, change Bettina, help both children to get dressed. My longing to flop down on the big bed is painful in its intensity, but first the children have to be fed and bundled up. The kitchen is hot and very lively, with four McNair children aged between six and ten getting ready for school. At eight-thirty I push the stroller across Yonge into the polite, hushed world of Forest Hill. There daily life is just beginning. In the school, mothers take tiny rubber boots off preschoolers, hang coats on hooks decorated with pictures instead of names. Bettina doesn't want me to leave and with a howl throws herself on the floor. Joan makes a sign to me to slip away quietly, and I do, tears in my eyes, great aching waves of fatigue sweeping over me, so that on the way home I nearly get run over.

In less than three hours I'm roused from sleep by the McNair children, back for lunch, merrily stampeding through the house. There's little peace until the school bell rings at one-thirty. I love these children, but I'm ready to wring their necks when they return, shortly after three, just when I've fallen asleep. It's no use trying to sleep again, for they're now home for good. I might as well get up, drink some strong tea, and get my children from school.

Supper is early, around five-thirty, a useful time. It gives me half an hour to eat, then put my children in the tub and read to them on the big bed. I put on my coveralls when I get up in the afternoon so that I don't have to change before going to work. The children are used to them now. One sees these factory coveralls everywhere on streetcars, even on residential streets in Forest Hill. By six-thirty I'm on the Yonge car again. I know I probably won't be able to keep up this kind of life. I'm looking forward feverishly to day shift next week.

~ October 15th ~

It was hard to find a moment for this journal while we were on night shift. We're on day shift now, and I have the evenings, sitting near the children as I always have in the evenings. The odd thing is that, out of habit, I now don't sleep at night, even

35

though I've got over the terrible nightmares I used to have in Barrie whenever trains came by, hooting like air-raid sirens. The trains that shunt on tracks just south of Merton don't disturb me. The street light outside throws the shadows of bare trees on the thin white blind, huge hands with long fingers. Bettina cries out in her sleep. What happens when I'm not home, nights?

For day shift I leave at six-thirty in the morning. Once I get to work, there is now little time to worry about the children – how they get across Yonge with Mrs McNair; are they picked up on time after school? – because during the day there is a much livelier demand for blueprints. We also have to take time off to have X-rays taken in the company's health office. Sweeney and Carol don't much like having X-rays. They both have smoker's coughs, and they're afraid the X-rays might reveal TB.

On our way home from day shift the streetcars are even more crowded, because, in addition to factory workers, there are people returning from offices and banks downtown. By the time I get home, the children have usually had their supper. I give them a bath and read to them in bed. My supper is cold, so it doesn't matter when I have it.

Sweeney thinks I should move closer to the factory, put my-self on the waiting list for public daycare, and find a landlady to mind the children until Bettina is two in March. But I know I'll never find a nursery school like Joan Hall's. Giving that up would be a terrible wrench. And the McNairs – where will I ever find such good people? Their children are noisy because they're loved.

Jean, Carol, and Sweeney have borrowed Dennis's paper to check ads – for me. Their three heads are bent over the newspa-per, and suddenly my heart contracts with the realization: they are my friends.

~ October 18th ~

I didn't get to see Joan Hall again until we were back on night shift. She's looked at me once or twice with concern. I'm always afraid that Bettina is too much trouble at the school. She's not completely toilet trained and still wears diapers. There's the additional chore of putting them aside for me to take home so

36

they can be washed. There's no other child that young. But Joan has not complained so far. I think she sees no other way for us to survive at present.

"You don't get enough sleep, do you?" she said once. "Can you really manage?"

"I'll get used to it. I've only had two full shifts so far."

We got back our X-ray results and I have a clean bill of health. So has Sweeney. But Carol, who looks healthier than any of us, has advanced TB. She is being sent to a sanatorium in Weston to have one lung collapsed. She may be there for a long time, no one knows how long. Why this, when so much has been taken from her?

So Sweeney and I ask ourselves. We have become friends. We have our coffee breaks together, and she'd like me to come to union meetings.

"You shouldn't be living that far away," she maintains. "Your day would be shorter if you lived, say, in Parkdale."

"But that's too far from the nursery school."

"Well, try for something like the West End Crèche. It's subsidized. You'd pay less."

I told her about the St Patrick's crèche. "They won't take the baby until she's two."

"Put her on a waiting list anyway. Just for a couple of months try to find someone to look after her."

Jean agrees. She's boarding with a woman whose daughter has a slight heart condition and makes most of her income from knitting at great speed. She's one of those people who should not work in factories, but she could look after children while doing her knitting.

Jean boards near Parkdale. She knows the streets there. She and Sweeney scanned the ads in Dennis's paper for days. They wouldn't give up. And today they found something: two rooms on MacDonell Avenue.

"Two rooms – I'd never be able to afford that."

"Yes, you will, if they're unfurnished."

"How's that?"

37

"The rent is a lot less. Most landlords rent furnished rooms because when they're furnished, you can give tenants a week's notice. Unfurnished, it's a month. For you, that would be an advantage."

~ October 20th ~

Saturday afternoon Sweeney took me to Parkdale. I didn't dare take the children along, so went at their nap time.

The house on MacDonell is a typical Toronto brick house, probably built around the same time as that on Merton but better preserved. The rooms for rent are on the ground floor, interconnected by double doors, the typical arrangement for living and dining rooms in old houses, with the kitchen in the back. Newly papered. Hardwood floors. I haven't a chance, I thought. The landlady will never accept children.

But this landlady has had a tenant who was an alcoholic. "A lovely girl, really, except for that. Two children couldn't be as bad as she was – when she was bad. I have a teenage girl, you see. That sort of person is a bad example. "

The teenage daughter is about fifteen. A bit young to mind children unless the mother is at home too. But it might work later, so I mention it.

The rent for the two unfurnished rooms is twenty dollars a month. I make a down payment at once. I can't believe it: I've been in Toronto for about a month and I have a place of my own. I can now bring my cabin trunk from Barrie, where it is stored in the school basement. It was packed in a tearing hurry during the London Blitz. The notice that we could travel, that the waiting list for boats going to Canada had suddenly become shorter, came as a surprise. We threw in my mother's monogrammed sheets, even some family silver. They'd come in handy now. By hook or by crook, I'll get hold of some beds and a card table. Shelves I can make from orange crates. If I put the children's beds in the back room and a couch for myself in the front room, which has a nice bay window, then for the first time in years, I'll have a room of my own.

Leaving Joan's nursery school and the McNairs will be a wrench. A terrible decision to make. But for the children's sake,

I must survive myself. I've ignored the Barrie doctor's command never to work more than part-time. I can't afford to be ill again.

If I manage to get portrait commissions, I'd now have the front room for my painting. I promised my fellow worker Jean a pastel portrait. I like her freckled face, the mane of dark curly hair, the large hazel eyes – she'll make a good subject.

My next move was to contact the daughter of Jean's landlady, the one who knits. She'd charge ten dollars a week for minding the children. My rent is down to five, but I have to make meals for myself, and there are still fares. All that has to come out of the ten dollars a week that remain. I hope I soon get a raise.

~ October 26th ~

Night shift is my greatest problem right now. I've inquired at the John Inglis personnel office to see if there are "steady day" jobs. There are, but it's office work, badly paid. Everyone wants that shift. Sweeney introduced me to the union steward on inspection. His name is Bill Sefton. It would be hard to imagine anyone who looks less like a typical working-class representative. Bill Sefton looks like a poet. He is tall and dark, with deepset blue eyes. A lock of black hair falls into his high forehead. He wears a fedora, not a cloth cap as most British working people do. He has a low, rather hollow voice and only a trace of an Irish accent.

While I lived in Barrie, I'd heard about the long strike at Kirkland Lake, from an engineer who'd worked there and was visiting the Smiths. That strike caused bitter divisions, not only up north but among the people who discussed it. During that strike Bill Sefton and his brother Larry had been organizers for the Steelworkers union – the very union that is now attempting to organize John Inglis. They are going to open a small union office on Queen Street, not too far from the factory, almost walking distance from MacDonell.

When Bill Sefton heard that I'd worked as a secretary, he asked would I work at the union office if I made the same salary as at John Inglis? Should I? Shouldn't I? I really hate office work, and it normally pays less. There will probably be

39

extra hours. But working at a union office should be a real challenge.

After Bill Sefton and Marguerite Sweeney had talked to me in the cafeteria, I argued with myself. We're on day shift and very busy, but I'd have to decide before we go on night shift again. What choice do I have anyway? From our glassed-in cubicle I looked out at the place where the inspectors sit, Sweeney among them, her head with its bandana bent over her microscope. She was examining a small gauge. These gauges are for Colt guns!

I don't believe in deadly weapons and I believe in unions. Unions were the backbone of any resistance against Hitler in Germany, the first organizations the Nazis tried to break. In Barcelona, unions had contributed to the concerts Pablo Casals played for working people, concerts so cheap that even I could go to them, though as an au pair with a family there, I never had any money. So at the next break I walked over to Bill Sefton and told him I'd be happy to work at the union office (though I've never seen it and don't know what my duties will be).

Sweeney's family have a garage in which all of them (she has eight siblings) store surplus cots and chairs. She also has a brother with a truck who could move some of these things to my new address. And on the way, he'll pick up a rusty couch that lives on Florence's narrow balcony, the kind that has two wings that drop down on either side if only the middle is used. So there's my furniture.

~ November 1st ~

We have moved to Parkdale. Saying goodbye to the McNairs was hard – they've been the best and kindest landlords. But I had to make a choice, and the choice was simply survival. For Fiona it meant leaving a nursery school where she's been in her element. On our last day there, Joan told me that she's often wondered how long I'd hold out. Every day I came to get the children, she noticed that I looked a little more hollow-eyed. She thinks that Bettina – who easily gets bronchitis – would be better off at home until March, when she will be two years old. The first year at nursery school a child gets all the colds

40

that go around. How often, I wonder, will I get to that part of Toronto again? It seems miles away from where we are now.

Our new landlady, Mrs Stubbs, also goes out to work. There's no husband around; perhaps he's overseas. Mrs Stubbs isn't communicative, and we don't often see her. I avoid using the telephone in the back hall. I don't want to intrude on her household.

Sylvia, the knitter – who looks after the children when I am at work – seems nice enough, good-natured and practical. She wears glasses, has a high colour, and looks robust (in spite of heart trouble). I know she'll never replace what Fiona had at the Halls', the painting and music. But for stories I have found a solution. I discovered a good public library just around the corner on Queen Street. They have story hours for children on Saturdays.

This evening Florence turned up at our new rooms with an old crank-up record player – small enough to be carried here on the Queen streetcar – together with some records from the Columbia series on the history of music. Bruce has bought a new, superior phonograph, very sensitive to scratches and background noises, so Florence has promised to bring more of their old records.

Fiona is enchanted by Handel's song "Where'er You Walk." She wants to hear it over and over again, never mind the scratches and tinny voice. Not nearly as tinny as the few records my sister and I had when we were teenagers – usually popular songs, for practising dance steps. Oh, for "Singing in the Rain"!

My parents thought music lessons essential. My mother had started playing the piano when she was five years old and still plays on her Steinway grand with that wonderful Clara Schumann touch. But I wasn't allowed near that instrument. I had to practise on an old upright piano donated by my godmother. My sister played the violin, one brother the clarinet, another the flute; only the youngest continued with this instrument professionally. Our family did not own a radio until the early 1930s' when more and more music by Wagner replaced Mendelssohn and Rachmaninov. Radio was still so new that some people thought what they heard there must be the

41

absolute truth, the voice of God. Whereas more and more of the time, it was a rasping voice I detested (it gave me great pleasure to turn off that voice whenever I could).

During the years I worked in Spain and Italy, records had come into their own. In our London artists' co-op, music meant jazz. There were regular jamming sessions that shook the old building even more than the Brompton road buses thundering past.

Then at the Barrie school, the music of my childhood came flooding back in great waves of recognition. The English music teacher would play Mozart symphonies for her classes, and I listened from a distance. How was it possible that Mozart, during my childhood, was still considered of lighter calibre than Beethoven and Brahms? Records changed all that.

At The Barn we spent whole evenings listening to records; I heard Mozart's clarinet concerto there for the first time. And

*David Smith
at the piano and Gunda
playing treble,
The Barn, Barrie, 1941*

〜〜

Bach's Brandenburg concertos – how could I have missed them till then? The first Bach I remember was the Christmas Oratorio, sung at the Darmstadt town church. Casals now plays Bach most of the time, but in Barcelona it was the Brahms double concerto he both played and conducted. He sometimes visits the United Sates, where I can't go to hear him. After the Spanish Civil War he has not set foot in Spain again; the French side of the Pyrenees has to be Catalan enough for him. The war chased him briefly to Latin America. He travelled there on the same liner as a handsome woman who came to Barrie while visiting sons at a Canadian boarding school – one of those tall women that look stunning in a large hat (I sketched her in one). She must have been almost twice Casal's size. He liked to kiss her hand, she said, and every morning practised Bach on the ship's piano. His morning exercise, he called it – gymnastics of the mind. (He's not a pianist.)

·~ November 3rd ~·

Florence and Frank Hines, who turned up while she was here, suggest we should have a housewarming at my new rooms. My cabin trunk is still in the school basement in Barrie. Frank mentioned that after a weekend in Barrie he would get a ride back to Toronto with David Smith, so I asked whether the two could bring my trunk in David's car. They are neither of them big strong men, but Frank promised they would. David would, I know.

I first saw David Smith when he was changing Bettina's diaper. I'd just come from hospital – she was a new baby. I'd never seen a man do such chores, for me – like breast-feeding – a woman's job entirely. Later he stood in front of the Smiths' huge stone fireplace, deep in thought, his head down so that a shock of his prematurely grey hair was hiding half his face. He wore a red woollen shirt and would have made a fine painting.

I don't think I ever in my life met people like David and Edith. I was used to a worldly, cynical, hesitantly left-of-centre attitude in Britain. I couldn't, at first, believe their earnest attempts to introduce social awareness in an ultra-conservative community. Their passion for all the arts was real. I'd never before heard Bach played and listened to with such abandon. There was an innocence in those evenings, listening to music, reading plays with overt social messages. They opened up whole cultural areas I'd lost or never known.

The background of Canadian socialism (the CCF) is religious; even when they lose contact

David Smith,
1941 (oil)

43

with the doctrines of organized religion, a social conscience remains. David's family is Scottish Presbyterian; Edith's parents were Saskatchewan Baptists. One might expect a narrow puritan view; and morally, their lifestyle is nothing like the bohemian one I knew in London. They were social workers at Toronto's University Settlement; then, with a Carnegie grant, started a Simcoe County project for the University of Toronto's Extension, ambitiously named "Community Life Training Institute." They taught hard-pressed farmers to form a credit union, encouraged meetings of the Women's Institutes, and were members of the Fellowship for Christian Social Order.

Now my Columbia records bring back those evenings, the scent of freshly brewed coffee, the crackling fire, the merry voices. Those evenings seldom ended before midnight. The Barn was open to everyone. No one wanted to leave early. David, who drove to rural meetings all over Simcoe County, often came back much later.

Edith, fair, vivid, always on the go, is a western Canadian, a mix of German and Scottish. David has the Celtic features of my mother's mainly Welsh family: straight nose; long upper lip; large, expressive blue eyes. His vigorous shock of hair is grey though he's only in his mid-thirties. Sweeney is even younger, and her hair is even whiter. Is there something in the Canadian climate that causes this?

When David dropped by to deliver my trunk, he was dressed as usual in grey: grey winter coat, grey fedora. His clothes never look warm enough for Canadian winters. Other men wear fur hats with earflaps, quilted windbreakers, felt-lined boots. Like Bill Sefton, he looks more like a poet than the image of a social democrat I've had up to now.

After placing the cabin trunk in the niche of the bay window, David and Frank stayed only long enough to inspect my (still almost empty) rooms and say hello to the children. They brought an invitation from Edith to visit The Barn for a few days after Christmas. David offered to drive us there after staying with his father in Hamilton.

As soon as they'd left, I started to unpack my trunk. I'd forgotten about the cotton cover with the Indian motif I've now draped over Florence's old couch. My mother's good linen sheets smell a bit musty. I never unpacked them in Barrie. Her silverware is still carefully wrapped in the soft chamois covers she made for me before I married. (The registrar's office in Florence, where this ceremony was performed, was in the famous Palazzo Signoria – the background for Michelangelo's *David*.) My mother's name was Maud Lee Williams. Marrying an artist by that name seemed like returning to my mother's family. How naive to think so!

Garth is having hard time in New York right now, and even in England he had not been able to find work. He is highly qualified, an RA graduate who earned the Prix de Rome. He's doing commercial photographs at present. He's found a studio and is hiding from his creditors and from military service. I wouldn't have known, but Frank Hines is a passionate admirer of New York, and that – at present – includes Garth. Frank wants to live there. What do Toronto people see in New York that so captures their imagination? The dynamic twenties of Edmund Wilson? Isn't its vitality due, at least in part, to the influx of artists and writers from Vienna, Berlin, and now Paris? According to Frank, the place is so fully alive, he wants to be part of that scene.

When the children had been tucked into bed in the back room, I sat on the newly covered couch and stared at my sturdy huckaback towels, so carefully embroidered with my mother's initials before she married in 1912. How could she have known that within two years her own country and the one she married into would be at war? She too spent a war in largely unfamiliar country with small children. For years, her beloved children did not have enough food, even though she lived in a good house and had servants. At least, I promised myself. this will not happen to my two; they will not starve.

~ November 6th ~

Went to my first union meeting, in a plain, overheated hall on the second floor of an old Bloor Street building. I had no idea what to expect. In Germany, unions (*Gewerkschaften*) were blamed for all the disasters of the German economy by my conservative relations (but the *Gewerkschaften* resisted Hitler). In Barcelona the syndicalists (also unions) managed to be nationalists as well. During the Asturian miners' strike the family with whom I'd come to Barcelona as au pair, all their Catalan relations, and all my student friends walked long distances through town with a sense of supporting the strike, (streetcar drivers had gone on strike in sympathy with the Asturians). Then, to our horror, we saw, from the height of the Tibidabo, the army of the Republic swarming in like ants from their headquarters on Mont Juic. That was when Franco was mentioned for the first time: he used Moorish troops to suppress the strike. In Asturias, of all places – the only part of Spain never conquered by the Moors.

In London towards the end of the Spanish Civil War, we stood in the dismal rain watching the return of the International Brigade, recalled in an effort to make the German and Italian fascists supporting Franco do likewise. That day we knew we'd be the next to be bombed. News of the fall of Madrid came the very day Casals was conducting a concert of the London Philharmonic, in March 1939, more than three years ago now.

People here have gone through a devastating Depression in the thirties, as bad as or worse than anything in Europe; but that didn't produce fascism here. I thought I might find some answers at this union meeting, but it was low-key and scantily attended, though it was scheduled for a time when people could come between shifts. Not all girls wore coveralls. Some had dressed up in skirts, and their furry overshoes hid high-heeled shoes. The curlers normally hidden under bandanas during shift work had been taken out. Beatrice, a big, hefty union steward, even wore a fur coat (unthinkable at a European union meeting).

The speaker at this meeting was Bill Sefton's brother Larry, who is a full-time union organizer. Tall, fair, freckled, Larry looks like everyone's favourite neighbourhood boy. His slightly husky voice is appealing; both he and Bill have this low, pleasant voice and radiate sincerity. Sweeney tells me that they often pay union dues out of their own pockets for people who they think can't afford them.

The Sefton brothers were in Kirkland Lake during the long strike in that mining town. Bill's slightly humped back is the result of a skiing accident there. I'd always thought of skiing as a rich people's sport (my wealthy cousins in Germany went skiing; we didn't). I just cannot imagine a union man in Germany or Britain going off to ski – think of Orwell's *Road to Wigan Pier*!

At the time of the strike Larry and Bill were probably the most unpopular men in all of Kirkland Lake. They were blamed when things went badly for the strikers. The strike was not caused by local conditions: the miners' welfare hinged on world prices for gold. During the Depression, Kirkland Lake had been one of the few places where people could find work. When the bottom fell out of gold prices, the strike became one of despair. Its only relief really came with war work for those who lost employment up north. Deeply discouraged, the Sefton brothers returned to Toronto, where they are now nagged because they are not in the army. They were not accepted for health reasons: Larry because of stomach ulcers, Bill because of his back.

I could place most of the people at the meeting, except for a nattily dressed businessman who sat in the back and who I thought at first must be one of the Inglis employers. I saw him again at the union's headquarters on Lansdowne and Bloor, where he has a small office. He is the American liaison with the Steelworkers and talks with a nasal twang I associate with the Midwest. So far, I have not seen him at the shabby little office on Queen Street, an abandoned store, where I am going to work full-time.

~ November 10th ~

During my last night shift at John Inglis the snow came to stay. It's snowed several times before this, but the snow quickly turned to slush. That morning, when we got out of the plant, I felt that something had changed. It had snowed all night. The streets were strangely hushed, except for the scraping of the snowploughs, with their revolving lights, and the clanking of the streetcars that could not move fast because of these churning monsters in their way. The plows built miniature alps on the side of the road on which, later in the morning, children would

47

climb and slide. The street lights were blurred by soft flakes that seemed to rise from the ground as well as fall from above in a slow, hypnotic rhythm.

It was a Saturday morning. On that day we go to the Queen Street public library for its story hour. The children's librarian, Alice Kane, has the true gift of the storyteller – few people have it. Even Bettina, who doesn't yet understand the words in the stories, sits spellbound when that red-headed librarian reads to the children.

Fiona has finally outgrown the little tweed coat and leggings I made for her, which on our arrival in Barrie had been too large, but she still wears the coat. The last two winters she wore a wonderful, waterproof light blue snowsuit. In such a one-piece suit children can roll in the snow without getting wet. This snowsuit now fits Bettina, and as I bundle her into it, I remember how we found it.

The first snow, that first winter in Barrie, had been a miracle. It transformed the world We woke up to brilliant light filtered into all windows, light that shone from below as well as from above. Shadows outside were intensely blue. The great evergreen trees around the school buildings were laden with a heavy, immaculate burden. The fierce white of the drifts almost hurt the eyes.

On the kitchen table outside our room sat a little blue figure as solid as a small person – a one-piece snowsuit with a pointed hood attached. At its feet stood a pair of tiny white rubber boots. The snowsuit was seated on a sleigh – a sleigh something like a baby carriage with runners. The handyman who looked after the school's furnace had found

~~

Fiona in the little tweed coat I made, in front of the house on MacDonell Avenue, Toronto, 1942

it in the basement and had re-
painted it. I never found out
where the snowsuit came from
– perhaps from the whole
school, perhaps from only one
well-wisher. Like the snow,
the gift filled me with a happiness and hope I'd not known
since the beginning of the war.

Fiona
in blue snowsuit
found outside our door
at Ovenden School

I've had a short letter from
Garth, who still hasn't found
work in New York, just the
odd photo asignment. He
thinks we should have stayed
at the school; of course, his
own responsibility would then have weighed less. But my shoulders are broad enough to carry the burden for us three. This
way I remain friends with the school. And with those in Barrie
who've helped us along for two whole years.

~ November 16th ~

To save transportation I walk to work, a fairly long way along
Queen Street - about twenty-five minutes – through, first, old
Parkdale, where the buildings have seen better days, then past
small stores, some of them with empty windows. At this time of
year, when even the snow and slush look dark grey, they seem
especially dismal.

Sylvia arrives around eight-thirty. It's a great relief not to have
to bundle up the children into snowsuits on cold days. She'll do
that when she takes them out of doors, for even in November
the sun appears more often here than it did in London. I take
time to dress and feed the children before I leave, and I'm back
to give them supper and put them to bed, a steady routine at
last after all the changes of the last months.

In the winter light the Steelworkers John Inglis office might
look depressing to anyone whose spirits are not as buoyed as

mine. There's a built-in store counter, now used as a shelf for files. A single light bulb illuminates a floor strewn with bits of plaster (some renovations have been attempted). The large store window is smeared with white paint to make it less transparent. There's a rickety table for my typewriter and a couple of hard chairs. But the place is warm, and it's much less noisy than at John Inglis. Still, though the noise was deafening, I miss the movement and life at the factory. It's only early November, but the loudspeaker there regaled us last week with Bing Crosby's "White Christmas." To Sweeney's great satisfaction: Bing Crosby is her absolute favourite.

During my first day at the union office, Bill and Larry Sefton brought files, chairs, and table from the main office using Larry's car. That's another surprise: working people with cars. They have car pools for going to work, and though gas is rationed, their war effort entitles them to drive. As I get to know people at the main office, I'm beginning to wonder whether my job is not part of Sefton generosity too. Everyone there is super efficient, types at great speed, and knows how to use the Gestetner machine, still new to me. I've worked for many years as secretary and translator, but I still make mistakes typing. Oh, it's so hard to correct mistakes on those filmy Gestetner copies. When there's a rush job, we all pitch in, stuffing hundreds of envelopes with newsletters and union pamphlets. Some of those then land down at my John Inglis office for distribution.

The main secretary at the Steelworkers headquarters is Vi, who types with dazzling speed and whips off mimeographed copies with a telephone receiver squeezed beteen her ear and shoulder. She works long hours at the office, while the organizers, including one woman, go out to factories to distribute leaflets. This woman, Eileen Tallman, was a promising student, and I hear that her business education was largely paid for by the CCF. When there's a rush, she helps Vi, as everyone else does, stuffing envelopes, running off mimeographed notices. I'll never be able to match the pace and dexterity of those two.

~ November 20th ~

The only money I ever earned at Barrie was for portraits. Now that I have a place where I can paint, I hope to find some portrait commissions. Most people like to have this done at their own place, they may not welcome my children. The university here in Toronto has a committee that looks after war guests, wives and children of academics. I phoned them when we first came to town. but they could not help me find a place to live. However, they put me in touch with a woman living in an apartment just off College Street who, like me, is a warguest with two children.

She invited me to visit her, something I couldn't do until we had a more regular routine. Now I've managed that. I found her apartment surprisingly large and comfortable – dark woodwork, walls painted turqoise. I think she gets a lot of help from the university, perhaps also from her husband, a Manchester surgeon. Her name is Margot. Her complexion is slighly sallow, a shade lighter than her dark blonde, almost olive-green hair, combed back tightly into a chignon. This severe hairstyle suits her – she has strong cheek bones. Her family is from Yorkshire, so maybe there's some Viking in her.

Margot's children, a boy and a girl older than mine, are pretty wild. I don't know whether I could paint their portraits, as she first suggested. I would very much like to paint her portrait, though, and to this she finally agreed. So on Sunday afternoon the three of us went there, equipped with paint and canvas board. Even without this extra burden, a streetcar trip remains a hassle. Bettina's stroller has to be folded before we climb the steep steps. Fiona has been trained to climb up first and give tickets or money to the conductor. I follow, carrying the stroller, Bettina (a heavy weight), and that day my paints, canvas board, and the diaper bag. It's something mothers with small children accomplish everywhere, but it needs special practice.

Margot that day wore a maroon trouser suit that enhanced her colouring. Now that so many women wear coveralls to work, trousers worn at home have become acceptable. She looked elegant in this outfit.

Bettina fell asleep in the cot of one of the children, and Fiona played with the girl, the younger of Margot's two. We talked while I made my first rough sketch. She told me that her husband is a doctor but not in the army. The apartment here was found for her by the university (I don't know whether financed as well). She hopes to find work, perhaps at Eaton's, when they are busiest, before Christmas.

When Bettina woke up around four, the children became rambunctious, so I stopped painting. I covered my palette with a damp cloth to preserve the paints on it. Even covered, the palette still fits into the paint box, and the cloth keeps the colours fresh for days. I can't afford to waste them.

When we got home, we had one of those peaceful hours that seem miraculous where there are small children. Fiona had Bemelmans's *Madeline* on her knees and pretended to read the story, as she had seen Alice Kane do it (she really knows it by heart):

> In an old house in Paris – all covered with vines
> there lived twelve little girls – in two straight lines.

Quietly, I opened my paint box, got out the palette with the left-over paints, and in about twenty minutes completed a little painting of Fiona that is better and fresher than most portraits I've done so far.

After the children were put to bed and I'd closed the door to their room, Florence dropped in. She had bought herself some new overshoes and insists that I must now wear her old ones with the furry edge: the kind you slip over your shoes. Luckily, Florence is as tall as I am and her shoe size is the same. She'd been horrified to learn that I walk to work in ordinary shoes. But then, no one in London wore overshoes.

She has a friend, a Cree, whose husband would like her portrait painted. "She's quite different from the Ojibwa children on the Rama Reserve you painted last summer," Florence said,

When we shared a cabin on Lake Couchiching, she and I had rowed over to Rama, towards its little white church, standing deserted among fields of goldenrod. Its steeple top had been shattered by lightning – a bad omen – and the building henceforth stood unused. The unpainted wooden homesteads nearby looked deserted too. We finally found a woman whom I asked whether I might be allowed to paint portraits of her two children for twenty-five cents each. The children who sat for me, Sam and Geraldine Snake, were marvellous models. I've never known children before or since who sat as still as they did.

I thought of Gauguin's paintings of softly moulded golden faces, inscrutable opaque eyes. Hard not to make these beautiful children look like girls in Tahiti. Neither of them spoke a word until they got back to their mother, a friendly woman who told us that she came from the Lake Simcoe island Georgina. She told us that her husband and many men on the reserve had joined the army.

~~

Fiona reading Madeline, *1942 (oil)*

"How about the children," I now asked Florence. "May I bring them along?"

"No," she said. "That's the problem. Sabina can't have children and longs for them. It would make her sad, I think, to have them around. But if your helper, Sylvia, can't come on Sunday, I could spend a few hours here. You'd make twenty-five dollars."

That's the equivalent of a week's wages, so I don't object. I'm curious to meet Sabina, who, Florence says, is married to a scientist of German origin whose parents (like Florence's own) worked in the Orient for years. He's not been interned, so perhaps he was also born there. As a scientist, he probably does useful work for the government.

~ November 28th ~

I now walk to work in my elegant overshoes and take them off at the door, as everyone does around here. Days at the small Queen Street office have been uneventful. Some Inglis workers drop in with union dues or grievances. I collect the first and send them on to the main office; the second I refer to the Seftons. New members are registered and get a file card each. On these cards, addresses have to be changed often, especially for women from out of town. Like me, they have trouble finding rooms and they have problems finding someone to mind their children. These women are strong union supporters. Their pay never equals that of male factory workers, even when they do the same job: welding, riveting, running machines. And where are the female lead hands?

Some Toronto women who do war work come from a sheltered background, have a house of their own, a husband in the army, an allowance as a soldier's wife or as a mother, and relations who help take care of the children. Some are the wives of professionals with quite high salaries. They work, not from dire necessity: their motives are patriotic. Some union women resent this privileged type. "They're playing at doing war work," Beatrice says.

"Maybe they just want to help in some way," I sigh. But I know what she means. At first, Bea took me for one of those women, though she knows better now.

Last Thursday Sweeney stayed overnight. She had, as she often does, volunteered to hand out union leaflets for the night shift. When she finished her day shift, she dropped in at our little office to put in time till the night shift came on. I asked her to come to supper and stay the night, to celebrate my new job and my front room decor.

I'd found some cotton on sale, a bit like my Indian bed cover, enough to make curtains for the bay window, cover a pad for the cabin trunk and cushions for the couch. The place looks cosy to me, but Sweeney finds it bohemian. She likes the kind of furniture one sees at Eaton's.

My cooking facilities are bohemian, that's true. A small gas burner on a card table in the back room, where I boil the cheapest vegetables I can find (potatoes, carrots, peas, beans) together in one pot. If I cook turnip, I put in an apple to sweeten the dish. I then set aside the vegetables in a double boiler with very hot water and quickly cook an omelette or some fish. In the stores there are many more packaged and canned soups and vegetables than one finds in England now. Baked beans are a favourite with the children; so are noodles. Sweeney, like many Americans, thinks a steak is the best dish. I'd have liked to get one for her, but we made do with small chops we bought on the way home.

Sweeney lives on Oakwood, in the northwest of Toronto. It's a long streetcar ride from John Inglis, but she continues living with her large family – her parents, brothers, and sisters. Her earnings helped them during the Depression and probably still do.

After supper she rushed off to distribute her union literature. When she came back, the children were in bed and we could talk. Sweeney is always curious about my childhood. She'd heard about the "Great Inflation" in Germany and somehow equates it with the Depression here, though I tell her it was much earlier, in the twenties. After the First World War, my mother used to get bones from the butcher to boil for soup. Sweeney's mother did the same during the Depression. "She'd pretend they were for the dog," Sweeney said. "The butchers knew better. They always put some aside for a large family like ours."

For sleeping, we pulled out Florence's old couch to its full width. The two sides normally hang down. Propping them up was more complicated than I expected. I put a pile of books under a corner that kept collapsing.

Sweeney curled up on the window seat, my cabin trunk. It's right beside the ventilator that blasts heat into our room from the basement furnace. Sweeney feels the cold; I don't. I usually turn the ventilator flaps so as to prevent the warm air from shooting up. The first thing Sweeney does when she visits me is to reverse their direction. "Heat's included in your rent. Make the most of it," is her advice. "Tell me more about your mother."

"Well, she had this great friend, my godmother, one of the people to whose school she'd come from England. That school was known as Internat: a bit like a convent, but the teachers were not nuns.

"This aunt was resourceful – she always saw the good side of a bad situation. After the war we had very little flour in the house, and every bit of it had to be used. She made soup with it. If the flour was lumpy, she'd call the soup dumpling soup. If it was burnt and brown, it became 'chocolate soup.'

"One day, Mother found mouse dirt in the flour and asked my aunt Lulu if it could be sifted out. 'You could make a cake,' my aunt suggested. 'And call it seedcake.'"

"And did they?"

"We never found out. They laughed so hard when they told that story."

"Your aunt sounds like a great woman. She could be Irish."

That is Sweeney's greatest compliment. It includes many things: a sense of humour, of the absurd and incongruous; a combination of the poetic and the practical; a kind of heroism; the voice of Bing Crosby.

"Our family name was Davidson. That's a Scottish name, but to the Nazis it sounded Jewish. Like most people, we had to produce a family tree. It turned out that our Scottish ancestors had settled in Poland, then moved west. But then my family could not move out as I did. I went to my English grandmother and married an English artist. So my nationality changed; theirs didn't."

Sweeney wanted to know more about the school to which my mother had come from Cheshire in 1903, when she was seventeen years old.

"It was run by Aunt Lulu's mother and aunt. She was brought up very strictly, Aunt Lulu. Young ladies had to sit bolt upright, wherever they went. But on a train trip back from Switzerland Lulu had become tired and leaned back against the upholstery. When she got back home, her mother found lice in her hair. She was fanatic about bugs. She used such a sharp lotion on Lulu's hair that the front part never grew back. Lulu had to wear a hairpiece all her life. The pompadour hair style made that easy for a while. She continued with that style all through her life."

"Ridiculous," Sweeney mumbled, half-asleep. "What kids don't get lice in their hair at school? You treat it with kerosene. Everyone knows that."

"That hairpiece had a name: Wilhelm."

"After the kaiser?"

"Maybe. Who knows? I never thought of that. This "Wilhelm" was taken off at night. For us children, my aunt then changed into another person. Her hair hung down her back in white whisps. And by the time we knew her, she also took out her teeth. They'd broken when she fell down the stairs."

"People call that accident-prone." Sweeney's head was drooping. "I think we should go to bed. Or have you some coffee somewhere to keep us awake?"

I tiptoed to the back room and by the dim glow of the night light put on the kettle. I have no coffee, just a substitute called Postum; it won't keep us awake. Anyway, Sweeney made preparations to go to bed, and we arranged bed clothes on the fully extended pull out couch.

"Will you be warm enough with those blankets? Wait, I'll put my winter coat over the foot end of the bed."

The kettle started to hiss. I went to get the coat and the hot drink from the back room. "Don't bother," Sweeney, said and for a moment I thought she meant the Postum. She hates it; she likes good coffee. But she took the cup. "I won't need the coat. I get very hot in bed." This is one of Sweeney's beer-parlour remarks. Another, milder one is "I feel naked without my earrings."

I went on with my own story: "When my aunt came to say goodnight to us, I always thought she'd changed into someone else, with a different mouth and different hair."

"Shut up about your aunt and get me some sort of nightgown. I could sleep in my underwear, of course; it wouldn't be the first time."

"I will if you get off my chest," I said. We started giggling again over this. "I mean, off my trunk."

From the cabin trunk I now pulled a heavy red flannel nightgown I brought from Britain, prepared for an icy climate. I haven't yet found a place cold enough to wear it. When Sweeney came back from the bathroom down the hall, she'd changed into a sort of Santa Claus with that red gown and the silvery knob of a head.

"All we need now is Bing's 'White Christmas.' You got enough records here. Why don't you have that? I'll get it for your Christmas present."

That was what I feared. "Sweeney, with all your relations, don't think of us, please. Think of them. And these records here are on loan. They're not mine. So's the player."

I put out the light by the main switch (I'm short of lamps), and we lay in the dark, a good atmosphere for personal questions about Sweeney's love life. I wanted to find out how much she cared for Bill Sefton. But when I approached the subject, she became even more sleepy.

"I have to get up at the crack of dawn," she murmured. "So, good-night."

Well.

I was woken by a crash and, from an air-raid habit, thought at first the room was shaking because of bombs. But it was only the bed. My covers were pulled sharply to Sweeney's side, and she herself had disappeared altogether. The rickety legs of the old couch had given way. She lay on the floor, convulsed with laughter, unharmed, to my great relief, and not even swearing in beer-parlour style.

I put on the light, and we reconstructed the bed. I shoved an orange crate full of books under Sweeney's side. "That bed never came from our garage," she remarked.

"No, it didn't. It got a little rusty on Florence's balcony."

I needn't have worried about giving Sweeney a decent breakfast (no coffee). When I woke up, she was gone. She'd left at six, when we were all still asleep. I knocked over the box of books as I jumped up to make our porridge.

~ December 14th ~

Went to see Sabina about the portrait. She and her husband live in the large, airy top flat of an old house. It's been beautifully redecorated and the objects in their rooms – chairs, tables, sideboard – look like antiques. They have that personal quality of old furniture lovingly made and lovingly used.

Florence told me that Sabina is eight years older than her husband, but you would never think it. She looks young and fragile and somehow oriental. Her features are more aquiline than those of the Rama Ojibwas. She has clear, light brown skin; her black eyes are rather small; her hair is dark brown rather than black; her wrists and ankles are fine-boned.

While I set out my paints, Sabina talked about a film starring Ingrid Bergman. "Swedish, like Garbo," I murmured absently. Garbo may have starred in lousy films, but to me she's unforgettable.

Sabina prefers Bergman: "She has the face of a child, those soft contours. That's what's so beautiful about her."

Keeping in mind Florence's warning, I tried to avoid the subject of childlike qualities. I am blessed with children; Sabina wants a child and can't have one.

Can one be both a mother and an artist? I have a sharp memory of the pianist Eileen Joyce, who from 1939 shared our co-op. She stopped briefly in her ten-hour daily practice of Rachmaninov's second piano concerto (the one used in Noel Coward's film *Brief Encounter*). I remember her standing outside her ground-floor room, which held nothing I more than her grand piano, her bed, and a vast Victorian wardrobe, as she watched me carrying Fiona, a heavy baby, down the stairs. "I have a child that age," she said. "I've left both the baby and my husband."

I was shaken by the news. I knew Eileen had been married, but nothing about a child. She was the daughter of an Australian miner whose fellow workers collected enough to send her to England to study music. When living with us, she practised almost non-stop for the noon-hour concerts at London's National Gallery, taking turns with Myra Hess, right through heavy air raids.

Here now was Sabina, who envied me my children.

As I was painting, she told me about her life. She had been married before; her first husband drowned in a sailing accident. Her second husband works overtime because there's such a demand for people with his qualifications. I'd wondered why I did not see him on Sunday, but he did come in later. He looks as young as a schoolboy, except for a wide, pleasant, determined mouth. There are two deep lines either side of it.

Sabina at once excused herself and went to turn on the bath. They always have a bath together, she said, when he gets home. I thought of bombed-out friends in London who'd come in for a bath (sometimes in pairs). Until we kept the tub permanently filled to facilitate pumping away incendiary bombs on the roof.

I took my leave. I didn't want to leave Florence with the children for more than a couple of hours anyway. When I got back, I did what I'd done after Margot's portrait session. I used the leftover paints on my palette to make an oil sketch of Florence. I want to do something for her. The painting did not go as well as that of Fiona though.

"How did you get on at Sabina's?" Florence wanted to know.

"Oh, I had to stop when her husband came home. They went and had a bath together. Is that common practice here?"

Florence shook her head. I began painting over parts of the sketch where perhaps I should not, if the oils had not dried. This is the danger point where one should stop and let the fresh colours dry first.

It was getting dark early, as it does before Christmas. The stores downtown are full of presents and Christmas music. "When we were children, we had to make our own presents. For every aunt and uncle and grandparent. The number of pen wipers and calendars we produced was staggering." I began to pack up my paints.

"Will you make a present for Florence, Fiona? With your crayons. But don't let Bettina have them. She will eat them. And don't let her have those little scissors. They're just for you."

Of course, Bettina now wanted those scissors and began to howl. Florence promised her a blunt little pair for Christmas, but that didn't mean much to someone so young, We gave her coloured Plasticine for the first time and she didn't eat that. So she must have learnt something from Sylvia.

~ December 19th ~

Sweeney invited me to go to midnight mass with her. I've never attended midnight mass at Christmas. In Germany the real candles on our tree were lit at dusk on Christmas Eve, and in that mystery-filled twilight we opened our presents. In England we waited until the morning of Christmas Day.

How solemn and festive Christmas nights had been in Spain without the commercial noise and glitter. Women in black shawls over their heads had quietly gone to mass. For presents and for the almond confection called Turon, you waited until January 7th, the Fiesta de los Reyes.

On Sunday I took the children to the Art Gallery of Toronto to have another look at Varley's portrait *Vera*. There was a festive Christmas atmosphere. Beautiful handmade Christmas cards by Canadian artists were displayed near the gallery entrance, linocuts and woodcuts, most of them in colour. There were also some in black and white, in an Expressionist style familiar to me. Fritz Brandtner's linocut *Christmas 1942* makes no pretense that there is "peace on earth." Above a battlefield of broken bodies, a scene of desolation, float three angels, shielding their eyes with their hands, mourning over the carnage. I am told that Brandtner has been influential in the contemporary art movements at Montreal. I found no other work by him. In Germany he would have been declared one of the "decadents," like all the Expressionists.

I asked about Varley's portrait *Vera* but found it is on tour. The person who told me this was also looking at the Brandtner linocut. She spoke English with a strong accent, a woman of perhaps forty, who had an extraordinary air of vigour about her. She seemed to know Brandtner quite well.

"He opened an art centre for children who can't afford art. Who haven't that privilege. Or any other."

Christmas 1942
*(linocut by
Fritz Brandtner)*

"It was Bethune who really started that." her companion re-marked. "He, and Marian Scott."

"Of course. I know," the woman snapped.

Her companion was a tall man with a very high forehead and very light eyes. He too spoke with a strong accent. "Let's look at your painting," he suggested.

So this woman was a painter. I wanted to see her work. If it was in this gallery, she must be fairly well known. For the moment I could not follow the pair, though, because of the children. All that space at the gallery made them want to run, and run they did. Only their unwieldy snowsuits and boots prevented them from escaping altogether. Still clumsy, Bettina runs faster than her short legs allow and falls over her toes. Then she starts to howl. I had to do some consoling, took off some of the children's heavy gear, and went back to the cloakroom.

When we caught up with the couple, they were standing in front of a bright sunny painting in a room that showed recent Canadian art. By the time I got there, walking slowly, holding each little girl by the hand, they were about to move on, but I could still hear the woman's unusual voice.

"People say to me, 'What fun it must be to paint.' It's not fun, It's mostly pain." Yes, I thought. It's pain because you nev-er achieve what you see in your mind.

When an artist comes close to the inner image, somehow you know it. The painting they looked at had that quality. There was something about it that struck me as essentially European, that I don't find in much Canadian art. Recent European, I should say. The painting is full of light, like a Monet, but it has moved beyond Monet in structure and authority. It has firm contours. This woman, I'm sure, studied Cézanne. There is only one artist in Canada who is that close to recent European movements, and that is Maurice. He evokes the Fauves, who are so much more joyful than the German Expressionists.

The woman's painting is of a clearing in the woods – an inti-mate clearing, seen close, no horizon line. One knows it's spring: the profusion of growth is due to that season, the sun, the amplitude of forest soil. None of the artist's pain shows. There is an almost ringing joy. The abstract nature of the

painting has the secret geom-
etry of music.

"Woods," Fiona said. She
too liked the painting.

I looked carefully at the
signature, but it was hard to
read. The surname of this
woman is Clark, an ordinary
English name. But the first
name, Paraskeva, is probably
Russian. Slav, certainly.

Paraskeva Clark

In the next room of the
gallery I felt a shock. I was con-
fronted with her true persona. The pair had moved on somewhere, but the painter had remained. She appeared in a magnificent self-portrait, the painting of a woman with a defiant spirit.
Dress and hat are black, accentuating the Slavic blond features
that in the bulky winter clothes of the woman I'd just seen were
less noticeable. The vigour of the painting was like a trumpet
call. Here was a woman not afraid to take on the world.

I was glad we'd come. I'd not seen *Vera*, but I'd seen a portrait I was not likely to forget. Painted recently, painted by a
woman I'd actually seen in person. She's from another country,
but there's none of the duality there of people whose minds are
divided, torn in two by this war. She's all of one piece.

I went back to the front desk to have another look at the
Brandtner linocut that so vividly reminds me of the carnage that
tears us in two. It's not for sale and I can't afford it anyway.

"There'll be a party at the Seftons," Sweeney told me at the
union office. "Christmas night, after midnight mass at
Sherbourne Street church. We're all invited."

"Me too?" I asked. "I'm not a Catholic."

"Nor is Charlie Millard. He'll be there."

I've not met Millard, the head of the Canadian Steelworkers,
but I've seen photographs of his square, good-natured,
shrewd face.

"And," Sweeney went on with special emphasis, "Clarence Gillis will be there. He's special. Member of Parliament for Antigonish in Nova Scotia. That's a coal-mining area. When Parliament is in session and he's in Ottawa, he comes here to visit."

"Is he from Cape Breton, where some people still speak Gaelic?" I asked.

"Search me. Why would so many Scots there be Catholic?" she wondered.

"They supported the wrong side: a Catholic pretender to the throne."

"Ask Clarie why they and the Irish there were the first union people in the coal mines. They had lots of troubles."

"Well, I'm relieved to know that not all union people in Canada are Irish. I was beginning to worry."

Sweeney saw that I'd adopted her style. "The best are," she topped my remark.

"OK. You convinced me. I'll go to midnight mass with you."

"I'll come by for you, at your house," Sweeney offered generously.

~ December 26th ~

There's more food and drink around here at Christmas, so more parties than in Europe. Sylvia is going to a party herself, so she recommended an old lady, Mrs Larkin, who will mind children on that particular night only. It's her contribution, Sylvia says, to the Christmas spirit. So that some of the many lonely mothers can get out one night. I arranged via Sylvia to have Mrs Larkin come in around nine, after the children's bedtime, to stay the whole night if ncessary. I didn't, then, think for even a moment that I'd be away that long. But I was.

When I returned just before eight on the morning of Christmas Day – yesterday, in fact – I felt that my life had changed. I was walking on air. And it wasn't due to love. It wasn't due to alcohol. It's hard to know the exact cause. There were times when I felt like this in Barcelona, when we'd talked through whole nights and walked down into town from below the Tibidabo to see the sun rise over the Mediterranean. But since then much has happened to shatter that belief in human goodness we held so firmly then.

It was almost ten p.m. before Sweeney and I left my apartment. By that time Mrs Larkin had settled in my only comfortable chair, a rocker sold to me by Frank Hines. I asked her to stretch out on the couch when she got tired.

"I'm a light sleeper," she said. "If there's a peep from the children, I'd hear that."

I told her where she could reach me by telephone and asked her to be careful about gas. The gas burner in the children's room is a constant worry for me. I always leave the window above it slightly open, to the landlady's dismay (it affects the thermostat of the furnace).

"I won't touch it. I brought a thermos with tea. I needn't put on a kettle. Anyway, I wouldn't want to use your sugar rations."

"Oh, rations aren't so bad here."

She nodded her head. "Yes. We have much to be thankful for. Compared with over there."

I thought of Brandtner's three angels, the carnage they mourn.

Sweeney and I stepped out into the clear night. Each street light had an aura, a rainbow mist, around it. A brightly lit, tightly packed streetcar took us along Queen to Church Street, where we had to change. In that section downtown there seems to be a bar at every corner. The air was saturated with an overpowering smell of alcohol. Loud singing came from the steamy entrance of one tavern.

"Soldiers on leave," Sweeney shrugged. She looked pretty, I thought, in a fitted black coat with a narrow fur collar. She wears her hair in what is called an "upsweep," and it could pass for platinum blond. Long earrings dangled from her ears (she "feels naked without them").

In the next streetcar our clothes began to steam. We had to walk a block to the large, brightly lit church. I had expected the hushed, candle-lit atmosphere of the old church where we used to listen to Bach's Christmas Oratorio.

There were candles here too, but in the brilliant light from other sources they hardly showed. A profusion of metallic ornaments reflected the light and doubled its impact. The high ceiling glittered, reminiscent of baroque churches in southern Germany, but without their exuberant paintings. I had never gone to church with my Catholic grandmother in the Rhineland, Her family had come from Alsace, where certain churches were shared by Protestants and Catholics – something Sweeney simply cannot believe. All Irish history is against it.

It seemed to me, though, that the Anglican Christmas service is not very different from the Catholic mass. I thought of the sedate rows of Ovenden schoolgirls in their dark blue uniforms walking to the Anglican church in Barrie on Sundays. Daylight and candles had mixed there too. Perhaps I simply miss the mysterious candle lit Christmas Eve of my own childhood, something that will never return. Who, these days, would have real candles on an inflammable evergreen in any living room?

I remained seated in the back row while people patiently lined up for communion and quietly returned, their eyes lowered. In Europe it would be morning now. The sun would rise and shine indiscriminately on peaceful scenes and scenes of carnage alike. In the trenches of the 1914 war they sang Christmas carols at night and murdered one another the next day. It will be no different this time.

The Seftons' apartment is not far from the church. I am still conditioned by the memory of miners' cottages in Wales. My Liverpool aunts ran a tea room in Wales. They spoke of miners as people who, "if you give them a bath tub, they fill it with coal." They complained, during the first war year, because they were asked to put up evacuated working-class children: "They brought in vermin." The children's diet had been "fish and chips" or "bread and cheese," and they would not eat anything else.

The orderly prosperity of the Seftons' apartment reminded me a little of the farmhouse where I spent two weeks after Bettina's birth. A large brick house on the outskirts of Barrie, it was owned by two retired nurses who did all their own housework, as even prosperous women here do. They kept their kitchen spanking clean, and their appliances were much like those the Seftons' have in their kitchen, though the farmhouse furniture was old, probably inherited, while here all was solid, well kept, new-looking. On the dining-room table there were platters of sandwiches and cakes, enough for a threshing party.

Mrs Sefton, though a city woman, reminded me a little of the women I met at the Barrie Women's Institute. That must be due to the long rural and short urban history of Canadian families, conditioned by a small-town atmosphere between both. A widow, tall, blue-eyed, soft-spoken, she courteously asked after my children. I, in my turn, asked her whether, during the Kirkland Lake strike, she had been worried about her sons. According to the newspapers, things could have turned ugly.

"So worried that I moved north to keep house for them. Strikes are very bad for any kind of home life. Bad for married couples, but also for those who are not married."

Seemingly never-ending quantities of beer appeared, taken from a gigantic icebox by the Sefton brothers. A girl who I thought must be Dutch came to offer me some. I thought I'd seen her somewhere. Her name is Elaine Melhuish. Sweeney tells me that she works in the office of the CCF "that liaises with the unions," as Sweeney puts it. So perhaps I've seen her at the Lansdowne office. She has that soft blondness, those delicate rounded facial contours, that make poets describe this type of girl as "a rose." Her voice too is soft, her speech cultured (Irish?).

Mr Walker, the American representative of the Steelworkers, was not at this party. Millard has some of his solidity but is also unmistakably Canadian. A down-to-earth union man, miles removed from the Welsh miners I've seen but never known, yet not an intellectual. He is said to mistrust the intellectuals in the CCF (Jolliffe, Coldwell?). People like Barker Fairley (communist intellectuals) would be anathema to him.

Sadly, naively, I at one time believed that, if the socialist and communists had made common cause in Germany, Hitler would never have come close to winning. But then, even in Spain that had never been possible.

Millard was treated with friendly respect by everyone at this party. But for Clarence Gillis, the MP from Nova Scotia, there was something like reverence. Elaine Melhuish listened with rapt attention to his stories of early union battles in the Maritimes.

"I knew there was someone in that hall who intended to shoot me. Before starting my speech, I laid a gun across the table in front of me (it wasn't loaded, but who would know?). A precaution, I said, should anyone break up the meeting." This kind of union history sounded more like Germany or Spain.

Bill and Larry brought plates with more food, and more drinks. Sweeney and I occupied the same easy chair, she in it, I on the wide armrest.

"Let me fill up your glass, Marguerite," Larry said in his husky voice.

"Don't mind if you do," she grinned. Larry is the only one among us who always calls Sweeney "Marguerite." He turned and reached Elaine with his tray, and for a moment these two beautiful young people stood as within a charmed circle. Probably not much younger than I am, but to me they seemed to belong to another generation. They were as yet unharmed by the destructive world that breaks up families and friendships. At that charmed moment they represented for me all that is lovable in a new and better world.

Elaine looked at a little watch that glinted on her wrist, protruding from the long sleeve of her dark green dress, a beautiful dress of soft wool that set off her rose and golden colouring. "I have to go home," she said. "It's morning. It's been morning for some time."

"Wait just a moment and I'll drive you home," Larry offered. "I'm one of the few lucky car owners."

"I was going to share a taxi with Clarence. He has to get back to his hotel."

"Taxis are hard to come by tonight. I'll take you both. Just a sec. I'll get your coats."

Sweeney extracted herself from the depth of her armchair. I sank into it as she walked over to talk to Larry.

"Of course, of course," he said. "And you, have you a ride home?"

"Yes. A bunch of us go to the far northwest of Toronto."

"You're certainly in the sticks, up there, "Larry grinned. "North of Eglinton, beyond Bathurst. Have they plowed the fields there yet?"

"Not any more," Sweeney said cheerfully. "Too many bungalows in the way."

Sweeney had suggested that Larry include me among his passengers. She knew I couldn't afford a taxi, and streetcars don't run between one and six in the morning, The morning of Christmas Day. Larry's car was parked at the front of the house, the engine kept warm by a couple of rugs. He helped Elaine and me into the back. Clarence sat in front as they drove north through dark and quiet streets.

The area around Elaine's house looked familiar. It is probably not far from John Hall's, where I'd taken my children from Merton Street – a prosperous part of Forest Hill. "Come in for some coffee," Elaine suggested.

We left our overshoes and coats in a conventional vestibule. A few lamps in the Melhuish living room gave a subdued light. Elaine turned them off so that only the electric bulbs on the Christmas tree remained, making a golden halo of her hair. I know real candles are a fire hazard and not allowed these days, but I still miss them.

Clarence Gillis settled in one of the deep easy chairs. In the dim light, lines of fatigue could be seen in his long face with its square jaw. I have a feeling that he does not trust me. It's quite a new experience. But I am a foreigner with a discernable accent. Perhaps in Nova Scotia, close to the Atlantic Ocean, spy scares, even threats of invasion, are more commonly accepted Perhaps small communities that have to fight for their life are more susceptible to suspicions of all kinds.

I have nothing to show any affiliation with parties of the left in Europe. Our London co-op vaguely supported a dimly perceived left, and there were Fabians in Bloomsbury who bought our art. Rudolf Steiner's anthroposophical movement, to which many of our German friends belonged, would not mean anything to a Nova Scotia union organizer. That movement had been outlawed by the organized Nazis, resisted only by even better organized social democrats. Clarence would have thought of Steiner adherents as "babes in the wood." And he would have been right.

While Larry and Elaine went to the kitchen to get a tray with coffee cups, Clarence asked me some careful questions about my background. What could I say? My mother is English. So is my husband. No, he's American now. They have the same name but are not related. I'm not Jewish, not a political refugee. An evacuee from the London Blitz with two small children. He still looked doubtful.

The atmosphere warmed as soon as the golden pair returned. Larry deposited the tray with the cups on a low table, and Elaine knelt down beside it, close to the tree, to pour the coffee from the pot she'd brought. A soft, pensive atmosphere enveloped us for the next hour or so. Time seemed to stand still. The conversation was desultory, a quiet drawing together that, to my surprise, included me, the stranger. The others knew each other through their work, but in those office hours there was always the pressure of time that now fell off them as if by magic.

Larry was at the centre. He talked about Kirkland Lake, the bitter atmosphere of the strike that had severed his relationship with a girl on the "other side," a lawyer's daughter.

Clarence talked of injured miners in the Cape Breton mines who never received compensation. Of their widows who received no pension. Inadequate safety in the mines was glossed over by the companies.

"A pit pony was worth ten miners. The miners used to shovel coal, lying on their backs in water."

"It was civil war, trying to unionize. The British Empire Steel Corporation – the company later known as Dominion Steel and Coal – they had their own police force. A network of spies. They were hand in glove with the government of that day. Still are."

"It was piecework, whether you shovelled coal into rail cars or worked in the steel plant. We paid for our own shovels, our own explosives, and when we got sick – as we all did – for our own doctor and hospital bills."

"And now they expect those underpaid people to work a seventh day free, loading convoy ships in Sydney harbour. Their war effort, as good patriots!"

I thought of the Asturian miners, of 1934 when I lived in Barcelona. How little has changed. I began to talk about that strike. Clarence asked how I had managed not to belong to any of the parties in Catalonia.

"Oh," I groaned. "There were so many. And I was so young. So dumb and confused. I came from a very conservative background."

"So does my family," Elaine consoled me.

"Have they checked you out?" Clarence finally asked outright. "Fingerprints and all that? They trust people who were in Spain even less than those who come from fascist countries."

"Oh yes, I went on my own to get all that done. One has to, for a visa to enter the United States. I wanted to join my husband there. American friends who'd known us in Europe offered to sponsor me. But no luck. They go by country of birth. Here I am a British subject, there an enemy alien. Yet my father's family, the Davidsons, had come from Scotland – probably around the time yours came to Cape Breton.

"My political education really started here, in a small Ontario town. I lived at a girls' boarding school, but I spent a lot of time with a family who started credit unions, that kind of thing. They didn't get much help from the government here for that. They had a grant from the Carnegie Institute."

"But look how Carnegie made his money," Clarence remarked into the deep silence.

Then the noise of buses and streetcars on wintry roads, however distant, reminded us that it was morning. "I have to get home," I said. "There's someone minding my children. She should go home now."

Clarence too had to be back at his hotel, to prepare for a train journey.

As Elaine helped me into my coat, Larry laid his hands on her shoulders for just a moment. Even more than at the Seftons I felt their connection and mine to them. An electrical charge seemed to go through us all. But overtired, over-sensitive, I may have imagined it.

The chain broke. Elaine stood in the light of the open door and waved to us as we struggled out into the snowy morning.

Larry scraped the windshield of his car. He turned up the heat, but it was still icy. He drove in silence along St Clair, then south. Suddenly, out of the blue, he remarked, "That girl, Marguerite Sweeney, I really like her."

"Yes, she's a wonderful friend," I agreed.

"A good organizer. A fine person. If only Bill ..."

He left this interesting sentence unfinished. We passed Dundas and he had to find our house on MacDonell.

There was a grey dawn now. The children, not yet conditioned to the excitement of Christmas morning, were still asleep. So was Mrs Larkin, on the rocker on which I'd left her.

"Oh, you should have made yourself comfortable on the couch," I reproached her. She rubbed her eyes.

"I did lie down," she said. "I just got up a little while ago in case the kids ... you know ... wanted their presents."

She glanced at the two tiny socks that hung above the unused fireplace. Their contents: an orange, three figs, some raisins. She gave me back some of the money I handed her.

"Buy something for the kiddies," she said.

"Thank you, I will. And why not have breakfast with us."

"No, I have to go. I have an old aunt who is dependent on me."

Age is relative, I thought. I could not imagine any one much older than Mrs Larkin, but she is probably only in her sixties, healthy and strong, a sturdy white-haired woman who, wrapped in a shawl and a heavy cloth coat, cheerfully marched out into the cold morning.

A branch Florence had cut from the bottom of her spruce tree was our only Christmas ornament, decorated with Fiona's paper cut-outs. Under it I'd placed the parcel that had arrived in the mail. The room was very warm; the slats of the register that blows hot air from the furnace into our room had been left open for Mrs Larkin. How wonderful to come back to a space all one's own and not to worry about being cold.

Mrs Larkin had probably needed the heat. It was so warm that the children could stay in their pyjamas while they opened their presents. The floor was soon covered with bits of paper. There's a colouring book from Florence, and a pair of those blunt little scissors I'd promised Bettina. And from Garth, two little dresses, beautifully made, not warm enough for winter. But later the little girls will be able to "dress up" as if going to a party.

I sat drinking the cocoa I'd made for breakfast and looked on, glowing within our own charmed circle of love.

1943

Our point of gravity has shifted. In Toronto I now feel like a
visitor from the country, instead of a "visitor from another
country." My Barrie friends now look to me like "my family in
the country." Going back there from a place where I am independent seems quite different from being there as a dependent
war guest. I'm beginning to understand the "ingratitude of the
poor" that English country families complained about, when,
during the first war years, poverty-stricken evacuees returned to
their slums. Their homes.

For our first trip back to Barrie, we were to meet David Smith
at Thornhill, a place where Highway 7 from Hamilton meets
Yonge Street. Up Yonge we took a rattling streetcar on tracks
that once served an old railway from Toronto to Lake Simcoe.
On long open stretches this tram speeds ups, swaying recklessly,
like a crazy old battleship.

David, who'd visited his father in Hamilton, was to meet us
at a historical roadside inn. This inn, a well-proportioned,
white clapboard building, doesn't really take advantage of its
fine Thornhill location, its quiet charm. We sat at a table covered by a checked, none-too-clean tablecloth and ordered the
only food available: hot dogs. In Germany these sausages made
from remnants of beef and pork are called *Frankfurters*; here
they're sometimes known as wieners. There they're served with
sauerkraut; here we ate them wrapped in long, white, tasteless
buns (you can have mustard with them, or pickles or ketchup).

David was late. In Hamilton he'd picked up an important
visitor: Agnes Macphail, at one time the only female MP in
Canada. I read somewhere that she was always plainly dressed,
always wore the same navy blue suit in Parliament. She must
have taken that criticism to heart. She looked stunning, almost
royal, enthroned on the front seat of David's old grey car. Like

royalty, she sat bolt upright, her black cloak, lined in bright red, contrasting dramatically with her strong, wavy, silvery hair.

The children and I crowded into the back seat. I reminded Fiona that she would soon see her little friend Marta Smith again. Marta is a year and half older than Fiona, just old enough to be an older sister. When Fiona played at pulling books out of the Smiths' well-stocked shelves, Marta dutifully put them all back again. Books were precious in that house. Some of Marta's useful clothes were passed on to Fiona (waterproof leggings and boots, warm socks, warm underwear). I am now able to buy some of these things myself, and every piece I buy fills me with pride.

Like many houses in Barrie, the Smiths' Barn is surrounded by tall trees. David parked the car under a huge maple, but as the house is built against a hillside, the tree forms a shelter just below it. We scrambled up the path to the front door, and Edith and Marta rushed out to meet us – without outdoor clothes or boots, as they often do.

The tumultuous welcome between the children was interrupted by sleigh bells from a cutter, a light one-horse sleigh that stopped at the gate. I recognized it at once as that of Ovenden's headmistress, Mary Elgood. She emerged from her fur wrappings just long enough to invite us to the school for tea the next day. Then she shook the reins, and the cutter gave a quick jerk and flew up the hill, as if defying gravity. Leo and Spring, Miss Elgood's two dogs, followed, barking merrily. The ringing of bells, dogs barking, children's voices, the clean glistening snow, and winter sunshine combined in one of those old fashioned winter scenes conjured up in old prints. As if winter nowadays is much greyer than it used to be.

In The Barn the large open spaces have been left undivided, so that there is, downstairs, a large living room with a fireplace, divided from the kitchen area only by bookshelves and a dining table. Upstairs there's a large bedroom to which Marta's little room and a bathroom have been added at the back, where the ground is a storey higher than in front (barns are often built that way to facilitate bringing in hay). The large, undivided space upstairs has always been a great temptation for the children to run back and forth. They did so after supper, stimulated by the high spirits that precede "going to bed." Bettina stumbled back and forth behind the two friends, Marta and Fiona, like a clumsy puppy.

The adults had not yet finished their early supper, timed so that Miss Macphail could attend a special meeting of the Women's Institute with David, who is often the only male at these meetings. I was afraid the children's rambunctuousness might disturb them and ran upstairs to quiet them down. From

Agnes Macphail
with fellow MPP
Eamon Park

up there I could hear Miss Macphail's stentorian tones (David was getting ready to drive her to the meeting): "Wherever David goes, I go."

Holding Bettina and taking Fiona's hand to stop her wild running, I watched from the window as David and Agnes Macphail walked down to the car.

There's no end to the Smiths' generosity as hosts. We three settled in Marta's room, and Marta slept with her parents.

⁓⁓⁓

At one time I'd wondered whether Ovenden School, in its experimental beginnings before World War I, had been a little like Prior's Field in Britain, the school started by Aldous Huxley's mother, Julia. The emancipated women, including Garth's mother (who spent all of World War I here), may have brought a special kind of philosophy to the school in its early days. I knew that Dé, my mother-in-law, had been a suffragette, that she'd known Bertrand Russell's educational experiments. But

76

the school is larger now and has become more conventional. Boarding schools are not common here. People who send their children to private schools are usually wealthy and often conservative.

I thought about this as we walked over to the school, across the main street of Barrie from The Barn, to have tea with Miss Elgood and Miss Ingram. I'd hardly ever visited their special drawing room, Senior School's holiest of holies, while I lived in the Junior House. Its chintz-covered furniture, the brass sparkling near the fireplace, conjured up my grandmother's sitting room in England.

I hoped the children would behave. They looked sweet, once their heavy winter gear had been peeled off. They wore the new dresses Garth had sent from New York. Those who remember Garth and his sister when they were small, during World War I, always point out Fiona's likeness to that earlier Fiona, whom I'd never met (she died aged thirteen at an English boarding school). Bettina, changed from a dark-haired baby to a plump, blond toddler, also reminds them of Garth. She's still restless and rambunctuous, so I was prepared not to stay long.

Neither of the two headmistresses cares especially for young children, so their relationship with the Junior House was at one remove. Mary Elgood has a strong relationship with the senior girls of the school. She teaches Latin and English and, with Elsie Raikes, has formed a drama group that last year performed *Twelfth Night* with real distinction. Miss Ingram, who teaches math, wears frilly blouses, and controls the school's housekeeping, evokes images of Gertrude Stein's Alice Toklas. Mary Elgood is not as heavy as Gertrude Stein but has a similar leonine head. The exterior of a horse-loving Englishwoman in her person hides a broad range: the politics of a Violet Bonham Carter, the dramatic speech of an Edith Sitwell.

The two are not unlike the spinsters who'd presided over my mother's school in Cheshire at the turn of the century. They encouraged her musical talent. They suggested her going to Germany to study the language and, if possible, the country's most renowned gift, its music. When Maud Lee Williams came to the Darmstadt finishing school for girls, she found that it was run by a pair of similarly intrepid women, two sisters who became her greatest friends.

Miss Elgood is tactful in her questions about Garth. She probably guesses that we may not be able to join him, though that was my official reason for leaving the school. Her old friend, Garth's mother, had come to Canada, leaving an artist husband in New York, and I think she guesses that our situation is somewhat the same.

One of Garth's most attractive watercolours, of children playing ball in a late afternoon light, hangs above her fireplace. His Prix de Rome had been for sculpture, and his London studio had been used mainly for sculpture portraits. The clay of unfinished works had to be moist so that he could continue working on them. They were covered by cloths moistened daily and, shrouded, looked mysterious, like ghosts. I'd brought a finished portrait of a Canadian girl with me on the boat. It broke on the way. Her parents, who commissioned it, refuse to accept it, though Garth has tried to rework it (Most probably because Garth didn't join the army and gave up his British citizenship).

It was late afternoon when we walked back to The Barn, on the little road I know so well, its great trees now bare. I wondered whether Agnes Macphail had left. There was no sign of her. Another visitor, a tall young man in soldier's uniform, sat by the fireplace, a visitor from nearby Camp Borden.

"This is David Woodsworth," Edith called over her shoulder, busy with supper, her hair flying as she moved quickly from oven to counter to icebox.

"Can't we help?" the young man and I asked in chorus.

"David has scrubbed the vegetables, and the roast is in the oven. You could start feeding the children, if you like."

This we did. We placed cushions on a couple of chairs, and Marta brought a big telephone book for Bettina to sit on. Edith handed plates of food across the partition between kitchen and living room (the bookshelves that had kept Fiona and Marta busy on former visits). The children went upstairs after their meal, while we had a leisurely dinner. We heard them running around up there, but Marta would see to it that they didn't fall down the steps.

After I put my two to bed, I helped David Woodworth wash the dishes. He's a nephew of the man who started the CCF in western Canada. His parents were missionaries in the East. He was brought up in Japan.

Recent papers had featured horror stories about Japanese atrocities. Similar stories were written about Germans earlier in the war. As I was drying the brown pottery plates and stacking them back on the shelf, I remarked that I had difficulty believing some of these stories. The teachers and neighbours I'd known in our small community would have been incapable of committing such atrocities. "I find it easier to believe such stories about the Japanese," I said. "Is that because I don't know them?"

"It surely is," David Woodsworth said. I could not fathom his expression – it was both fierce and sad. "The neighbours we had in Japan were the kindest, gentlest, most sensitive people I've known."

I thought that by now I'd overcome most prejudices. Prejudices make life simple; they prevent doubt and duality. Things are either right or wrong, black or white.

After young Woodsworth had gone back to camp, Edith told me that he'd suffered from shell shock earlier in the war. Shell shock is treated with more understanding these days than in World War I. It is surely one of the major war wounds. In David Woodsworth's case, the military authorities discovered, just in time, his knowledge of Japanese and made him a translator.

Edith is a westerner. The Japanese in British Columbia, she said, had not supported the enemy. They were born and raised in Canada and considered themselves loyal citizens. In a fit of national hysteria, they were deprived of all they owned: their houses, land, boats, all property. Families were separated and herded into camps. I listened with distress. I seldom read the papers and only vaguely understood that some Germans had also been interned, even some Canadians who sympathized with fascism. Was it because the Japanese could be easily identified that they had undergone such harsh treatment? Or had it some-

thing to do with the prime minister's political motives? (He'd
admired Hitler at one time.)

∿

The next morning, Elsie Raikes
came in her small car to take us
out to her log cabin. Elsie went
to Ovenden School when my
mother-in-law taught art there.
She was encouraged by the
school to go university in the
early twenties, and later came
back to teach. She's also the
school nurse. She was one of
the first people I met after we

*Elsie Raikes, 1941
(oil, painted with
Fiona's help)*

arrived. Fiona had to stay in bed because of bronchitis, and I
was slow to recover from our trip across the Atlantic. Suddenly,
a grey-haired woman with a fine-boned, wide face and beautiful
dark eyes stood inside our doorway. I had not heard her enter;
she walks very quietly.

"I've come to see if you need help." Her voice is low. I've
never heard it raised. During our many bouts of illness she was
a soothing presence, different from the shrill, bossy, spick-and-
span nurses I'd known in English hospitals.

When we'd settled, she was one of the first people I asked to
sit for a portrait. Fiona, then not quite two years old, watched
with interest as I squeezed oil paints on my palette from various tubes and set my canvas board against the back of a chair
(I had no easel).

Elsie was called away on a nurse's errand, and I went to the
school kitchen for just a moment to get some water. When I
came back to my canvas board, on which recognizable outlines had been drawn in wash, I found that my young daughter
had not been idle. She had managed to get hold of one of
the larger brushes and had covered half the board in brilliant
colours, mostly Prussian blue and emerald green. I had to let

these colours dry before I could continue the portrait, and I never quite managed to get rid of them, however many layers of duller, darker colours I put on top.

Elsie Raikes is the daughter of pioneer settlers in Shanty Bay, a couple of miles north of Barrie on a dirt road. The old Raikes farm stretches down to Lake Simcoe from higher land with better soil. Elsie's brother Cam lives in the large farmhouse. Her married sister has built a modern house on the other side of the township road. A rail line separates these two houses from the cabin Elsie and her brother built during the Depression, on a rocky promontory overlooking the lake. They used inexpensive, left-over hemlock slabs that in the sun turn a warm red.

This cabin, where Elsie lives during holidays and weekends, is a focal point for school outings, community picnics, and the theatre groups David and Edith have started. It's also a place of refuge for some of the school staff, though I could not make use

Elsie Raikes's cabin,
Shanty Bay,
Ontario

~~

of it often during my two years in Barrie. Fiona is allergic to poison ivy, rampant on that shore, so that I could not take the children there in summer.

Now, in winter, the cabin under its tall red pines had a different character, isolated as it was from the snowplowed road. We had to leave Elsie's small, draughty car by the gate and walk the rest of the way. Her brother had made a lane, but I had to carry Bettina; the snow's too deep for her.

Shanty Bay was named after the shanties of refugee slaves who had fled to Canada from the United States. There's still a tiny African church to commemorate that settlement. Winters must have been too hard for the refugee settlers – they all returned south after the Civil War (or perhaps settled near Niagara somewhere). Earlier in the nineteenth century, officers retiring on half pay were given farmland, and many made the mistake of choosing land close to the lakeshore, easy to reach by water. But the land close to the lake often had the poorest, rockiest soil.

Elsie returned from university when her mother died and ran the farm household for her widowed father for many years, but she now lives at Ovenden during the school term. The cabin was a heavenly escape for teachers and older students. The place was so isolated that on summer mornings Elsie and her visitors could "skinny-dip" undisturbed. I'll never forget the scent of the outdoor fires, lit for corn roasts on summer evenings, on the promontory above the lake.

This scent of wood smoke permeates the cabin. A large fieldstone fireplace heats the living room, divided only by a curtain from a small bedroom and even smaller kitchen. Everything inside this cabin – chair covers, cushions, curtains – seems to have taken on the rust colour of the hemlock slabs of the inside walls. A porch in front of the living room, where summer meals are taken, darkens the cabin in summer, but now, in winter, the brilliant white of the snow on all surfaces outside throws reflected light into the windows.

In summer there is an unforgettable sound associated with this cabin: that of the screen door to the porch swinging back. Every time someone enters or leaves, to hang a wet bathing suit over the porch rails, to get a towel for swimming, to bring food out to the porch table, there is this sound of the door slamming back on its hinges, the unique cottage sound of Canadian summers.

I stood on the porch and looked out over the frozen lake. I marvelled that this place, no larger than my two rooms in town, could have given so much pleasure to so many people. There are Barrie people who think of Elsie Raikes, unmarried, a heavy smoker, "someone who lives out there alone, playing Bach, drinking beer," as an eccentric.

For me she is, like certain Canadian painters, a truly nature-related person. All were probably influenced by Thoreau; the road sign directing you to the cabin indistinctly spells out the word "Walden." The first settlers saw nature as an enemy to be subdued. Later, nature became more than a friend, something like an orienting idol: you see it in the paintings of the 1920s.

Two such paintings have pride of place on these hemlock walls. They are by Lawren Harris. The small oil panels show a northern landscape in late fall – one particularly, with its background of heavy, dark clouds and grey rocks, the last golden poplar leaves trembling in front.

Elsie saw me looking at the paintings. We were sitting as close as possible to the new fire she had just lit. We were still wearing our outdoor coats. "Lawren Harris came to Barrie when I was at school," she explained. "He was visiting Camp Borden, then gave a brief talk at Ovenden. He really impressed us with his talk about Canadian painting.

"When I came to Toronto as a student, I got up the courage to visit his studio. I thought I'd saved enough to buy a very small painting.

"He showed me around. It was hard to make a choice, there were so many wonderful paintings. He'd started to paint out west by then and in the Arctic. I didn't realize that, though Lawren Harris was wealthy and could have given away his paintings, he would not reduce his prices; he was setting a standard to benefit others in his group.

"I could only afford one painting but liked both of these. I found it hard to decide. In the end I bought this one. Then as I was leaving, Lawren Harris gave me the other one as a gift."

In this cabin the paintings looked at home.

Driving back to Toronto the next day, I listened with distress to David's account of the way Japanese Canadians, most of them born in this country, were rounded up and sent to camps, dividing whole families. I still don't read the papers.

In the back of the car the children had gone to sleep on either side of my old skis. They were too long to fit into the trunk.

Anticipating snowy winters, Garth had added them to the luggage I was allowed on my trip over from Britain. These skis date back to the time of Garth's Prix de Rome studies, when I worked as au pair for an Italian family in Florence. In the Apennines skiing was still a rich people's sport, a status symbol. When we tried our luck on the nursery slopes, the March sun and night frosts had made them so icy that I at once lost one of my skis. It took hours to retrieve my new ski from the depth of that Apennine valley.

I wondered whether I would ever be able to use these skis in Toronto. But David said that some of the ravines that intersect this city have pleasant slopes – the Rosedale golf course, for instance, and High Park. He drove us all the way to Parkdale instead of turning west at Thornhill to take the highway to Hamilton. But he had to leave in a hurry. I dragged the sleepy children, the skis, the stroller, and our overnight bag into the house on my own. The chimney of the small tiled fireplace in our front room is closed off. My tall skis lean against its ugly green and brown tiles, looking out of place – elegant, if incongruous, visitors.

~ January 10th ~

There's been no time for skiing this last week. Our schedule at the union office is hectic. They're close to signing a contract, and I had to make out dozens of new membership cards. There's been a rush for more pamphlets too. Twice I paid Sylvia to come back after supper so I could help Sweeney handing them out when the night shift came on.

After one of those cold evenings by the factory gate, Larry, Bill, and Sweeney drove me home in Larry's car. They came in for a moment because I'd brought something precious with me from Barrie: a small package of real coffee. I know how much Sweeney loves good coffee.

My place looks nice now (I think), with new cotton curtains and orange-crate bookshelves. Bill and Larry seemed to have eyes mainly for the skis that still stood against the fireplace. Bill sat down gingerly on the padded trunk in the bay window, Larry on the rocker, Sweeney on my rickety couch.

"How do you like my new place?" I asked proudly, bringing in coffee from the back room.

"Oh well," Bill grinned. "We like camping too."

So they saw my homemade decor, my orange-crate furniture, as makeshift, probably as bohemian.

When they were about to leave, rummaging for their overshoes in the vestibule by the front door, Bill suddenly turned to me and asked, "Could we borrow your skis, next Sunday?"

"Yes, of course," I said at once. They work so hard, they deserve time off. Good for them, I told myself. Then why this sudden heartache? After they left, I sat rocking in my only chair and the coffee in my mug tasted bitter. They had not asked me to come skiing with them.

~ January 16th ~

Bill called for my skis around noon on Sunday. The children and I watched him from the bay window, as he loaded them onto the top of Larry's car. There were two pair of skis on the roof rack, so why did they need mine? Then I saw that Larry was not alone. At his side a red tuque on a blond head was just visible. Elaine. They were taking Elaine skiing.

I could imagine her on the High Park hills, rosy, laughing, tumbling in the snow. While I'd take the children tobogganing in a nearby park. But then, I thought, I've known since Christmas about Larry and Elaine. Maybe Bill Sefton felt as left out as I did.

~ January 24th ~

I have no radio and don't buy a newspaper. But people bring papers to the union office, and there are newspapers in the library where we go on Saturdays. The radio in Mrs Stubbs's kitchen is often loud enough to make me aware of the latest news. And there are letters. Grannie and my aunts in England write regularly. Garth's mother has sent tiny gifts for the children. Mail is probably censored, but somehow one gathers that there are fewer raids in England (though raids over Liverpool seem to be heavy still). Their rationing is more severe than ours, but they remain cheerful. The Allies are now doing well in

Africa. In Russia the seemingly invincible German front has come to a halt.

~ February 2nd ~

John Inglis is fully organized now, and our small union office on Queen Street will be closed. My work continues at the Steelworkers' main office on Lansdowne and Bloor. Files, shelves, typewriter have been taken up there. I'll have a desk, a corner only, instead of an entire office. And it's not walking distance. I have to take two streetcars. Up there I often feel like a fifth wheel. What they really need is someone who can work like a well-oiled office machine. I know nothing about Addressographs, for instance, used for all the new addresses of union members to whom our newsletters are mailed.

I have less time for portrait commissions now. Luckily, I finished the painting of Sabina fairly quickly, but I haven't gone back to Margot's again. Florence has now found someone who wants an old painting (of an ancestor) copied. I have never done any copying. It might be hard to reproduce the style and patina of a nineteenth-century painting, but I must try. The old painting is not really valuable; it's by an unknown portraitist. There has been a family squabble over its possession until someone came up with the idea of having the painting copied, if that would satisfied the heirs. They agreed, and Florence suggested that I do the work.

While the children listened to Alice Kane telling stories, I tried to find library books on the technique of Old Masters. A specialty library in an art college would be better, but I took home a book on techniques by Hilaire describing the old method of preparing the ground and using the correct sequence of viscosity (less oil in the first coats), so that the oil colours remain luminous. It even explains the demanding technique of egg tempera.

~ February 7th ~

The person who brought the painting to be copied is a social worker, Marjorie Johnston. I've met her somewhere, probably at the Y camp on Lake Couchiching, at one of the conferences there. She is in charge of personnel at the Neighbourhood Workers. I'd say that she's about forty-five, Elsie's age, but she looks younger. She has a fine aquiline profile, and her hair is still dark and nicely cut.

The portrait she brought to our apartment is of a young man in mid-nineteenth-century clothing: stocks and a dark jacket. It's painted in a brownish Rembrandt style that was then popular. Luckily, the subject has good skin colour, reddish blond hair, sparkling brown eyes. Copying old paintings, my German aunts told me, was the way to study art in their time. They would get special permission to copy in the Louvre, where well-dressed ladies with bustles, gingerly perched on folding stools, were a common sight then.

Pre-Impressionist techniques are difficult for someone who, like me, has been taught by a Neo-Impressionist. Light was all-important for the artist who admitted me as the youngest student to her private classes. She painted in Seurat's pointillist style, putting contrasting colours side by side to achieve a scintillating effect. She admired Monet.

The town where I went to school had been a centre for art nouveau. Anything after that was declared decadent. Paula Modersohn Becker, for instance, who'd discovered Cézanne and whose diary I brought with me in our trunk. This young woman left a conventional artist-husband in northern Germany. In Paris she was befriended by the poet Rainer Maria Rilke, who worked as Rodin's secretary during those years. He wrote a moving obituary for Paula Modersohn, when, aged thirty-one, she died in childbirth.

Paula Modersohn's writing is as personal and vivid as her painting. She preceded the Expressionists and is often classed with them, as Emily Carr, another spontaneous writer, is classed with the Group of Seven. But they're not really part of any group.

~ February 9th ~

Marjorie Johnston has invited us to visit her. I'd mentioned that in London I'd lived in an artists' co-operative. Housing co-operatives exist here too, she said. She lives on the top floor of a house owned co-operatively by three occupant families. They don't share household expenses though, as we did in London. Each have their own floor.

The middle floor of that large Rosedale house is occupied by the Cass-Beggses, a family with three children who, like Marjorie, are Unitarians and CCFers. Like Mary Elgood, they came from England on the *Athenia*, the first ship torpedoed at the beginning of the war. During the time of rescue they were separated from their five year-old-daughter, a harrowing experience. Since then they had twins, a boy and girl, still in a playpen.

When Marjorie took me downstairs to introduce me to the Cass-Beggses, I remembered seeing them, like Marjorie herself, at a conference of the Fellowship for Christian Social Order, held at the Y camp on Lake Couchiching in the summer when I shared a cabin with Florence and Bruce Morris.

The Cass-Beggses had other visitors that Sunday afternoon. I recognized Jarvis McCurdy, a professor of philosophy who had been at the same conference. I remembered the rather heated discussions over Marxist politics at that conference. Florence and I attended some but not all of those discussions. The children, swimming, and canoeing lured us out of doors.

Party lines were severely drawn during that conference, but here they must have given way to personal friendships, I recognized the painter Paraskeva Clark, whom I'd briefly seen at the art gallery, and the light-eyed man with the high forehead who'd accompanied her then. His name is Infeld. He's scientist – a highly respected one, it seems – who, I gather, occupies the ground floor of this large Rosedale house.

Paraskeva Clark talked about the Russian constructivists with whom she'd studied. They were interested in machines, like the French painter Fernand Léger, now in New York. She herself has lately been commissioned to paint munition workers in an armament factory. She found the space and the structures there as interesting as I had, but I was too shy to tell her that.

Barbara Cass-Beggs asked me whether I'd consider painting her twins, still small and rather restless. They might not keep still for long. She'd heard from Marjorie that I painted portraits. I said I would try. It might be easier now than later, when those two little toddlers will be out of their playpen. She's a musician; I heard her sing and conduct choirs at the Y camp. Marjorie had told her about my children; she said I could bring them some Sunday afternoon to make a preliminary sketch of the twins.

Her husband is an engineer. I am surprised that in this swanky area they are allowed to divide up a house as they have done, sharing it with others. These Rosedale houses have beautiful large rooms and high ceilings. Hard to heat in wartime, but the Cass-Beggses are English and do not overheat. Luckily for Marjorie, much of the heat goes to the top of the house, where she lives.

~ February 14th ~

I have carefully grounded the canvas board for my copy of the young man's portrait. The first attempt of this copy seems to go quite well. It's hack work, of course, but then, even artists as original as Schwitters had to paint portraits to survive.

Marjorie, for whom I'm doing this, has become a good friend meanwhile. On Saturday afternoon, when her office was closed, she took us to the building of the Neighbourhood Workers, to a room where they store second-hand clothes. I found quite a few useful things there, warm ones for winter, all quite clean and new-looking.

The best thing she's done for us, though, is to introduce us to the West End Crèche. She is quite experienced when it comes to such institutions and thinks the children will do better in a nursery school than with Sylvia. And a crèche is much less expensive. Bettina will soon be two, so I should put the children on a waiting list. She telephoned her friend Sophie Boyd, who is in charge of the West End Crèche.

This crèche is on Dundas, a street just up from Queen. We'd have to walk that far, then take a streetcar along Dundas. This walk is heavy going because Bettina is not a good walker yet. I have to take her in a stroller, fold it when the streetcar comes, lift her and the stroller into it, and drag Fiona behind me. Some conductors are grumpily disapproving of this time-consuming procedure. They won't allow me to put the heavy toddler on the shelf in the front window while I pay for the tickets. Luckily, Fiona has learned to go ahead and pay for the tickets, graciously handing the conductor the right change, melting his grumpiness with her sunny smile.

Sophie Boyd is a quiet-spoken, sympathetic person. It turns out she knows Elsie Raikes. She went to university with Elsie's sister. She has to know the income of those who bring their children to this subsidized crèche, for it is to serve those who really need it. "You have no income other than your salary? No mother's allowance? No soldier's pay? What about your husband? What if you're ill?"

"I can't afford to get ill."

"There's something to that," she smiled. "But a helper like your Sylvia is useful in times of illness – the children's or yours. More expensive than a crèche, but not to be dismissed out of hand."

"Mine has decided on factory work after all. The pay is so much better, I can't say I blame her."

"We could take your eldest child right away, of course. I'll register both for March."

I watched the children at play. Those of Fiona's age have a delightful teacher, Miss Weaver, who reads to them, sings with them, and gives them clay and paints. Fiona has only used crayons at home lately; Sylvia is a strong believer in colouring books. Fiona will be in her element, as she was at Joan Hall's little school, months ago now.

March can't come soon enough for me.

~ February 20th ~

Just when I need them most, I'm running out of materials for painting. Miss Elgood's oil paints lasted just long enough for the copy I'm making for Marjorie. I bought new canvas board for it, and that's expensive. A kind of canvas-textured heavy paper is much cheaper, but has to have some support – cardboard or wood. And now there's something new and even cheaper: a textured board called Masonite, smooth on one side, textured on the other. A kind of fibre board, that comes in large sizes only: you have to cut it yourself to the size you want.

I'd tried this for Florence's portrait. But I found that the colours get absorbed quickly and lose some of their brilliance. The material is deceptive. I have to double the grounding, make it thicker. Haven't quite solved that problem. For the time being, I've gone back to pastels. I always liked them for children's portraits. At Ovenden I'd used them for that purpose until I had oils. One can charge more for oils, of course.

Last Sunday afternoon I took the children with me to the Cass-Beggses' house. The twins are a boy and a girl, Michael and Ruth, surprisingly docile and well behaved in their large playpen. (Bettina was much more boisterous, restricted like that.) The older girl, Rosemary, took Fiona along to her room. Bettina, meanwhile, sat outside the playpen and tried to get at the twins' toys. This, in the end, caused howls of protest and put an end to the sketching I attempted. Still, I managed a rough outline for each child.

The twins are almost white-blond, even fairer than Bettina. Their eyes and eyebrows are light too, while hers are fairly dark. They have quite distinct personalities: Ruth is gentle and gives in to Michael. Good as they are, bringing my children will not work. Next time I'll come alone: Sylvia may manage to come in at nap time on Saturdays. That will eat up most of my portrait money.

After my session with the twins, we briefly dropped in on Marjorie Johnston in the top-storey apartment of their shared house. She thinks I should put down my name for a translator's job, better paid than that of a secretary. There are many refugees from various countries who are doing this, but most of the time it means moving to Ottawa, where we have no friends.

~ March 7th ~

Finally, Bettina is old enough to go to the West End Crèche. Her second birthday came and went, uneventful except for a visit from Florence. I used my plain gouache colours to paint some blocks of wood, remnants from a nearby lumber yard that looked nicely polished. I shellacked them to make them water-proof. While Bettina was sitting on the floor, playing with her new blocks, I made a few sketches of her with the remnants of gouache in my paint box.

The weather is springlike. The snow has not entirely disappeared, but turned grey and hard in the patches that are left. But I remember from the day Bettina was born that snowstorms may arrive unexpectedly in March.

Bettina
on her second birthday
(pen-and-ink sketch)

The week Bettina was expected I was boarding with two nurses in a farm house outside Barrie (Miss Elgood's idea, in case the baby arrived unexpectedly). When a snowstorm was forecast, I spent the evening at The Barn, minding Marta and Fiona while the Smiths were at a meeting. I was not quite alone – the secretary-treasurer of our credit union was also present, catching up on some bookkeeping.

My labour pains started around nine-thirty. Gordon McKay, a big solid man, looked out at the snowstorm with apprehension. He heard me telephone the doctor at closer and closer intervals. When I got to "ten minutes," he nervously suggested getting a taxi before they were all snowbound. He was tremendously relieved when I finally drove off into the blinding storm. The taxi got through all right, but at the hospital my labour pains suddenly stopped. Bettina was not born until eight the next morning. A big baby – big even now.

"I wish I could do without the stroller," I said to Florence.

She had a brain wave: "Ask people who live near the first streetcar stop if you can leave the stroller in their backyard. There may be a shed or something there."

There's an old house at the corner of Dundas that has such a shed. We walked up there to have a look. The shed door was swinging open, revealing a few broken flower pots. We walked to the front of the house and knocked at the door. A tall shuttered house with paint peeling. Some of the frail wooden ornaments around the windows and door are broken. No one came to the door. I pressed what I took to be a button for an indoor bell and waited. No sound. It was probably broken. I knocked again. No response.

"They're out," Florence said. "Try again tomorrow."

On my way to work in the morning, there's never enough time. When there was again no reply to my knock, I simply left the stroller in the shed, closing the door a little to conceal it. *I'll explain later, and ask permission.* I simply could not face the streetcar hassle again with both children and the stroller.

There was another hassle at the West End Crèche. Bettina, who never turned a hair when I left home for work, at the crèche protested with a howl. As before at Joan Hall's, she threw herself on the floor. Miss Weaver, who'd taken Fiona's hand, motioned that I should leave. I did, but during my working hours I made even more typing mistakes than usual. But when I came to collect the children, I was told they'd had a happy day. Fiona was radiant, Bettina mollified. She's quite capable of repeating her protest again the next morning.

~ March 20th ~

All these last weeks I've left the stroller in the little backyard shed at the corner of Dundas. It's always there when I return. I don't know how many times I knocked at the front door, rang the bell. Eventually I climbed the delapidated porch steps that lead to the back door of the corner house. It too is shuttered and looks unused. But I noticed that on garbage day a trash can is put outside the gate of the yard. Someone must live in that house.

I've taken to hiring our landlady's teenage daughter to look after the children on evenings when we distribute union literature. Only when Mrs Stubbs too is home in the evenings, though. Her kitchen is at the far back of the ground floor, behind our rooms. So far, Jane, a rather heavy, round-faced teenager, seems reliable.

One such evening, before going out to the factory gates, Sweeney came home with me after work. We picked up the children on the way, and as usual, I got the stroller out of the shed. I'd given up knocking at the door of the corner house. "That's neat – leaving the thing there," Sweeney remarked. "Do you know who lives here?"

I explained. "I'm afraid I never got permission, There's a chance the stroller may disappear any Tuesday with the garbage."

"Bettina's eating something," Fiona shrilled.

My toddler, strapped into her stroller, was bending her face, rosy with the cold, over something round and shiny. Her hands clutched a shape like a crystal ball, larger than the largest marble, too large (luckily) to swallow. That her sister should get a toy – she alone – seemed even worse to Fiona than her eating the wrong thing. She tried to pry it loose, but those little fists had an iron grip on their new find.

"We're nearly home, sweetie. Let's look at it in the house."

Fiona pushed hard to get the stroller home as fast as possible – downhill most of the way from Dundas. She helped to pull the buggy up the steps. Sweeney unlocked the door with my keys while I freed Bettina from her harness. We all rushed into the front room to examine the shining object my toddler would still not relinquish.

"Found it." Her voice, deep and loud, folded around the few words she masters, clutching them as she clutched the glass ball. Even when I peeled off her outdoor clothes, she wouldn't let go.

The glass or crystal ball turned out to be the kind in which, when you shake it, a miniature snowstorm develops. Only in this one, tiny flowers opened up. "Will you look at that," Sweeney remarked. "Here you leave a buggy in a totally strange place, without permission, expecting daily to find it gone. And not only has it never been missing, but something has now been added to it."

Fiona, who'd finally got hold of the ball, shook it and turned it. Her sister protested with a howl. As soon as Fiona saw tears, she gave up her treasure. "Tomorrow," she said. "Tomorrow there'll be something for me in the buggy, don't you think?"

My heart contracted seeing her expression, so sad and wise. "I'll let you look first, tomorrow," I promised. Secretly, because unlike my four-year-old, I don't expect miracles, I made up my mind to buy her a small present.

Peace was restored. I frantically boiled instant noodles in our small pan, made a cheese sauce, then scrambled eggs. Hungry children are cranky. Fed, they're easily lured into pyjamas with the promise of a good story.

Jane Stubbs appeared punctually at seven. She is now almost sixteen, but looks younger with that singularly bland, round face. The children like her: she brings comic books.

"We found a cute toy-ball." Fiona pointed out the part of the crystal ball visible between her sister's pudgy fingers.

"Yeah, cute." Jane plumped down on my couch, a child on either side. "There used to be a corner store near here where you could buy things like that. From a Jap couple."

"What happened to it?" I asked, gingerly slipping into my coat. So far, no protest from the children. They were intrigued by the garish pink and green illustrations in Jane's comic book. On one page, long-jawed, noble-looking cowboy types were fighting yellow-toothed Japanese soldiers. They were the enemies in the war that hung over our heads, and nothing was too nasty for them. Large balloons with short, simplistic explanations bulged above both warring factions.

"They closed it," Jane mumbled without interest. "After Pearl Harbor. You know …"

"Jane, if the children want a story, will you read them one from their new library books? The comics are OK for you, but they're too grown-up for them."

Jane looked surprised, my tone was so emphatic. I left before there were any arguments.

"So, what was all that about," Sweeney asked as we hurried to the streetcar.

"Oh, it's these comic books," I sighed, thinking of David Woodsworth. Sweeney, who likes comic books, shrugged her shoulders.

For early spring, it was still cold outside the plant gates.

"Keep stamping your feet." Sweeney's nose was turning red as we stood there, handing out leaflets to unwilling people who came trudging in, heads bent against the wind, their hands in their pockets, so we didn't know where to put the pamphlets. Many of them, printed at some cost to us all, fluttered to the ground, into mud and slush.

The next day Fiona, on our way home, carefully examined the stroller before I harnessed her sister into it. I had a small rubber ball in my pocket, just for her. But to my surprise, something had again been added to the stroller. Deep in one of the cracks of its padding (it's beginning to disintegrate) a tiny fan had been stuck – a fan delicately painted with flowers and birds. Fiona would not let her sister get even close to this treasure.

I've never seen a light in that tall, shuttered house. I wondered, all the same, whether someone was watching us from behind those closed blinds. What would they see out in the yard? A tall, thin girl, her tousled hair never quite held in by her kerchief. Two little girls, one dainty and fragile, the other a fat joyful toddler.

Who could it be in there? Someone who has to hide from a ruined reputation? Someone who wants children, who has become hysterical without them? Someone crippled, very old, perhaps deaf, paralyzed? No, not paralyzed, for whoever lived there managed to get out into the yard. Knew about the stroller in the shed. One of these days I'll find out.

We've established a routine that depends entirely on all going
well. If no one is sick, if I don't have to work extra hours,
then our day works out something like this: I get up before
the children; dress (more or less) while I make breakfast; dress
Bettina. Fiona manages on her own, but often wants to wear
her best clothes instead of the play clothes laid out for her.
Bettina wants to do the same – there are few mornings without
a small battle of some kind. Luckily, dressing for out of doors
is easier now. though the children still need to wear boots on
slushy days. We push the stroller up to Dundas and stack it in
the shed, then take the streetcar to the crèche. For me, there are
two more streetcar rides before I arrive at Bloor and Lansdowne.

There's a new secretary at the union office, an efficient little
person, a real whizz in shorthand-typing. In our short lunch
hour I've talked to this girl. She's not at all interested in politics
and unions. Ideological convictions don't seem to interest those
at the office (always excepting the Seftons). Eileen knows this
girl from way back at business school. I've a suspicion she's
been hired because I can't cope with the hectic workload, a depressing thought. She's friendly, though, interested in my children – she has a little girl of her own. Offered me ten dollars for
a portrait of her. How can I say, No, that's not enough?

If the day is normal, I get back to the crèche between five and
six. During rush hours, streetcars are crammed full, morning
and evening. One always has to stand, and children are seen as
a nuisance. At Dundas we pick up the stroller, strap Bettina into
it, and push it home. If necessary, we get milk and groceries on
our way. Most shopping, though, and all the washing is done
on Saturdays. I pay Mrs Stubbs a bit extra to use the washing
machine in the basement. Doing this and hiring Jane for minding the children I see as some kind of insurance, a bonus that I
hope will keep our rooms for us. We're out of the house so
much, we might be considered model tenants.

Sundays I take the children to the park, or in bad weather, we
read the new library books we get on Saturdays from our friend,
Alice Kane. Since the crèche is cheaper than Sylvia has been,

I've saved a little and managed to buy new tubes of oil paint to finish Margot's portrait.

She had hoped to get work at Eaton's in the winter, but the children had bronchitis, and she had to stay home for weeks.

"And your family in England?" I asked.

"Oh, they have the usual war troubles: restrictions, raids, rations. My husband has taken up with someone else. But what do you expect? He's handsome – and a doctor."

Neither Florence nor Sweeney know what I told her then, while finishing the painting. During my last year in London – the time of the phony war – we adopted a beautiful Jewish girl who was very unhappy, living with a strictly Orthodox East London family. She's the daughter of a wealthy, liberal Viennese lawyer (she brought trunks full of clothes with her). Her sponsors in London were fur merchants who expected a puny fourteen-year-old and were presented with a fully grown young woman looking like a film star. They were afraid to let her go about in town and, for her own protection, confined her so strictly that she became quite miserable. Friends of ours who'd taken up the cause of refugees finally managed to get her evacuated to their country house, where I too spent some weeks as evacuee.

Fiona was a small baby then, and we were glad to find someone who could help with chores at the co-op household, since most of its members were now on air-raid patrol. So we took over the sponsorship for this girl. She came to live with us some months before I left. During the Blitz we sent her back to our friends in the country. But she was bored there, and shortly after my departure, she returned to our house. She fell in love with my husband. The way he tells the story, she seduced him.

"I'm in a similar boat, you see," I told Margot. "And I'm German and racked with guilt over all that's been done to the Jews. I'll not stand in their way. He – I mean Garth – should marry her, don't you think?"

Margot shook her head. "I think you're not the only one to whom this happened," she said. "But that's no consolation."

"What will you do?" I asked.

98

"I'll probably go back," Margot shrugged. "I had a torrid love affair last winter, but I'd never marry the man who so wildly attracted me. It's behind me now. You should probably do the same."

"I don't know," I said. "I found out that I like being independent. I lived in Italy when we first married. It should have been ideal, but I was unhappy all the time. In London too. Garth is a much more accomplished artist than I am. That at first was very important to me, then it overwhelmed me. He was years ahead in every way. But in London I was the one who managed to get a job while he, with an RA and a Prix de Rome, could not find work. Now in New York he's finally managed to get some small commissions for the *New Yorker*. His father was illustrator for the paper preceding that magazine. So perhaps he can help a little."

"You speak all those languages, Spanish, French, Italian. You should get a better job," Margot suggested.

"Yes, I made four pounds a week in London."

"Better than what they'd have paid me at Eaton's," Margot sighed. "But then, I'm lucky. I have an allowance and a decent apartment." (She's never visited mine.)

Margot paid me ten dollars for her portrait. I earned another ten dollars painting Frannie's little girl, at her neat little house in an uninteresting housing development west along Bloor. Frannie, the new typist at the union office, is the wife of a soldier overseas and of course gets some of his pay in addition to her office salary. She could probably afford more for the painting, but how am I to tell her? Or Margot?

~ April 16th ~

The fragile equilibrium – crèche, work, home – I should have known it couldn't last. We had a few days off over Easter, but all that weekend Fiona was not well at all, so we didn't go anywhere. She doesn't have a temperature but complains of a sore throat. On Tuesday she seemed better, so I took her back to the West End Crèche.

Miss Weaver took one look at Fiona, asked her assistant to take over the group of other children, and whisked us into a little room – a kind of nursing station, where they keep first-aid equipment. She deftly examined Fiona's glands and looked into her throat, a painful procedure I could see.

"There's an epidemic of mumps," she said. "Fiona has it. She has to be quarantined. You have to keep the children at home."

"Should I see a doctor?" I asked. "And how will I get the children home?"

"We have a visiting pediatrician. You can see him when he comes here. But I can tell you what he'll say. Can you afford a taxi?"

What could I say? That a taxi fare would swallow my savings? No more paints. But I nodded.

"Then I'll call one."

While we waited for the taxi I tried to take stock of our situation. It couldn't be much worse.

As through a fog, I heard Miss Weaver explain what the doctor would advise: to put Fiona to bed, keep her on liquids, and, if her throat was very sore, dissolve a children's aspirin so that she could swallow it. Keep her warm.

"Bettina has to be quarantined too, I'm afraid. For the next three weeks, or rather, for three weeks after Fiona has recovered, she can't come here. The best thing for you would be that she gets mumps tomorrow or the next day."

I began to realize that if Bettina would get mumps on the last day of Fiona's quarantine, this could mean six weeks away from work. Six weeks! I could not ask for leave of absence that long, even without pay. And if there's no pay, what then?

After I paid the taxi and got the children into the house and Fiona to bed, I sat down to calculate our chances of survival. I'll have to try and find work I can do at home. I telephoned the union office to explain my absence. Vi was sympathetic. She would phone back, she said. But when she did, the news was not good. I was not to return to work until the children's quarantine was over. I explained that I'd had mumps as a child and was not a carrier. That I might find someone who was also immune and would mind the children.

Then I telephoned Florence, who luckily has had mumps and was willing to come over. When she did, I found out why they had been so emphatic about my staying away, at the union office. Men who contract mumps may become sterile. It's not an old wives' tale, she said; it's what happened to Bruce. They can't have any children. It explains a lot about her, about the unhappiness that nags at their married life.

~ April 18th ~

Fiona now has a high temperature, and her little face and neck are hugely swollen. The small children's aspirins I dissolve in juice for her to drink don't seem to do much good. I keep Bettina in the same room, so that if she gets mumps, she will get it as soon as possible. So far she seems perfectly healthy and shows no sign of swelling.

One thing I should be thankful for: everybody in the Stubbs household has had mumps, so that Jane can stay in my front room to do homework after school, while I dash out to get a few groceries. I have to use the telephone in Mrs Stubbs's hall more often than usual, which makes me uncomfortable. It adds to the kind of commotion I've tried hard to avoid. I offered to pay for my calls. She insists that I need not. It's not like England, where a local call costs twopence.

I called Mrs Larkin, who had looked after the children at Christmas, but she's down with the flu and not at all well. I telephoned the office again to ask, officially, for sick leave, if I'm allowed such a thing. It seems I am – a couple of weeks, even with pay – so that may help a little. As much as if I myself had been ill, Vi says. All the same, knowing the pressures there, few people will make use of sick leave as I have to do now.

For a couple of weeks I can draw a salary I don't deserve. Then what? I should find a factory job again. I'm not really good enough at the demanding work of the union office.

~ April 26th ~

I finally got through to Sweeney on the phone. She's almost always out. It turns out that she's never had mumps and that, as she still lives with her large family, the danger of passing it on cannot be ruled out. She offered to lend me money to tide me over, but paying back debts is something I can't face. It would make life even harder later.

I scraped together the rent for May. Florence has come to bring some cans of soup, something Fiona can swallow. She's on liquids – milk and orange juice mostly. While Florence sat in the front room talking to her little friend through the sliding doors, I took Bettina for a much needed outing. She's walking much better now. She can't be taken into buildings, though, while she's quarantined, so I brought her back and made a separate trip to get more juice and milk for Fiona and to exchange our library books.

Alice Kane seems to know exactly what the children like, what's right for each age group. I don't know what we'd do without these library books and this sympathetic adviser.

I worked a short time on Florence's portrait. She too offered to lend me money, but she does more than enough for us as it is. I don't want to charge her for the portrait, especially as I'm not totally satisfied with it.

Fiona can now sit up and crayon colouring books and scrap paper. She has never spoilt any library books by scribbling in them, as some children do. But yesterday afternoon, while Jane was doing her homework in the front room, I went out for a few minutes to get milk. When I came back, I found that Fiona, who'd run out of scrap paper, had made a design on the wall-paper instead. Thank heavens she didn't call Jane, who was entertaining Bettina in the front room. I sent Jane home, my heart in my mouth. I had no idea how to deal with this dilemma. Can one replace wallpaper? How seriously will Mrs Stubbs take this disfigurement of her property? I have to erase it somehow. What if Mrs Stubbs finds it before I get rid of it?

I'd heard that pellets of bread are used for cleaning. I tried to rub out the marks with bits of our precious supply of bread. It did no good. Washing with soapy water only created a greater smudge. Is there some kind of cleaner one could get? Will I have to pay for repapering the room?

Fiona was very upset because I was. Somehow it had never occurred to me that she would be creative in this way. There are so many don'ts in a child's life, I could not add to them, enumerating all the unforeseen. She is so good and so responsible for her age. She cried when she saw the effect of what she'd done – the effect on me, that is. I ended up consoling her.

~ May 3rd ~

Yesterday, when there was no one in the house, the front door bell rang. I looked out of our bay window, and there was Elaine Melhuish. I opened the front door, glad to see her but ready to warn her: "Wait, wait, don't come right in. The children are in quarantine for mumps."

"That's why I came. I know about it. I've had mumps, don't worry."

"Actually, Fiona is quite well now. It's Bettina – she doesn't seem to get it. I've tried everything."

"Some people never get it," Elaine said. She looked radiant. She'd come, she said, because she heard about my predicament, and because she wanted to tell me her news. She and Larry are engaged to be married. I knew since last Christmas that they would.

She had not come in on the Sunday the Seftons borrowed my skis for her. They brought them back a week later. She works at a downtown office, and I've not seen her since. Did she want to make up for this? Would she even have noticed that I minded, staying home while they all went out to ski? Or did she just want to share her overflowing happiness?

She wanted to present Larry with a pastel portait, if I could do it fairly soon. She would sit for me right now, if that was all right. I nodded, grateful for her generosity, and got out my box of pastels. I was out of canvas board, but still had some rough grey paper.

Elaine's beauty has to be captured in nuances of Renoir, who knew just how to portray women and girls, children, their soft glow. Her features are not definite; even her colouring comes and goes according to the light. No one, I thought as I worked on my sketch, no one has ever been able to paint a rose. I have an aunt who tried and tried. The walls of her apartment are covered by awful oil paintings of roses.

I told Elaine that I'd applied for translation work, on the advice of a friend (Marjorie). But that I'd really prefer factory work.

"You could try Lever Brothers," she suggested. "They're well unionized."

"How will your life change, as the wife of a union organizer?" I asked.

"I'll go on with my job for the time being," Elaine said. "I know union organizers are hardly ever at home. But I'm happy. If Larry loves me only half as much as I love him, that's enough for me."

I tried to do justice to her evanescent loveliness, that special colouring. But I knew I was failing. I wondered, did I ever have this completeness of love? Had I imagined all that when I left my family to go to Italy? I didn't know it at the time, but I was escaping, not only from a bourgeois family but from a country where nothing, nothing, was as it had been.

Outside the bay window a little ornamental tree (cherry? crabapple?) had begun to open its blossoms, white and deep rose, a delicate wonder impossible to paint. Like Elaine herself.

~ May 15th ~

Fiona is perfectly well now, and Bettina still shows no signs of getting mumps. I could easily go back to work, but they keep putting me off. Meanwhile, there's been a note from Selective Service, suggesting an interview for a translation job. It would be from Spanish and in Ottawa, so I don't know whether I should apply. But I'll go to an interview with the person in charge, who'll be here from Ottawa some day next week.

I ran out to post my reply. When I came back from the mail box, disaster had struck. I had left the back window open, and in the breeze the children's drawings, which I'd carefully hung over the disfigured wallpaper, had fluttered down. I'd taken both children with me to the mailbox. Mrs Stubbs saw the open window, across the backyard from her kitchen. She does not like leaving windows open at any time. It affects the heating, for one thing. It invites curious eyes, for another. So she came into our rooms to close it and discovered the damage on the wallpaper.

She gave us notice. In addition to all other uncertainties, we have to look for a place to live by the first of June.

I promised to replace the wallpaper. I'd do anything, if only we could stay.

Mrs Stubbs is determined. No more children. She's decided to take adults only. Single men, who are out of the house most of the time.

She could not be moved. I know she's tired and irritable, like everyone who works all day and then does housework, not only for a lazy teenage daughter and herself but also for an old father who lives upstairs. I think she is separated from her husband. There's never any mention of him. He's not in the army or oversees, or if he is, she doesn't talk about it.

So we're back to square one, where we were last September – no rooms and, for the moment, no work.

The children will, finally, be out of quarantine next week. I'll be able to take them back to the West End Crèche, where they get one meal at least, while I go house hunting. I should live walking distance from the West End Crèche, so that if I only find shift work, someone in the household could take them to the crèche, the arrangement we had at the McNairs.

~ May 20th ~

I've been out every evening, up and down Dundas, looking for vacancy signs. In this area there are many immigrants. The way of showing a vacancy here is a cardboard sign in the window: "Room for rent." Usually, the door is opened cautiously, and as soon as I mention children, it is closed. I'd quite forgotten about the stroller because we hadn't needed it since Fiona was diagnosed with mumps and we'd taken a taxi home.

It's now fairly light in the evenings, so I made an early supper, asked Jane to come in, then walked up to Dundas again. It was just beginning to turn dark when I reached the tall, shuttered house where we'd left the stroller, weeks ago now.

I slipped into the backyard. The door to the shed was closed, and I wondered whether I would attract attention opening it. I had never been at this corner as late as this evening. As I stood in the yard gazing at the back door, I noticed that the blind was not quite down and that there was a faint light, as from a distant room, coming from below the blind. Of course, that was it. Those who lived in the house were only there evenings; they worked during the day. No wonder no one ever answered the door.

I walked up the rickety steps to the back door and knocked. I wanted to thank the owner or tenant, who must have seen our stroller in the shed every night. I knocked again. A faint out-door light, a single weak bulb, came on in the porch. The door opened a crack, revealing a slight figure, a mere silhouette. The figure withdrew immediately, and I stood quite still, so as not to frighten this shy person.

"I just want to thank you," I blurted out. "We kept our stroller in your shed and I could never get permission. I knocked many times. Is it still there?"

The head, a dark smooth head, nodded.

I tried to explain the hassle on the streetcar. The figure came closer to listen. The light now fell on a soft round face, a golden colour, the eyes a dark glow. A small mouth. This must be a Japanese woman perhaps my age, and, like me, from an enemy country. Or perhaps born in Canada, as I was not. I thought of David Woodsworth.

"You may keep your stroller in the shed as long as you wish," an astonishingly mature voice said in faultless English – not the kind of English one can learn. It was free of any inflection, except perhaps the slightly western one Florence too has in her speech.

"But how are your children? Are they ill? I have not seen them for a long time."

From the bottom steps of the porch, I explained what had happened to us, why I had not got the stroller any earlier. While I talked, I pictured her watching us out in the yard. wondering about us, about the children. As I had wondered about the oc-cupant of the house.

106

Then it dawned on me: "It's you. It's you who put those toys in the stroller. Oh, you don't know how much the children enjoyed those. I tried to thank you. I knocked, I rang. There was never any reply."

"No." The voice sounded more subdued now. "I don't normally answer the bell. Or any knocking. And I work long hours, often till dark. So I don't often go out in daylight. I work for my uncle. He's a doctor."

"Oh, I wish I had an uncle," I burst out. "I have no relations at all in this country. I'm one of those horrible Germans we're fighting."

She gazed at me with wide, round eyes, a gleam in their darkness. And I realized that to her I looked like all other white Canadians (just as I had difficulty distinguishing between Chinese and Japanese – an insult to both nations).

Then suddenly her face brightened, and she started to laugh. "And I'm one of those horrible Japs," she said. "My parents are in a camp out west, but both were born and raised in Canada. I was lucky. I had gone to work for my uncle by then. I am always worried about them. We seldom hear how they are."

She is less of an enemy alien than I am, I thought. She does not even know Japan as I know the Germany of my childhood, a country that seems to have disappeared, swallowed up by a military machine. It was on the tip of my tongue to ask her if she had rooms to rent. Then I thought of what that might lead to: more problems for her, if we were both thought of as enemy aliens (though neither of us is).

So I thanked her again, and the door closed. I took the stroller from the shed and pushed it, empty, down Lansdowne towards MacDonell. I walked fast, deep in thought. There was still a late, golden light on the trees that now had tiny green leaves, fresh, soft leaves springing from red buds, regardly of war, regardless of all other troubles. Inexorably, spring had moved in.

She must have seen us quite often. And to her, we looked like everybody else, like the square-jawed cowboy types in Jane's comics. They shoot at Japs. My heart ached for her. Our worries seemed insignificant compared to hers. I thought of her parents, herded into camps; and my mother, from whom I never hear, in enemy country. She's English, an enemy in Germany as much as Japanese are thought of as enemies here. During the First World War she was somehow protected by her husband's status. But now?

The door was never opened again, though I knocked several times. I never found out what happened to our small angel.

Only one of the angels in this town. There are more than I can count, so I'm sure we'll be all right in the end. Our predicament is tiny, after all, compared to what happens right now, in this war, in the rest of the world. Do I have any idea of what happened to my Jewish school mates? As far as I know, both got away in time, one to England, the other to America. But their families? Some may still be there.

There are bombed and destroyed towns on both sides. One knows as little as one knew about Spain during the Civil War, when many still believed that Guernica had been destroyed by the Basques themselves. A veil of lies and secrets hangs over everything military.

~ May 25th ~

The children are out of quarantine and back at the crèche. Talking to Sophie Boyd has done me good. She sees things in proportion.

The weather has turned to steam heat suddenly, and it's much harder walking up and down streets, looking for rooms. One room – I've given up on apartments, even unfurnished rooms. They're impossible to find in the area near the crèche. I've given up on ads too. I knock on doors or ring bells where I find a sign: "Rooms for rent."

It was again Elaine who brought me the news, though Larry or Sweeney may be behind this: Charles Millard, the head of the Steelworkers union, needs an office worker at his election office on Bloor West. Elaine, who works at the downtown office of the CCF, suggested me for the time the committee rooms will be open before the election – that is, most of June. It would be, mainly, the work of a receptionist, dealing with people, dealing with membership and announcements, finding out what riding visitors belong to – that kind of thing.

A month of grace – at the same salary. And then what?

Meanwhile, I had my interview for the translation job in a downtown hotel where the civil servant from Ottawa stayed overnight. It happened to be the King Edward Hotel, where a CCF convention was taking place. I was foolish enough to mention to the interviewer that I hoped to attend some of the sessions because of my present job (at a union office and, later, a CCF election office). I was given a test in Spanish and was asked a lot of questions about my position in this country (war guest), my husband's job (was he in the army?), my place of birth, etc. I don't think for a minute that I'll get the job. And I don't really want to move to Ottawa and start all over again. Ottawa may not have the angels that have watched over us here and in Barrie.

~ May 28th ~

Sophie Boyd suggested asking parents who brought their children to the crèche about rooms for rent. That had some results. A Polish woman, whose curly-haired little boy is Bettina's age, told me that a tenant has just left a large attic room in their house. She lives in an area where Ukrainian immigrants have settled. They don't advertise; they operate mainly by word of mouth among their own community. They too prefer single men who do war work, but Anna is allowed to make some decisions in the house where she lives; the landlord lives elsewhere and leaves renting arrangements to her.

She doesn't speak English well, and none of us speak Polish. There's something very nice about her. She wears her hair long, in a chignon. I mentioned to Sophie Boyd that I admired the embroidered blouse she wore, and Sophie told me that Anna earns something by doing fine needlework. It may have ruined her eyes: she wears glasses. Her little boy, Sonny, is a delicate child, beautifully dressed always.

They live only two blocks from the crèche, so I went to the house right away. It's on one of the side streets going north from Dundas that has a little park on the west side, a great attraction. The house itself is a typical Toronto brick house with a deep porch. The street has shade trees, but they're not tall enough to cool the top floor of the house. The room for rent is in the attic, though, and it is boiling hot. But I really have no choice, so I decided to take that large sparsely furnished room. Bettina's crib would probably fit in there, as well as my rocker and Fiona's little desk.

A narrow hall divides that attic room from another, occupied by a Ukrainian couple with a little boy younger than Sonny. His father, Anna said, is seldom at home. He works long shifts and overtime. There's a two-burner electric stove in the hall and an icebox, both shared by the top-floor tenants. Reluctant as Anna seems to talk about the husband, she regards the wife, Lecia, as a friend. She herself has a large apartment with a bay window on the second floor.

In this attic, then, I might have a close neighbour, glad, perhaps, to earn something caring for my children in the evenings. Millard's committee rooms will have to be open long hours because people visit election offices after work. And I might reciprocate sometimes, looking after Lecia's small boy, who is younger than Bettina and with whom she stays home most of the time. Anna tells me that she and Lecia take the children to the park across the road whenever the weather allows it.

I made a down payment – the rent is reasonable. I have to take the room furnished, even though there's only a metal bed and dresser in it. It's not only the cheapest room I could find, it's the only one.

I have no time to mourn the loss of our apartment, of my own private room. Somehow before I get my first paycheque for work at the election office, I have to make some money. So over the weekend I went to finish the portraits of the Cass-Beggs twins. I would not be able to come the next weekend, they said, as they were going to an FCSO conference, the kind I'd witnessed on Lake Couchiching.

Avis McCurdy. the wife of a professor of philosophy at the University of Toronto, was at the Cass-Beggses' the afternoon I tried to finish the portraits (impossible – the twins were too lively that day). She and her husband, Jarvis, mean to attend the same conference if she can find someone to mind their household (four children) for the weekend. I offered to do this, if I may bring my own little girls.

Avis McCurdy offered to drive me to their house in Forest Hill, so I can see what's involved. The McCurdys have two girls, nine and seven. They also have adopted two little boys, both Fiona's age. Dorothy and Janet are good at doing things around the house and know where things are kept. The McCurdys have a "victory garden" growing vegetables, down in the ravine. Theirs is a rambling house, low-roofed, slightly art nouveau, and the feeling of space around it is increased by the ravine behind it.

When I told Avis McCurdy that I was about to start work at Millard's election office on Bloor West, she said that she herself is a volunteer at the CCF committee rooms north of St Clair. "Volunteers are the backbone of your election work," she advised me. "It's important to develop a good memory for people. Check their names on the voters' list. Listen to complaints. Keep track of their interests."

I told her about my predicament, moving from two rooms to one, and she offered to store my big trunk in their basement. I think I can manage the rest, if I return Sweeney's and Florence's furniture.

~ May 30th ~

The heat has abated a little, or perhaps it's just that at the McCurdys' house one doesn't feel it as much. The space around us made a wonderful balance to six lively children. Their meals, reading to them at bedtime (getting as far as bedtime!) – all that did not seem too exhausting, didn't even take all my time. Dorothy, the nine-year-old, is a responsible little person who bravely weeded some of the victory garden. She is also motherly towards Fiona, Bettina, and the two little boys. Bettina can now run, and she made full use of the space, both in the house and in the garden.

Returning to our apartment and my packing was a wrench. I had hoped to finish Elaine's portrait before we move, but I'm not satisfied with it, and she seldom has the time to sit for me.

~ May 31st ~

So here I am, our last evening in a place where I finally had a room of my own. I'm going back to the way we've lived for years, all three in one room. Everything is packed. Sweeney's brother will pick up the beds in his truck and take our few belongings to the new attic room. Moving costs a fortune if it's done by a moving truck. But Sweeney won't let him charge anything. It's impossible to find out from her whether she herself finances him or whether he helps us out of the goodness of his heart.

Sweeney herself is moving to the Toronto Island for the summer. She invited us to come and see her there.

I told her about our attic room: "Boiling hot in summer, I'm afraid."

"Still, you get a breeze up there that you don't get in the lower floors," Sweeney said, and I thought how we'd laughed about my aunt Lulu, who always saw the good side of things. Our rooms on MacDonell are on the ground floor, shaded by trees. I will miss that coolness and space.

~ June 2nd ~

We're now installed in our attic room, and it's hot. Still, the mornings are fresh. It's pleasant walking the children to the crèche before I take the Dundas car a long way west. Dundas is one of those old streets that, like the old English ridge roads, follow the terrain, rather than a town plan. I think it was once an Indian trail. It changes direction from east-west to northwest and becomes a diagonal that eventually cuts across Bloor Street. From that intersection I take the Bloor car as far as Runnymede, just before Jane, the end of the line. It's a fairly long ride, but the streetcar is never packed because most people move towards downtown rather than away from it.

The committee rooms are in a vacant Bloor Street store. Some posters, one with a photograph of Millard, and a lot of CCF literature fill the window space. To the north of Bloor, South York is a working-class riding, but to the south, Etobicoke is middle-class. Still, it looks as if Millard may get some support there too. The people who come in during the day are mainly from that area.

Florence too is working in committee rooms for the lawyer Andrew Brewin, the candidate in her riding. Agnes Macphail is running for East York. High Park, which I pass daily in the street-car, is the riding of the leader of the Conservatives, George Drew.

C.H. Millard and
Andrew Brewin
in 1940

There the CCF candidate, William Temple, an army officer who on the posters looks most attractive, will have his work cut out.

The Conservatives, tired of their role of upholding tradition, have lately added the word "progressive" to their name. Millard calls them the "Pro-Cons." In spite of this new name, they rely heavily on old-fashioned patriotism and hope to gain many votes in the armed forces. However, many of those who enlisted have experienced the Depression first-hand and, a surprising number have indicated that they'll vote CCF. Their vote may come in late, but it will count and it may make all the difference in the end.

I'd like to tell them that in Germany the conservatives supported Hitler, and those working most strongly against the Nazis were the social democrats, known here as the CCF.

~ June 10th ~

In the mornings the committee rooms are fairly quiet. House-wives wander in, pushing strollers with small children. The way that factory workers dress, in coveralls and bandanas, has caught on somehow. Slacks are worn these days, and kerchiefs, often hiding a bulk of curlers.

Lenny (pastel)

In the afternoons, people who work night shift arrive. A volunteer takes over for me around five so I can take the children home and feed them. It's so hot that I seldom cook. Often we take a little jelly or some sandwiches into the small park across the road. It's a comfort to know that the children get lunch at the crèche.

In this heat it's hard for them to go to sleep. There are no screens on the windows and I haven't seen mosquitoes, but some must have come in, for the children itch and scratch occasionally.

In the evenings the committee rooms get really busy, so once the children are in bed, I go back there. Lecia, Lenny's mother, who shares the attic with me, keeps an eye on them. Her toddler goes to bed at the same time as my children, and we keep all doors open to create a through draught. It helps, as I know from those evenings when I stay in the hot darkened room.

Towards evening the streets are cooler, and going back and forth in the streetcar is pleasant when the windows are open. Then there's a wonderful breeze.

When I'm home on weekends, I offer to mind Lenny while Lecia goes out to shop or visits her friend Anna downstairs. Sitting in the bay window, Anna sews and embroiders the most beautiful clothes. mostly lingerie, lace-trimmed slips, nightgowns, blouses that go to expensive stores. She gets only a fraction of the price they bring. Sometimes, especially now, for weddings, she sits up late at night to finish urgent commissions.

~ June 16th ~

One of the volunteers at the committee rooms, who often takes my place around suppertime, has shown a special interest in our family. She is the wife of a professor of English at Victoria College, John D. Robins. She's one of the people I most rely on: robust, white-haired, though only middle-aged. I feel confident when she takes over. She has a son, Peter, a few years older than Fiona, who sometimes comes with her.

Last Saturday the Robinses gave a party for the CCF campaigners. They live next to High Park but are still in Millard's riding. Charlie M. was there, of course, as well as the High Park candidate, Bill Temple. Larry and Elaine came briefly, looking blissfully happy. Sweeney now lives on Toronto Island, so she was not there, and I miss her.

The party, on a beautiful afternoon, for the most part took place in the Robinses' large garden. People sat around out of doors in bright summer clothes. Fiona and Bettina, who had both been invited, looked like butterflies in their sundresses and fitted perfectly into the bright mixture of flowers and summer prints. Picnic tables were laden with food, and Bettina ate enormously – sandwiches, cakes, and cookies – but luckily didn't get sick. Fiona was more reticent, perhaps because eight-year-old Peter was acting superior towards little girls. And she fell in love.

The object of this, her first passion was not a boy Peter's age, but a grown man, his father: John Daniel Robins of Victoria College. I never met Stephen Leacock, though for a few weeks I lived across from his home on Lake Couchiching. I imagine Leacock's voice and manner to be like John Robins's. He even resembles Leacock photographs.

I tried to help our hostess, carrying platters of food from the house to the garden. In the dining room, above a sideboard, was a portrait of John Robins, painted by Lawren Harris, whose landscape paintings I had admired at Elsie's cabin. The portrait has the fine structure of Harris's paintings, but like the northern paintings,

John D. Robins

115

it has a coldness totally absent in the real John Robins, who exudes warmth.

Fiona told everyone that she will be four next week. Professor Robins, her new friend, has invited her to spend her birthday at his house if her mother will allow it. Mrs Robins even promised a cake (perhaps to make up the balance between the amounts of cake consumed by Bettina and the smaller helpings Fiona took, politely holding back). All the way home on the streetcar, Fiona chatted away about "the man I love."

~ June 20th ~

We set out for Fiona's birthday party decked out in our best clothes. I wore my slim mustard-coloured dress, the children their New York dresses – blue-green with white trim. I brushed their hair until it shone. Bettina's golden blond, Fiona's light brown and very fine, easily tangled.

We were to take the Dundas streetcar only as far as the junction with Bloor Street. There Professor Robins would meet us by car. When our stop came, we moved to the exit doors at the centre of the streetcar. I saw Mr Robins in his car alongside the exit and stepped down quickly to hand him Bettina. When our weight left the steps, the door began to close. Fiona, who was behind me, was not heavy enough to make a difference. Perhaps the conductor had not looked back or was in a hurry. Anyway, the doors inexorably closed and the streetcar moved on, Fiona's small, tearful face gliding past us, her mouth open though we could not hear her cries.

The man she loved leaped into action. We were pushed into the back seat, the door slammed, and we were off to rescue my daughter. We raced the monster that had carried her off to an intersection where there was, luckily, a red light to prolong the stop. A sympathetic passenger, about to get off, helped to keep open the centre doors until Fiona was with us. She was still weeping, but her tears were soon wiped away. She was given the place of honour in the front seat, beside the man she loved.

"And now, we're going to drive through my park," John Robins said. "We'll see my flamingoes first. Then my camels."

Fiona did not doubt for a moment that her noble rescuer in his shiny car had a park with camels and flamingoes. We had never been as far west as High Park from our Parkdale rooms, so she knew nothing of its zoo. I don't think she would have been surprised if John Robins had indicated that all of Toronto belonged to him, or even the whole world.

Slowly, we drove down the winding road through High Park. We saw – and smelt – the camels behind their high fences. These dromedaries, single-humped, regarded us with disdain. Next came fenced areas in which elegant deer and antelopes stood, eyeing us with large eyes, chewing their cud like cattle.

When we reached the ponds at the end of the drive, there were the salmon-coloured flamingoes, standing as still as statues, most of them on one leg, watching the water. Beneath the great shade trees it was wonderfully cool. The flamingoes looked as if they were dreaming, gazing at their rose-pink reflections. Alice Kane had introduced us to the Babar stories, and Fiona takes it for granted that elephants live like people, wear clothes, fly airplanes. John Robins's flamingoes and camels were no surprise to her. He is a magician.

At the Robinses' house there is a cake with four pink candles, which she's allowed to blow out. The Robinses' son, Peter, poses no threat and politely eats only one piece of the cake, albeit a large one.

The man she loves has written a book. The illustrations for it are wood engravings by Frank Carmichael, a member of the Group of Seven. He and Holgate seem to be the only ones in this group seriously interested in graphic art. So far, I've seen few paintings by Carmichael.

That whole afternoon and evening remain in my mind as a paradise, a short time of bliss, when ideas and music were more important than washing clothes or the next meal. For a few hours I was transported – like Fiona in her way – into another unearthly realm.

When the mosquitoes finally drove us into the house, John Robins mentioned a book, now out of print, by an early woman visitor to Canada, Anna Jameson, an art critic, writer, and herself an artist. This woman, he told me, had a strong connection with Goethe's Germany. After the old poet's death, his daughter, Ottilie, became her friend and they corresponded during the rather bleak months Anna Jameson spent in Toronto. During that winter Jameson translated Goethe's talks with his secretary, *Gespräche mit Eckermann*. She named this part of the book her "winter studies."

I opened the book and was startled by the poem that introduces *Winter Studies and Summer Rambles*:

> Sind denn die Baüme auch so trostlos, so verzweiflunsvoll, in ihrem Winter, wie das Herz in seiner Verlassenheit.
> (Are the trees as inconsolable, as desperate, in their winter, as the heart in its desolation.)

The poem is by Bettina von Arnim, one of Goethe's many female admirers. A tiny, passionate, highly intelligent woman of Italian origin (who later went for walks in the Rhineland with the journalist Karl Marx), she married Achim von Arnim, a Prussian aristocrat and romantic poet, the friend of her brother, Clement Brentano. These two romantic poets collected fairy tales and folk songs. Goethe did not particularly like them.

Bettina von Arnim wrote many letters to Goethe. He seldom replied, but after his death she had the nerve to publish their correspondence as *Goethe's Letters to a Child*. Because of Goethe's immense reputation, the book did quite well. (Few people knew that the famous old poet had once described Bettina as "a wasp disturbing my peace with its buzzing.")

I knew all this, yet the poem struck me with the force of something totally genuine, from the heart. Anna Jameson had chosen it because it expressed her own despair and isolation during that Toronto winter, a sad phrase like the reedy tune of a shepherd's flute.

For a moment it conjured up the lost world of my childhood, and I was in some danger of self-pity, something I must avoid at all costs. To regain my balance, I picked up I another dog-eared book. Its cover looked strangely familiar, and I plunged still deeper into that lost world. It was a copy of the *Zupfgeigenhansl*, a collection of German folk songs as well worn as that in my childhood home. Its cover showed the same silhouette of a lute-plucking *Wandervogel*. ("plucking violin" would be the exact translation of *Zupfgeige*). The *Wandervögel* were nature-loving people who tried to get back to a simpler life. They wore plain clothes and sensible shoes, carried their few belongings in ruck-sacks, played the mouth organ or the lute, and during their long hikes through nature, they sang. They camped before youth hostels sprang up. (As teenagers, we youth-hostelled until youth organizations were replaced by the Hitler Jugend.) The songs were good to walk to, and we sang them, walking to school through the Odenwald. Most songs were old, and some harked back to times when young men walked from town to town, mill to mill, as journeymen.

The Robinses, it turns out, are folklore specialists. They know some *Zupfgeigenhansl* songs almost as well as I do. Before long, Mrs Robins sat at the piano, and we three adults were singing one song after another. Fiona, whom nothing surprised on this day of magic, listened with wide eyes. Bettina fell asleep on the couch.

My mother used to play some of these songs, accompanying my father's sister Louise's beautiful rich contralto. We children would listen at night, upstairs in our rooms. The saddest of these songs, "In Stiller Nacht, Auf Hoher Wacht," to us seemed to be the most melancholy song in the world; a sadness shared (in the song) by wild animals listening, and by the moon and stars that refuse to shine. There is no explanation for the voice that mourns at midnight in the wilderness. The cause of the sadness is *Weltschmerz*: the pain of knowing what's wrong with the world. Here I stood, singing, beside people who knew what this word means.

Most of the *Zupfgeigenhansl* songs are lively, though. There are love songs, merry marching songs, songs of wandering and of leave-taking, of betrayal and distant wars. These songs led to Schubert's *Winterreise*, his song cycle based on the lives of wandering journeymen (like many in the *Zupfgeigenhansl*). Mrs Robins played the demanding piano accompaniment of these

119

songs, and we went on singing. The Robinses seemed to know all the words. The most moving of that cycle, *Der Lindenbaum,* was, finally, my undoing:

> Am Brunnen vor them Tore
> Da steht ein Lindenbaum.

When they reached the last verse:

> Und seine Zweige rauschten
> Als riefen sie mir zu
> Komm her zu mir, Geselle,
> Hier findst Du Deine Ruh.

I wiped tears from my face. Fiona's eyes opened even wider. She's never seen me cry. Her eyes too filled with tears, and I had to assure her that it was only the music that made me feel sad.

I knew this was dangerous territory, to be left alone. I'd been there as a teenager when the world around me collapsed (the good, the dependable world) and later, during times of illness. That dark realm I must avoid at all cost. The children keep me on top of despair most of the time. And now, these extraordinary friends.

It was time to take the children home. Bettina hardly woke up when we carried her out to the car. Both children soon dozed in the back seat as John Robins drove us through the dark streets. Blurred ribbons of lights glided by, first Bloor Street, then Dundas, right downtown to our own house, only a a few buildings up from Dundas.

The heat still hung heavy in the downtown street and in the dark porch to which I carried Bettina. Fiona took my hand, sleepy now after this full day. The "man she loved" pressed something into her other hand, a small parcel, then left quickly as if he did not want to hear my thanks.

When the children were both in bed, I unwrapped the flat brown-paper parcel. And there was the little lute player, the *Zupfgeigenhansl,* the beloved dog-eared book, its title page inscribed by its former owner: John D. Robins.

Election fever is at its height now, and I have to work almost every evening. One gets caught up in the excitement. Things, for the first time in years, look good for the CCF in Toronto, perhaps all over Ontario. In Canada, socialists are still considered an unrealistic minority, vaguely communist except perhaps, in the west. In the United States there are journals like the *New Republic*. The *Canadian Forum* comes closest to that, but its circulation is not as wide.

I have to pay Lecia almost every evening to mind the children. I had hoped to put by a few dollars so that we could take a short holiday away from this heat, perhaps in August. But I'm afraid there will be nothing left. The cheapest holiday would be camping. Garth brought a large canvas tent over from England, once used by his mother for their family outings. He's offered to send it to us. I asked Anna whether I could store this and the metal pegs in the basement of this house, which contains little except the furnace and washing machine. She said, "Why not?"

I like talking to her as she sits in her bay window, bent over incredibly delicate embroidery on baby clothes, nightgowns, silk underwear. Her husband, like Lecia's husband, does shift work, but there the resemblance ends. Anna's family life is quiet and harmonious. Lecia's husband is seldom home, and his manner is strangely offhand, aggressive, demanding, He wants to be the undisputed decision-maker, but he has little to give. He demands special meals, always on time, but is seldom reliable in his hours. He is irritated by the noise and liveliness of children. Sometimes there are angry voices coming from their room, and I occasionally hear a crash. I hope he does not beat her. He swaggers in after his shift, and I'm never sure whether he is sober and naturally overbearing. Anna has told me that he's told Lecia that, at twenty-three, she's over the hill; he likes very young girls.

When I started working at the committee rooms, I'd hoped that my working hours would coincide with those of the crèche, but they seldom do entirely. I take the children there on my way to work, collect them when the crèche closes, but I usually have to leave them again in the evenings. And when I'm at the election office then, I keep on thinking: "What happens at home? Lecia can't even protect herself and Lenny. But then, the fact that she makes money is the only thing that impresses her brute of a husband.

It can't last. I'll have to look for other work in July. I have been on leave of absence from the union office, first during the children's quarantine, then to work for Millard (on loan so to speak). I decided to give formal notice last week, with the excuse that I'd applied for a translation job. They seemed to be relieved. What is certain is that they managed very well without me and that Frannie has really taken my place.

Less than a week till the election now, and the atmosphere at the committee rooms is electric, hopeful, and excited. Millard may well get South York; Agnes Macphail, East York – both are working-class districts. For the rest, much depends on the votes from the armed forces, where young men, away from their hometowns, are beginning to find out what goes on in the world.

~ June 28th ~

On Sunday we have volunteers at the committee rooms, and I managed to get away to visit Sweeney on the Island. We felt a fresh breeze from the lake as soon as we stepped on the ferry. This is Lake Ontario's cool north shore, where the water is not as warm as it is on the Niagara side. Gulls screamed around us; sail boats glided in the distance.

Sweeney shares a cottage made of clapboard painted a yellow ochre. It has a large screened porch, useful against mosquitoes, though there are few left now. We all wore shorts. The whole atmosphere reminded me of cottage country on Lake Couchiching.

Sweeney walked with us to a little store to buy ice cream cones for the children. We passed a beach with a marvellous view of the Toronto shore. There are few high buildings, none higher than the Royal York Hotel. The muddy little town where Anna Jameson spent so bleak a winter has certainly changed.

Before we got to the store, I noticed, to my surprise, the Cass-Beggs twins on a porch similar to Sweeney's. I hadn't known they were here on holiday, and they probably wouldn't welcome interruptions, so I held Fiona back from joining the twins. I sensed a chilly lack of welcome when their parents came to the screen door, as if we were trying to bring with us the turmoil of the city they were trying to avoid.

I quickly assured them that we were here to visit a friend and had only seen them by accident. We walked on a little and were joined by our old friend, Marjorie Johnston, who was visiting the Cass-Beggses and stepped down quickly from their cottage when she saw us. She'd been trying to get in touch with us, but didn't have our new address.

I told her about my work at the committee rooms. "I don't know what I'll do after that."

"That's what I wanted to talk to you about. One of our staff members is going on holiday, and I wondered if you could take her place for a few weeks. It's not very demanding work if you can type from a dictaphone."

I hesitated. I'm not sure that I want to do office work again – I'm not good at it. But for a short time – before I find another factory job – to work for someone as sympathetic as Marjorie … It might help. The hours, she pointed out, are exactly those of the crèche. Perhaps if I take this job, I can save enough to get away for a week or so.

"I've never typed from a dictaphone," I confessed. "I'd like to try, though."

"It's like typing to dictation. But if you can't keep up, you can turn it back. That helps."

It sounded better than trying to decipher one's shorthand scribbling. "Could I try? I could come right after the election. I haven't heard about the translation job in Ottawa."

Marjorie's office at the Neighbourhood Workers is just east of the centre of town (Yonge Street), a shorter streetcar ride than that to the election office. And there would be no further worry about evening hours. We arranged that I'd come by for a trial session with the dictaphone, and Marjorie went back to the Cass-Beggses' cottage.

Sweeney and I continued down to the beach. She spread out towels, and we sat watching the children playing in the sand. I made a quick sketch of the Toronto skyline. Sweeney sat quietly smoking, and I thought I noticed a change in her, a sadness for which she makes up by extra heartiness. But her gaiety rings hollow.

Bill Sefton has got engaged to a handsome Protestant girl. I knew this from Elaine. Neither Larry nor Bill's mother approves of Bill's choice. Sweeney does not discuss it. But after a long silence, while I was sketching, she suddenly said that she thought of getting a job in another town.

"But where, Sweeney. Everyone's coming to Toronto these days."

"That's just why. I am an experienced inspector now. My brother's driving south, through Windsor, into the States. I thought I might go with him. It's time I saw the world. If I want to settle, there are some good jobs in Windsor too."

"Oh, Sweeney."

How can I tell her how much her wit has helped me, her defiance in the face of obstacles, her faith in her union work? Helped my own badly shaken faith in what people can accomplish. She's been one of the first and strongest links in our safety net. "You'll be missed," I said at last. How inadequate it sounded. "You'll never write, I know."

"I'm not much good at writing. You have to come and see me."

I shook my head. Too complicated to explain our status as enemy aliens in the U.S.

"My parents will keep track. I'll keep in touch with the Steelworkers. They exist in the States too."

Yeah, I thought, *like Mr Walker in his business suit. Who indicated, with a few encouraging words, how welcome my departure would be.*

~ July 3rd ~

The election last week now seems a long way away, and it's hard now to relive the tensions of that day. Hundreds of new names had been added to the voters' lists, and there were many more volunteers showing up.

The important day started so early that I had to ask Lecia to take the children to the crèche for me. As soon as I opened the office, volunteers came in to help, arranging car pools to drive people to the polls. Scrutineers went off to check on the voting in each riding. The other parties paid scrutineers quite handsomely; in the CCF they're all volunteers. The telephone rang all day, and the radio blared forth voting results in hourly bulletins.

In some ridings the CCF did so well that for a few hours we believed it might become the leading party. Bill Temple won the High Park riding from George Drew, the Pro-Con leader, who will have to look for another seat. It was about ten at night when we finally knew that Millard had made it in South York. Agnes Macphail was elected in East York, Andy Brewin in Florence's riding. Nobody could be quite sure of the end results until midnight. Votes from soldiers overseas came in even after that, but they only confirmed the general trend: the CCF became the official opposition.

There were parties, celebrations, at the Millards, the Seftons, the McCurdys. We sang some of the old union songs we'd sung earlier, at the Robinses' garden party:

> Old Paint, Old Paint, a finer horse there ain't
> Than Paint, Old Paint – the horse with the union label.

Or the cheerful:

> There was a union maid, she never was afraid ...

And the slower, moving song:

> I dreamt I saw Joe Hill last night, the same as you and me.
> I said, But Joe, you're ten years dead
> I never died, said he. I never died, said he.

The next few days were an anti-climax. The committee rooms were packed up, the lists and cards and posters taken away. Suddenly, there was only an empty store.

I started my replacement job at the Neighbourhood Workers the very day after our election office had been tidied up. It has rained and is a little cooler now. From the West End Crèche I now take streetcars east, then north. The building where the Neihbourhood Workers have their headquarters – like many of the old houses in formerly prosperous areas – is slightly dark inside.

I had a session with the dictaphone before starting full-time. The blurred, tinny sound of the voices dictating their caseworkers' records seemed hard to understand at first. The other secretaries, who are very friendly, said they had the same trouble at the beginning. They showed me how to turn back the dictaphone so that one can hear the sentence again. They are so familiar with the material in general, and with the style of each caseworker dictating, that they have less trouble with the obscure parts.

These caseworkers refer to those they visit as "clients," a word reminiscent, at least to me, of business people, doctors, real estate agents. "Client said she has not received her husband's allowance for the children …" (a common complaint). "Client's children in poor health. Dirty (or is that sturdy?)." "Husband alcoholic. Bruises indicate abuse …" Most accounts describe hopeless people, dreary housing, sick or uncontrollable children, alcoholism, abuse. Lecia should seek the help of these social workers. But she won't, I know. And there are probably many like her.

One of the middle-aged typists, who's enviably fluent in her dictaphone interpretations, quite openly admits that she writes stories for a woman's magazine based on the accounts we hear. It's supposed to be fiction, of course. Is this ethical? Does Marjorie know? She's separate from us, in her own office. The person who writes these stories is convinced that she's doing a useful service by drawing public attention to the misery of others. There's no denying that Dickens did the same.

I try to see my little family with their eyes, as "clients": war guests without any resources. Would our background stand up to scrutiny? Of British stock and citizenship, but brought up in an alien country with which we're at war. I should be less suspect because of my convictions, but here the leftist CCF is seen as almost as bad as communists (officially our allies – both opposed Hitler). I share a small attic with an entire family (husband suspected of abuse) and have two preschool kids at a subsidized crèche.

What we hear on dictaphones does not seem to spoil our lunch breaks. Then, we talk mainly about hometowns and holidays. The typist who writes fiction is from Wiarton, a little town on Georgian Bay. On that town's sheltered lakeshore, she says, the Women's Institute sponsors cheap housekeeping cabins, a family camp. They have wooden tent floors for rent that share services with other cabins: electric light, picnic tables, drinking water, a communal cookhouse. The beach is shallow, suitable for children. For a couple of dollars a week you could have a safe holiday place. There's a small store at this camp office, where one can purchase milk and groceries for no more, probably, than what we'd spend on food in the city.

And there's no poison ivy. I had thought of camping at Elsie's in Shanty Bay, but Fiona is so allergic to poison ivy that a place without it seems ideal. The train fare to Wiarton is eight dollars return. Children under five travel free. Mrs Roach gave me the address of the Wiarton Women's Institute (she's a member). I wrote there right away to reserve a tent floor for the last two weeks of July.

~ July 10th ~

Florence has come to the rescue again. She and Bruce took a canoeing holiday right after the election, so they can now spare a lilo that blows up as a bed and takes very little space, as well as a small folding cot. I went to get both and found her and Bruce looking tanned and on easier terms than during the winter. They had canoed down the Severn River, ending up in Georgian Bay, not too far from where we're heading.

I have no sleeping bags, so I'll have to take the few blankets I own and the family linen that came with us across the Atlantic. They'll fit into my duffle bag if tightly rolled. My rucksack

127

(cooking gear and paintbox) may travel in the train compartment, but the heavy tent bundle (stored at present in Anna's section of our basement) and the duffle bag will have to travel in the train's baggage car. I managed to save thirty-three dollars these last weeks. That should be enough for train fare, camping, and food. With the money for the twins' portrait, we should have a carefree holiday.

Having furnished rooms, one can give a week's notice. Much as I like Anna and Lecia, I've decided to give up this attic room and look for another place. I can save rent money for almost a month: the McCurdys have to go to a ten-day conference in August and asked me to look after their house and children again. It will mean six children in all, but it's such a help to us that I gladly promised to do it. Saving rent and board for us three just then will give me time for job and apartment hunting.

Anna will let me store our few belongings (rocker, cot, and small desk) in her part of the basement, where the tent has been stored ever since it arrived from New York. It really looks as if, in a few days, we'll be off, travelling north to clean air, clear water, sun on rocks, the summer sound of screen doors.

After the election office closed I've seen the Robinses just once, before they went to their own cottage for the summer, where John Robins hopes to revise his book, *The Incomplete Angler*. He has lent me Anna Jameson's *Winter Studies and Summer Rambles* because, he says, it describes Lake Huron in the summer section. He insists that the *Zupfgeigenhansl* he gave us is not a loan but a gift. A gift I shall always treasure.

~ July 16th ~

I am scribbling this on our picnic table in Wiarton. The part of Georgian Bay one sees from this camp does not evoke the scenes painted by the Group of Seven. It's very tame and sheltered. I brought my paintbox, some small pieces of canvas paper, and some pieces of Masonite, the cheapest material I could find. But I'll have to get out of the camp to do my painting.

To get all our camping gear to Toronto's Union Station in one taxi proved to be quite a hassle. Even though the metal tent poles were severely shortened (the upper part slips into the hollow lower section), the taxi driver did not like them any more than the heavy tent bundle. Unceremoniously, he dropped us – tent and accessories, duffle bag, rucksack, small children, et all – near the place where we had to register our luggage for the train's baggage car. He drove off while I was still counting my pieces. I found that I'd left behind the bag with the tent pegs, either in the cellar or in the taxi. So I had to drag both children to the nearest pay phone to call Anna. She looked for the bag in the basement but couldn't find it. Meanwhile it was time to board the train. Luckily, tent pegs could be homemade when we reached the camp. We have enough luggage as it is.

The children fell asleep in the train, so I had time to leaf through Anna Jameson's book. The summer part, away from Toronto, is much more enthusiastic than that describing winter – not only about the landscape around Lake Huron but about the Ojibwas with whom Mrs Jameson was staying. She formed a strong friendship with a Native woman, Mrs Johnston, the mother of the missionary Henry Schoolcraft's Ojibwa wife. Plump, citified Anna undauntedly shot the Sault rapids with her new friends, and for this was given a special Ojibwa name.

When I got to this point, the conductor came along and told us Wiarton would be the next stop. I reminded him that we had a large bundle in the baggage van. I'd have to get it out at the station, or we'd not have a roof over our heads. He promised to see to it, as the train would not stop for long at Wiarton. I dragged my rucksack down from the luggage rack and alerted my sleepy children. At the Wiarton station we just had time to retrieve the tent and duffle bag before the train steamed north to meet the Manitoulin ferry.

The children, wide awake and hungry now, sat on our bundles while I looked for a taxi. There didn't seem to be such a thing, no vehicles of any kind, other than a truck, parked near the refrigerator cars that stood on a siding – storage, perhaps, for fish and other produce to be shipped south.

A short man in a lumberjack's shirt alighted from the truck and limped to the platform. He asked if we needed a ride.

"We have to get to the camp, the one run by the Women's Institute. Is it far?"

"It's on my way," he said. "I'll bring the truck over."

This was better than a taxi. There was plenty of room for our large bundles in the empty back of the truck. The children revived at the very idea of driving in a truck – a red one at that – for the first time in their lives. They squeezed in between the driver and myself. I looked across them at this man, whom I saw more clearly now that he'd pushed back his battered fedora. He was Indian, probably Ojibwa, like the children I'd met at Rama.

The deep-set eyes in his wide face were hidden by glasses. It's hard to guess his age. In spite of his limp, he seemed vigorous and quick-moving when he helped us load our luggage. He introduced himself: his name is Tom Jones, and he is the chief of the Cape Croker Reserve.

He drove us to the camp office and waited until we were shown to the wooden tent floor, where he helped us unload our gear. I was still taking stock of our space, which is surrounded by gnarled old apple trees, when Tom Jones backed out his red truck and rattled away, not waiting to be properly thanked. The woman from the camp office who took us to our reserved space was surprised to hear we'd come by train. Most people come by car, she said. That's why a taxi was not around. Private cars are parked near almost every one of the housekeeping cabins.

The bulk of our canvas tent looked daunting. I had never attempted to put it up. I pulled out the ridgepole to its full length and did the same for the upright poles that would have to hold it at each end. I laid them more or less where they should go, then spread the mass of canvas over the arrangement of poles and crawled underneath. The children, wide awake now, developed the energies that possess them towards evening. They began to jump around on top of the undulating mass that covered me. From the outside this mass must have looked like the hide of a collapsed elephant. When they found the entrance flap, they crawled in to join me. I chased them out and tried to put up the entrance pole. It remained vertical until I crawled to the other end to put up the other pole. Then it collapsed. It was almost totally dark in there, and I sweated with the exertion. Outside I heard voices mingling with the children's high chirp.

My arms clutching the pole, I looked out and saw several men in lumbermen's shirts whittling away at wooden spikes. "Dint' see no pegs around," one of them said. "But there's plenty of applewood."

I admitted having left the metal pegs in Toronto. But the whittled pegs soon found their places in the grass all around, and the ropes from the tent corners and sides were laid loosely beside them. The men helped me to erect the poles and fasten the ridgepole across the top. Then they tightened the ropes and fastened them to the pegs. The tent now stood, as solid as a house. Only the flysheet had to be fastened above it, and my helpers, neighbours in the camp, did not think it would be needed on a calm evening.

They were there mainly for the fishing, they said. Their families occupied the cabins near those rowboats close to the shore, and they now rowed out for their evening jaunt. Lights went on all over the camp. I too have a light bulb on a long extension, clamped to the ridgepole inside the tent. It makes quite a good lamp.

We explored the camp and found the washrooms and cookhouse. There are even a few showers in the washroom section. We bought milk at the little store where we'd registered. It does not seem to have fixed closing hours. Our tent, with the light left on inside, looks like a huge heavily, shaded lantern. We crawled inside like so many moths.

I'd brought a cardboard box from the store. In it I now placed my cooking gear and inherited family silver (I had no ordinary spoons and forks, couldn't afford even those at Woolworth's). All I had to do now was blow up the lilo and the children could go to bed, one on each end. They're small enough so their feet don't touch in the centre, and if they roll off, they can't fall far.

I placed the box as a kind of table between them and the camp cot I assembled for myself. It's quite low, but there's enough space under it to store the rest of our belongings – whatever does not hang from tent poles. It's surprisingly warm. We don't need more than one blanket for each bed.

There were small noises all through the night – dogs barking, voices from the cabins, radio music. Once or twice, a green apple fell on the top of our tent. I resolved to collect these intruders to make applesauce the next day.

The morning was dewy and fresh. A shred of mist hung over the bay, on which there were early fishing boats even now. We had our breakfast, cornflakes and milk, out on the nearest picnic table.

The table was between us and the nearest housekeeping cabin, and I wondered whether perhaps it was there for the use of the middle-aged couple who now returned from their early morning fishing. So I asked and was told that they used a table closer to the cookhouse, on the other side of their cabin.

The woman introduced herself as Mrs Harvey and showed me how to fry the fish in the cookhouse, when we took our turn there. This fish is known as lake trout: its flesh is salmon-coloured and quite delicious. They come every year, she said, from London, Ontario, where her husband is a professor of economics.

When I took the children down to the beach, I found it very shallow – good for the children but boring for those who don't want to walk out a mile for a proper swim. I got out my paints and did a little sketching, mostly of the children while they built sandcastles. The sand is dark, not really suitable for the children to play in. And I felt a little embarassed sketching, with all the people around.

Fiona and Bettina started to collect green apples, and I asked at the camp office if that was all right. "Take as many as you want," the woman there said. I bought extra sugar to make applesauce and went back to the cookhouse. In daytime, it's not much used,

Mrs Harvey saw my paintbox on our table and told me that she understood my disappointment in this bay. "The real splendour of Georgian Bay is just a few miles away, at Cape Croker and Manitoulin. We're driving to the cape tomorrow, if you'd like to come."

~ July 19th ~

The Harveys, who, like most of the campers, have come by car, took us up the Bruce Peninsula the next day. One can't drive as far as the Cape Croker lighthouse, which sits on the very end of a rocky point by that name, but we had a wonderful drive along a bay opening out to blue-green water, a transparent turquoise flecked with amethyst and rose. In the distance the lake was a deep indigo blue, shimmering through a curtain of birch trees on our right.

We stopped for a picnic near a large dock, used, the Harveys explained, by the lighthouse to get provisions. There were many canoes and rowboats milling around. The only motorboat belonged to the lighthouse, we were told. A teenaged Indian boy jumped on to the dock, fastened the boat, and began to take on boxes handed to him by women and children, also probably Ojibwa like him. The orange and red of the women's and children's clothes, the golden brown of arms and legs, added patches of warm colour to this scene. I wished I'd brought my paints.

~ July 21st ~

The Harveys had to leave this weekend, and I decided to do some painting on my own, from a cliff that seemed within walking distance from the camp. On our outing I'd noticed a path leaving the main road on top of a hill just above the town. It should get me to that cliff, and I'd have privacy there for painting. So this morning I packed my rucksack with paintbox and lunch and the deflated lilo for Bettina's nap. The three of us set out and slowly climbed the hill. The road was empty.

I'd thought it best not to leave money in the tent, so I took my cash in a change purse stuck in the rather small pocket of my shorts. There was no room for our railway tickets. I left those between pieces of sketching paper, taking only one canvas board with me and some scrap paper for Fiona to crayon.

The cliff was a little disappointing. There was not anything like the view we had at Cape Croker, though the water here too had that wonderful varied hue. I found a dry, grassy area among shrubs, mainly sumac, blew up the lilo, and tried to get Bettina to sleep after we had our picnic. Then I got out my oils and worked rapidly. The light changed. I was tempted to correct what I'd painted, but remembered how easy it is to make a painting look muddy if one paints on top of wet oil colours.

We couldn't see the road from our promontory, but we could hear the traffic. It seemed to get much louder as the day wore on. I'd forgotten that it was Sunday, and that there would be cars coming back from the Manitoulin ferry. This might get worse in late afternoon, so I decided to pack up and get back to camp before then.

I put the paintbox into the rucksack, rolled up the lilo, and decided to carry Bettina, while Fiona would hold my hand. But no, I needed that hand to hold my wet painting. Fiona would have to hang on to the pocket of my shorts. She did, for dear life, as we walked down hill on the narrow shoulder of the road. There's no sidewalk and, far closer than comfortable, car after car passed us on that road, at speeds that seemed aggressive. Cars could not pass each other here. Perhaps they could not for some time on this narrow road, yet had to get all the way back to Toronto or Waterloo or Windsor.

My arms began to ache fiercely, but I never stopped until we got near the camp. Then I set Bettina down. Fiona let go and I searched my pocket for the small change purse. I wanted to buy milk.

The purse was gone.

Oh, why had I not put it in the side pocket of the rucksack. I searched there also, just to make sure. Nothing. With a sinking feeling, I then searched through our tent from top to bottom. My books, the tickets, our family silver, were untouched, exactly where I'd left them. I stared at the silver forks and spoons? Should I sell them. I could, if it came to the worst.

For Fiona's sake, I put up a brave front. It was not the end of the world. We'd stocked up on cans and staples. I'd paid the rent. I went to the store and told them of our predicament, and they allowed me credit for milk for the rest of the week.

That very evening I wrote to the Cass-Beggses, hoping they were not on holidays too. The pastel of the twins is finished. Even if the change purse was found somewhere on the road, it would be good to have extra funds. We could extend our holidays for another week.

As the other campers came in from fishing, I asked them, if they drove north, to look out for a small red leather purse. Several of them set out right away but found nothing. They drove further than the path from the main road to the cliff, even stopped some cars returning from the ferry. Still nothing.

~ July 22nd ~

This morning, other campers searched the road again. But I now think that the purse was picked up right away by a passing car. I'll never see it again. Luckily, I had stamps with my writing paper, so I could mail my letter. I then called on the *Wiarton Echo*, published once a week, to see if they would insert an ad that I'd pay for later. They insisted on putting one in the "Lost and Found" section free of charge.

Even before the ad appeared, word must have spread. School children from all over town searched the highway once again, joined by local inhabitants and tourists. At our tent and picnic table, food began to appear as if by magic. Almost everyone in the camp seemed to have caught more fish than they needed. People about to leave brought remnants of their staples – breakfast cereal, potatoes, lentils, bread – which, they said, would only be left behind anyway. I still had enough sugar to make applesauce from the apples all around us.

~ July 23rd ~

Today the red truck reappeared. I thought it must be Tom Jones's day to deliver fish to the refrigerator cars, but the truck made straight for the camp, as far as our tent. Tom Jones had read the *Echo*. Schoolchildren from the reserve had set out with their teacher to look for our small purse, but found nothing.

"We have a camping area at Cape Croker," he began. "Would you like to use it, rent free, for a time? It's a really nice place."

"You mean right near the dock?" I asked.

"No, further north, below the Indian agent's house. It has as fine a view as the docks, but it's more sheltered. And there are good clean restrooms."

I had noticed people using this euphemism for outhouses, an important part of camping life. I wondered whether he mentioned the Indian agent (a white man from the Department of Indian Affairs) because he thought I might be nervous. I was not in the least nervous. It would be a wonderful chance, staying right in the centre of the reserve.

"I have a general store," he went on." You can have credit there."

"I've written to friends for money," I said. "But it may take more than a week to get here."

I made some rapid calculations. Our rent is paid up until the end of the week. I should pay the camp store before leaving, if my letter has any result. I could write to Florence too. But I don't really want to charge her for her portrait. And friendships are easily damaged if you borrow money.

Tom Jones's offer was too tempting to turn down. I told him that I had to wait for an important letter I hoped to get before the end of the week. After that, I'd be glad to accept. He said he'd be back and limped to his truck. Then only did he drive to the station and the refrigerator cars.

~ July 27th ~

Well, I didn't have to sell my godmother's silver spoons and ivory-handled knives. A letter from Barbara Cass-Beggs came today, enclosing a cheque for twenty-five dollars for the twins' portrait. She must have written by return. Her note was not free of admonitions about my carelessness with money. And she asked whether I could paint the twins in oils for the same twenty-five dollars, as they preferred my oils to pastels. Right now I didn't mind. I could now pay the store, after cashing the cheque at the small local bank. There was little money left, but I had our tickets and would only have to pay for food the next week.

When I announced that I was going to stay at the reserve, there were some raised eyebrows at the camp. But I'm gripped by the spirit of adventure. We're off to Cape Croker tomorrow.

~ July 28th ~

Taking down the tent took a much shorter time than putting it up, so that we were packed and ready long before the red truck came into view. This time I made sure the pegs whittled for us came along as well. We had a last shower, for I assumed there would be no running water in the restrooms mentioned by Tom Jones. And we thanked the many new friends we'd made at the camp, the children especially.

As Mr Jones drove us up the Cape Croker road, he talked about his childhood. His limp is due to polio. He was lucky, he said, to get to the hospital. He learned to read and did well at school. Eventually he became a teacher.

At the dock where we'd stopped with the Harveys' the truck turned north. We passed several sturdy log houses, some with garden patches of sweet corn. The houses looked more prosperous than the weather-stained board buildings on Rama. When I mentioned that I'd been there, Tom Jones said that the Protestants at Cape Croker had relatives there. Those that are Orangemen. I thought I hadn't heard right. "Orangemen? Aren't they Irish?"

"The Protestants here, the ones with the neat houses you see, those are Orangemen. They have more sense of progress than the Catholics. They voted for me."

I had to think this over. How extraordinary to find the Protestant work ethic way out here. How did the puritans invade this area? Where had they come from? Wasn't it Father Brébeuf and the Jesuits who had the first missions on Lake Huron? "Are there many Catholics?" I asked.

"All of the former chief's family," he said. "And many more."

He then explained his notions of progress. What made him "get ahead," he said, was his introduction of refrigerator sheds where fish could keep fresh until he took it to the train, to be transported to Windsor, Detroit, the States. Most of the reserve's income had come from fishing lake trout. "A family

137

could make eight hundred dollars, spring and fall, and that was enough for the whole year. But there's fewer fish now. And fewer men. So many are overseas."

Before coming here, I had tried to get some information on the history of the Bruce Peninsula. It had not been acquired for white settlers until the 1870s, when in western Ontario the feuds between Protestant and Catholic Irish were at their height. Why would the Ojibwas have become involved in this ancient religious (and political) feud? Did the division stand for something else? Something quite different, a way of living?

Manitoulin Island had been a holy place. In *Summer Rambles* Anna Jameson witnessed the annual ceremony of great numbers of Ojibwa coming to the island from all around Lake Huron, to collect government money meant to compensate them for their loss of land. The land they chose to keep was usually the best for hunting and fishing. Then agriculture came to western Ontario, the great forests were cut, and the abundance of game decreased. At the same time, Ojibwas who had lived as far west as Wisconsin were moved to Lake Huron. Perhaps this new faction had introduced the Protestant ethic. Or the other way around. There had, originally, been great resentment among the Ojibwas that the sacred island of Manitoulin was to be settled at all.

At a corner where a new road turned west, Tom Jones pointed out his general store, dwarfed by his refrigerator shed. We left the main road and descended a lane to a sheltered peninsula. Only one building could be seen here, a modern house some distance above this hollow, sitting snugly between trees. Its shutters were closed.

"The Indian agent's house," Mr Jones explained, but did not tell us whether or not the agent was at home. Perhaps he was on holiday. There was no sign of life.

The lane continued to the wooded tip of the peninsula. Here there were some picnic tables under the great trees and a modest, newly painted outhouse. Our camp site. Tom Jones would not have exaggerated if, instead of "a nice place," he'd called it "breathtakingly beautiful." Tall birches and evergreens framed a wide view of the open bay, its headlands and islands stretching into a shimmering distance. This really was a place for painting.

Between the rough-hewn picnic tables there is a small stone circle for cooking, and beside the outhouse a stack of firewood. "The wood is dry. You can get more at the store," Mr Jones explained, as he helped us to unload the tent.

"What about drinking water? Is there a pump somewhere?"

"That too you can get at the store, bottled. Or boil the lake water. Come to the store later and you can have a container. Five gallons may be too heavy, but there are one gallon ones too."

He turned the truck and it clattered uphill towards the main road. The children had immediately made for the beach. I ran after them, as enchanted as they were. The sand here is pure white, the water crystal clear, the colours of Georgian Bay as varied – sapphire, amethyst, turquoise – as the jewel colours I'd first seen at the Cape Croker dock.

I was determined to put up the tent on my own this time and, first, to find a really good place for it, level, mossy, with few rocks and undergrowth. I pushed one of the picnic tables to such a place and over it I laid the ridgepole and canvas. I then stood up the two end poles and tied them loosely to nearby trees. I asked the children to stick the wooden pegs into the ground while I raised the ridgepole and fastened it to the two upright supports. This worked. The heavy canvas slowly rose to the proper height.

I moved the tent pegs further away so that the tent was tautly tied down on all sides. It was large enough to leave the table in there as support for all our gear. Standing at the centre, it separated the lilo and folding cot on either side and provided us with a proper room.

Looking back from the beach that had once more attracted my little girls, I admired my handiwork. Our shabby old tent had taken on a homelike appearance, dwarfed by majestic cedars, ruler-straight balsam firs, silver birches that still had the perfect bark from which voyageur canoes had been made.

Across the bay, I could see a few buildings at a still further extension of our peninsula. This would be where the right fork of our road must lead. There are a few sheds there and some boats. I could see some movement, but it's too far to recognize details.

Now, for our drinking water. Mr Jones's store is no different from Ontario country stores I'd seen in Shanty Bay and Barrie. Baling wire, binder twine, tools, dishes, fly swatters, rolls of screening sit cheek by jowl with canned foods and dry goods. Somewhere behind the counter and even shorter than her husband was Mrs Jones, whose speech is as soft and low as that of Indian women I've encountered at Rama. There is no fresh milk; people on the reserve use evaporated milk, she explained. A little can of this is easier to carry anyway, when I had to carry a gallon water container as well, and a small hatchet to split wood.

I'm sitting at the picnic table now. The sun has left our clearing, and the water in our cooking pot on the stone ring shows signs of boiling. I've put a can of beans inside the water to heat. I'm using every scrap of paper I still have for these notes. But I don't have much time for writing. I have to keep a very sharp eye on the children, who so love this sandy beach. I took soap and towels down to the water – luckily very shallow – and we had our evening wash there. The evenings are drawing in earlier now, and that helps to get these tired little girls to sleep.

~ July 30th ~

Here I am, sitting at the same table in the morning, after our first day at the new campsite. Last night we'd collected sticks to replenish the firewood, and the water in our cooking pot was again showing signs of boiling. We were so intent on watching it that neither the children nor I noticed that someone had come, very quietly, and was now standing by our table, watching us squat around the erratic fire.

The children saw her first: a girl of about thirteen or fourteen, even-featured, golden-skinned, with tranquil inscrutable eyes. It struck me at once that I'd seen this girl before: she had been with the women and children on the Cape Croker dock the day we saw the lighthouse boat come in. I remembered the red cardigan over the cotton dress, the beauty of the tranquil face.

Then, too, I thought I'd seen her before, many times, painted by Gauguin, carrying Tahitian fruit. This girl too carried something in her arms: cobs of sweet corn. She laid them on our table.

"Corn!" Fiona cried, overjoyed. "Put it in the pot, Mummy."

"What perfect corn," I said. "Early, isn't it? Where does it come from?"

"My aunt sends it," the girl said. "Mrs Johnston."

She smiled, seeing the children's excitement. The corn went into the pot and in a few minutes was cooked to perfection, a sign that it was completely fresh. In even fewer minutes there were only empty cobs on our tin plates. I put them aside to dry, for fire-lighting.

"Won't you sit down," I asked the girl. "These children are called Fiona and Bettina. What is your name?"

"Lorraine," she said. "Lorraine Johnston."

Only now I realized that she had not come by road but by boat. Hidden by the cedars down along the bay there was a rowboat. A boy sat down there, on a rock, motionless, the painter of the boat under his bare feet.

"That's my cousin," Lorraine said. "We came from over there." She pointed to the sheds across the bay.

"Ah," I said. "So your aunt lives there."

She shook her head, smiling at my ignorance.

"My grandfather lives there," she explained. "He's away. But my grandmother is home."

I wished I had binoculars to study the distance, the birds, the islands. I thought I could detect small figures moving about near the sheds across the bay. "Are those children?" I asked.

She nodded. "My grandfather has many children. And then there are others ..." her voice trailed off as if the task of explaining all this was too much for her.

"I must go," she said abruptly. "Goodbye."

She was gone before I could properly thank her. The boat detached itself from the deepening shadows and moved soundlessly through the shining water. Splashes from the oars caught the last sunlight. It got smaller and smaller until it was swallowed by the shadows on the opposite shore.

We have no electric light here, so I have to give in to the earlier evening hours. I have to be careful with flashlight batteries too. Our flashlight is precious and for emergencies only. I miss the useful light bulb at the Wiarton camp.

We all go to bed early and I lie awake, listening, looking out through the tent flap at the moon rising over the trees. Crickets chirp in a steady rhythm. There are many other sounds; a yapping bark at a distance might be a fox. There may also be wolves around, bears probably too. The rustling in the bushes could be caused by rabbits, by coons or porcupines. Indians hunt year-round, I told myself, so animals know better than to come close to their habitations. Deer and coons are attracted by corn, though, and so are bears. I was surprised that this thought did not cause me greater anxiety.

I hadn't panicked when we lost our money. We are so far from the greatest anxieties, the war and terror in this world, that all I could feel was peace.

~ August 2nd ~

The wood fire blackens our hands, sheets and towels turn grey, and so do our clothes. Our socks, everything, needs washing. We don't go barefoot here, we've been warned that there are still some rattlers on Georgian Bay.

I decided to scrub and slap our laundry as Spanish women do, getting their linen snow-white in clear, cold water. Anna Jameson described the water of Lake Huron as so clear that you could see the white stones thirty fathoms below.

Our sheets, thrown into the water of this shallow bay, form bulges here and there like the backs of white whales. The children in their tiny bathing suits, ready to help, jumped on these bulges and they came up in another place. They shrieked with delight. I had to watch carefully so they would not slip and disappear under these white undulating tents of washing.

Towels were next. I keep our clothing to a minimum. We wear sunsuits or bathing suits all day. If it is chilly, evenings or early mornings, we put overalls or sweaters on top. My own bathing suit has narrow blue and white stripes and a ballerina skirt. I'd chosen it when we were still in Barrie, where everybody did their shopping from Eaton's catalogue. It had been a thrill, unpacking the Eaton's parcel when it arrived.

When I draped the laundry over rocks and bushes to dry, I made the children put on their sneakers (because of snakes) and settled them on a patch of sand with some tin cups and wooden spoons. Several towels had got muddy when we dragged them out of the water. I ran up to the tent to get a pail, so I could pour water over them.

Near the stone circle something like a short rope slithered through the moss. I picked up the hatchet, still stuck in a piece of firewood, raised it in blind panic, and brought it down on the head of a striped snake. It was dead at once. This, I thought, is what war is like. I killed. Why? Because I panicked. This was probably a harmless garter snake. I was shaking as I looked towards the beach, where the two children were still crouched over their mud pies.

I buried the snake before I brought the children up to the picnic table for their lunch. The day was hot now, but we were in the shade. From the crossroads a dusty blue Ford rattled downhill into our lane, the one that skirts the bay. It stopped above our camp.

A sturdy woman in a blue cotton dress got out and walked down to our table. A bit like our friend Elsie, I thought: the amused dark eyes, the rather square face. Sunburnt, but lighter than Lorraine, her dark hair in a short bob. "I am Verna Patronella Johnston," she said in a low calm voice, also like Elsie's.

"A countenance open, benevolent and intelligent and a manner perfectly easy, simple, yet with something of motherly dignity" – that was how Anna Jameson had described her Mrs Johnston, and it perfectly described this woman, though she would be younger than that other, nineteenth-century Mrs Johnston. Thirty-five, perhaps. And instead of the soft, musical Ojibwa Anna liked so well, this woman spoke English.

"Oh, was it you who sent the corn? Thank you. It was so good."

Unlike Lorraine, Mrs Johnston sat down with us when invited. She looked with interest at our tent and the cooking stones. Our pots and pans and cans and bottles. "How do you store your food," she asked. "Has someone told you to store it as high as possible?" She said this with some reticence, as if she was reluctant to interfere.

"High?"

"Well, hanging from the ridgepole, say. There are dogs around that might go after meat, if you had any."

"I have mostly cans. Bread or eggs I could probably suspend that way, maybe in a covered pot. Would that do?"

"It might," she smiled. "The coons would still manage. But they're around at night, and then you'd be sleeping in there."

"No bears? Or wolves?"

"Well – probably not. They're shy because we hunt them. "

Her farm, she said, is about three miles west from the store by the crossroads. "We have sheep, so we have to keep the wolves at bay. Dogs too, and bears. We bring the sheep to a shelter near the house every night."

She has five children. Lorraine, her niece, lives with her most of the time, but often stays at the house across the bay, that of the former chief, Charles Jones, her father. "He's gone travelling," she said. "He's in Utah, in the States."

"There are so few men here, so many boats that aren't used much."

"The men are in the army. My husband is."

"But in Toronto there are lots of men of all ages, still."

"They don't have to join up to get the vote."

"You mean you can't vote here?"

"No, not here. If you leave the reserve, you may. Another way is to join up. If you join up, you don't have to leave this place for life."

"I see." I looked out across the bay. "I understand not wanting to leave. This is the most beautiful place I've seen in Canada."

"You should try to see this bay from the cliffs behind our house."

144

There must be a local grapevine, the store probably. She seemed to be well informed about us, knew we were war guests, that we'd lost our money, that I painted. We arranged that she would pick us up some day soon to visit her farm, so that I could paint up on those cliffs.

I said that Lorraine would make a good model and that I hoped to paint her portrait. The children like her too.

"I'll send her," Mrs Johnston said. Verna Patronella, not an Ojibwa name. I wondered whether she had one. Whether Ojibwa was still spoken.

She left a gap, even after this short acquaintance. Her car disappeared in a cloud of dust, not back to the main road but continueing on the lane to the tip of the peninsula – the old chief's house.

Lorraine came from there by boat in the afternoon. She sat very still, as quietly as the Rama children had. But she was not as shy; when the children talked to her, she replied in a gentle voice. For her portrait, I'm using my last piece of canvas paper, pinned to Masonite. After this I'll have to use Masonite only, and it needs heavy priming. I'm running short of gesso primer too.

This existence on the border of owning nothing is surprisingly satisfying. Even when one thinks: there are the children; they should have enough to eat, clothes, books, toys. The children adapt amazingly; they have no expensive dolls or cuddly toys; they use sticks and sand; they love pouring water, whether from a toy pail or a cooking pot. Stones that have an intriguing shape or bits of glitter, they will see as small animals, pieces of bread. I've heard Fiona talk of bacon stones, yet don't remember ever giving her any bacon to eat. They're constantly occupied. A visitor like Lorraine makes their day.

Lorraine did not shift her position, even when her cousin Jim came down from the store, the boy who'd rowed her across the first time she came. He is Verna Patronella's oldest son and had walked over from their farm. He had a telephone message – for me, of all people. Not from anyone we know, though.

The bush telegraph has reached the lighthouse. Jim's friend Francis, the boy who takes the lighthouse motorboat to the dock for provisions, brought an invitation: Would we like to visit the Cape Croker lighthouse, next time he came with the boat? Wednesday. If we accepted, Tom Jones would pass on the message.

~ August 5th ~

Yesterday morning Lorraine came to say that her aunt would pick us up around noon. We spent an hour or so on the portrait. In her position as model she is the children's captive, but manages very well.

"She's not bossy," Fiona said.

I have to be careful not to make the painting too Gauginesque. This is not Tahiti, and I shouldn't romanticize. (Did Anna Jameson perhaps romanticize?) I placed the girl so that her background would be the very light bay shining through between birches and cedars. It makes the foreground dark in comparison and I'm not satisfied with this balance. Even the red cardigan seems too dark.

The blue Ford turned up as promised. Mrs Johnston was wearing a man's corduroy trousers tucked into boots, so that they looked like riding breeches. Her faded khaki shirt too was a man's, the colour of the uniforms one sees on Toronto streets. A leather belt was drawn tightly below her bosom.

As we drove west on the main road, the shape of the peninsula surrounding our bay became clearer, but the buildings at its tip were now dwarfed by distance. As the lake opened up, other headlands and islands appeared. High, round clouds sent swift shadows across the water that changed the luminous colours to dark indigo.

Along the shore some docks lay half-submerged, unused, the fishing boats tied to them filled with water. "Fewer fish," Mrs. Johnston explained. "It's not only that the men are away. Some women fish and trap. But there's so much else to do, if you have livestock, grow corn, look after kids.

"And lately the salmon hasn't run as it once did."

"Is it the lamprey? Come in with Great Lakes shipping?"

She nodded. "Tom Jones with his big refrigerator shed can't change that." Her tone was derisive. Jones, she said, built the shed from insurance money he got when his store burned down. While he and his wife were away, teaching on one of the islands. It looked suspicious, but nothing could be proved.

There it was, this hostility. I'd noticed it in Tom Jones too. What was behind this story? The man seemed all right to me. Had been voted in as chief. By Orangemen, though. Mrs Johnston and her father, the former chief, are Catholics. "Tom Jones acts like a white man," she said, and I thought of his remarks about progress.

She pointed out her house, tall and a little bleak, in its corn patch. An ochre-coloured frame house that rose abruptly without the hedges, borders, flower beds one usually sees around a farmhouse. A field nearby was cropped short by a herd of sheep.

Lorraine, who had sat quietly between the two little girls in the back of the car, was welcomed by younger children who ran out from the large, bare kitchen, then stood petrified as strangers emerged from their mother's car. They slipped away while we were offered strong, dark tea. Lorraine set the filled cups, sugar, and evaporated milk on a table covered with oilcloth. Fiona and Bettina gazed at her, then at me, in wonder. They were offered tea for the first time in their lives.

"Those cliffs are too steep for the kids," Mrs Johnston said. "Lorraine will look after them." We were shown a bedroom where Bettina could nap for the afternoon. There was no furniture in it other than a metal bed with a quilted cover.

Jim, the twelve-year-old boy who was to come with us, took a game bag from a high shelf, and his mother slung a rifle over one shoulder and handed me a sharp knife. She started to laugh when she saw my perplexed expression and nodded at my piece of Masonite. "The view across the bay is so wide, you'll have to do two paintings. You can't get it all into one piece. And two small pieces are easier to carry than one large one."

I had to admit that this was a practical idea. The two narrow pieces, after I cut the Masonite, fitted well on top of my paintbox. I tied them on with twine. Strands of binder twine were hanging on the back door.

We walked away from the house, the sheep, the shining water of the bay, following Jim towards a tall pink and white cliff. As we got closer I could see a narrow path among the berry bushes and shrubs that had taken root in the crevices. There were small trees, tough enough to hang on to, climbing up.

Mrs Johnston saw me looking at her rifle. "You never know about bears, when the berries are ripe," she remarked nonchalantly.

The path got steeper and we climbed in silence. Behind us I sensed a vast expanse of bay and islands, but I didn't dare look back. A dizzying space seemed to press me forward against the rocks.

Towards the cliff top the path levelled off. Larger, windswept trees had sunk their roots deep into the crevices up here, the ragged, expressive Jack pines of Group of Seven paintings. Mrs Johnston looked around. Apparently, we'd arrived at the place she'd chosen.

Gnarled trees, bent double by the wind, gave us some shade. I turned to look towards the bay and faced an unlimited expanse, bay beyond bay, headland beyond headland, islands, promontories as far as the eye could see.

Verna Patronella and her son Jim settled at the foot of the Jack pine, the gun between them. She nodded towards the north of the Bruce Peninsula. "Those are our hunting lands," she said. " We go hunting there every fall, women and children, all of us."

It was a great joyful session for them, like Christmas.

"If you hunt," she said. "If you have tasted the meat of wild animals, deer, moose, beaver, the meat of cows and pigs is very insipid. We started keeping sheep for the wool, not the meat. But now the hunting is down we also eat mutton sometimes."

"The hunting is down?"

"Parties of white hunters come north in the fall, loaded with liquor. They're not supposed to hunt on our land. But they chase the deer and moose out of it to places where they can shoot them, just outside the reserve."

While we were talking, I arranged my paints on the palette (the lid of the paintbox) and took out the small bottles of linseed oil and turpentine. I'd given my boards two coats of primer, but they still seemed porous. The first quick sketch, just using burnt sienna and turps, sank right in.

I would never be able to do this view the justice that it deserved, and that my new friend expected. It would be impossible. One has to limit oneself to what paints can achieve. But then I thought of Turner, the wild, impossible impressions of atmosphere and weather. Perhaps the constant change of light, the feeling of vastness, would eventually enter into what my two small boards could hold, even though the sketch looked so tame right now. The distant headlands changed constantly, looking now hazy, now sharp and clear. The water took on all the evasive colours of precious jewels: sodalite, opal, emerald, sapphire, amethyst, jade, ruby. How could mere oil colours in tubes capture this evanescent glory?

Those two behind me remained perfectly silent. In front and below us a buzzard was gliding on the warm air currents. Still further below and closer to the water, seagulls rose and fell, shrilly complaining. All around me was the aromatic scent of herbs, of pine needles and other plants I couldn't identify. My head began to feel heavy. I lost track of time.

There are few places in the world where you get a sense of infinity. I understood why this was Verna Patronella's chosen place. For a moment it seemed as if I had left my body for another world, a world I had not entered since my childhood, when we had lived on an isolated farm. There are no words for what you feel then. I wondered whether Europeans truly have this sense of place here, or whether the only people who really have it are those who've always lived here.

The two boards in front of me began to show shapes and colours, though they seemed dull beside the reality of the constantly changing bay. I was running out of rose madder, out of viridian too.

I came to with a start – my heart beating wildly. A loud crack, a boom, like that of a plane diving too close, shattered the web of soft noises around us. I closed my eyes for a moment, and inside my red lids saw the shape of a black bear.

When I turned, there was no such shape. Jim was standing, gun in hand, watching a small feathery shape, a spruce grouse, running in circles like a beheaded chicken. Mrs Johnston had not risen. When Jim handed her the bird, she felt its chest. "Not much meat on it," she said. "It hasn't found our corn."

She laid the grouse on the game bag. "We'll find some herbs to go with it," she promised.

I wiped my hands on my paint rag. Impatient with brushes, I'd used my fingers to smooth the paint. Oh well.

The shadows below were long now. It must be late afternoon. I felt as if I had taken an intoxicating drug. I was ready to throw myself off the cliff and glide like the buzzard. My painting didn't amount to much, but that was not what I cared about any more.

I packed up my tubes and scraped my palette. My mouth felt dry. Jim and his mother helped me strap the panels to my rucksack, facing outwards so they'd not be smudged. Jim tied two sticks together, making a kind of clamp to hold the paintings away from anything they might touch. The bottom of this arrangement he stuck into my rucksack, the ends tied so that they reared up like Bedouin tent poles. This left my hands free for the descent.

When we reached the house, the sun was low over the lake. The water assumed a blinding glow. The whole kitchen was golden in this light. Mrs Johnston had stopped during our descent to pick a plant here, a leaf there. She put a handful of these herbs with the parcel Lorraine was making of the grouse she'd plucked in a jiffy, after Jim had taken out the entrails. All this was done smoothly, quickly, as a matter of course, while the children and I sat at the table drinking tea again.

"When I was a little girl," Mrs Johnston said, "my grandmother told us stories of the pine, king of the forest, whipping the birch for its vanity. And of the corn spirit, fought by a brave boy who broke it into kernels. So many stories, of good and evil spirits, I can't remember them all."

"Write them down, before you forget."

The smaller children had come in and were listening. All of us were eating thick slices of homemade bread with blackberry jam. "Did you bake this bread?" I asked.

"My stepmother did. She bakes for all of us. She was a nurse once. A white woman. She's been married to my father for so long, she's taken on our customs. She adopts all the children who have no home. Who have no parents, or sick parents. Whose mothers, like Lorraine's, died of TB."

"Do many still die of TB?"

"Many. My own mother did. My stepmother can tell you more. She'd like you to visit her. Maybe on the weekend?"

"Our last weekend here, I'm sorry to say. I have to go and mind a family in town, I promised.

"And we're expected at the lighthouse on Wednesday. But we'll be back before the weekend. Could you let her know we'd like to come?"

Mrs Johnston nodded. She looked at the sky like an old, weather-wise farmer. I could see no heavy clouds there. The clouds there seemed ethereal, tinted by the sinking sun to brilliant orange, in a pale green sky that close to the horizon began to turn purple.

Lorraine and Jimmy went out to bring the sheep close to the house. They brought in more corncobs for us to take along and took them to Mrs Johnston's car for us. We followed, carrying my paintings and the parcel with the grouse.

Mrs Johnston was looking at the ground as if she saw the future inscribed there. "Insects tell us there'll be a storm," she said.

That was yesterday. We managed to cook the grouse and corn together in one pot. I cleared the picnic table in the tent and laid my paintings there to dry. Already they've lost some of their brilliance, but so far haven't smudged.

This morning I packed a few extra clothes in the rucksack, and we are now sitting outside the tent, waiting for Tom Jones to pick us up. He always meets the lighthouse boat with provisions on Wednesdays..

~ August 10th ~

The insects were right. We had a heavy storm.

The lighthouse boat that picked us up on Wednesday crossed a mirror-still bay, not a ripple. The headlands looked close and sharp, and I thought no more about Mrs Johnston's warning until, that evening, all headlands were obliterated from our view by one of those sudden Georgian Bay squalls that spring up in seconds. We had gone for the day, with extra sweaters for the evening. We stayed for almost three days because no boat as small as the lighthouse boat, even though it has a strong motor, could venture out.

The lead-coloured masses of water rose as if to meet the pounding rain, as if two bodies of water were about to unite around us. All evening, all that night, all the next day, the foghorn sent its coded message into that seemingly impenetrable grey mass. It has a strangely haunting sound, a foghorn, and for a long time it kept me from sleeping. I listened with all my might for the muted reply from other, distant foghorns (ships? other headlands?) in their own special code. Each lighthouse has its own.

The lighthouse keeper and his boy took turns through the night. Lean, sandy-haired, of Scandinavian origin, he took it all in his stride. He'd asked us to visit, he said, because he'd read about us in the *Wiarton Echo*. He reads all the papers he can get – it's a lonely life; days and months go by when nothing much happens. Now, during a storm, he was in his element.

Even before the storm broke, while we were still sitting in his large, neat, bare but bright kitchen, he'd informed me that the Allies have invaded Sicily. "Not like Dieppe," he said, waving the newspaper our boat had brought. I had not read it yet.

"That was a disaster," he said. "But now, now they're going from strength to strength. Moving north."

"And Mussolini has really been captured?"

"Captured; yes. But somehow later freed by some German parachutists. It won't do him any good, though. He's lost the support of his own country."

"I was in Sicily once," I said. "Five years ago. A year before the war broke out. It seems like a dream now. Those Greek temples on the island – the carpets of tiny iris all around them.

"My husband had just finished his studies in Rome. If you were newly married, you could travel anywhere in Italy for twenty per cent of the fare. Musso's idea to encourage large families."

We studied every inch of the newspapers for more news of Allied victories. Then the storm broke and all Mr Jensen's energies were concentrated on the revolving lights, the mournful blasts of near and distant foghorns. He had barely time to indicate that we would have to stay, that there was plenty of room, plenty of provisions. The boat could not venture out.

The living quarters for the lighthouse are in a clapboard building that could easily house a large family. Most of the rooms are sparsely furnished or entirely bare. Ours contained cots and cupboards, little else. There were no curtains on the windows, so that the room was brilliantly lit every time the lighthouse beam flashed to that side of the house.

The children liked the sense of space, the wooden floors on which they could run back and forth. The storage shelves were piled high with old magazines. I pulled out the most colourful, found a pair of kitchen scissors, and cut out pictures for them to play with. Mr Jensen had little time to play host. He told me to help myself to something to eat. I easily found the staples to make a meal: rice, noodles, flour, sugar. Canned soup, canned juice, canned beans – not much different from our usual fare, camping.

In the morning, when the storm abated a little, I ventured outside to pick up the green apples that had been shaken down from an old tree. I had to stop the children from following me: the entire area outside the house was covered by a carpet of poison ivy. Fiona is so allergic to poison ivy that I would not let her touch the apples until I'd washed and peeled them. But she was happy rolling out dough for apple pies.

Whenever Mr Jenson or Francis darted into the kitchen for a bite to eat, they found something made from these apples: apple fritters, applesauce, apple pie. I found enough jars and a large sieve to make juice and used up another bag of sugar for apple jelly.

It was cool enough to cook on the wood stove, but electric appliances had not ceased to function because of the storm; the lighthouse has its own generator. Nothing could be allowed to break down. All mechanisms in the lighthouse had to be in perfect order, so that Mr Jensen could be in constant communication with a world he could not see. This world depended on his equipment, the programmed code of light and sound to lead those out there to safety.

Even when the heavy rain abated, the lake still moved wildly. Waves thundered against the rocks and spilled their foam high up on the shingles and stones, the only beach at the lighthouse point. Fiona listened to the mournful messages from distant foghorns, now faint, now startlingly close, while I explained that out there on the wild lake there were ships. Our foghorn, like the bird in Hansel and Gretel, was guiding them to safety. On these ships there were people: a captain, a telegrapher who could talk to the lighthouse keeper, a crew in wet Mackinaws slipping about on a wet deck as the lake tossed the ship about. Lifeboats would be readied, and everyone hoped they would not have to be used. Fiona did not remember, as I did, our lifeboat practices when we crossed the Atlantic. Daily, we stood there in our lifebelts, ready for inspection. She looked tiny in that large lifebelt, only her little head protruding at the top and those tiny feet beneath. She was smaller than Bettina is now.

The lake still churned for another day. We had to wait until the whitecaps subsided completely before we were allowed to take the boat back to the Cape Croker dock. Tom Jones was there to meet the boat. He'd been asked by telephone to bring fresh provisions. I asked him if the tent had been damaged in the storm.

No, he said. The advantage of the camping place was its sheltered position. I had left the flysheet fairly tight, and he noticed that someone had loosened the ropes a little, so the dampness would not pull the canvas too taut. Lorraine? I wondered. Or Jimmy? Or Verna Patronella herself?

When we got there, we found the flaps tightly shut as we had left them. Our food hung, untouched, from the ridgepole, and the two small paintings on the table, almost dry, had lost even more of their brilliance. On our beds were my mother's monogramed sheets. Our family silver lay untouched among the cooking gear under the cot. How many places in the world are there, I wondered, where one can leave all this and find it all intact, days later.

The sun has reappeared today, and the few things that got damp in the storm have dried. We have changed into our last lot of clean clothes and packed up most of our gear. In about an hour Jimmy will row us over to the old chief's house. Lorraine is waiting for us there. On Monday we have to go back to Toronto.

It is mid-August now, and the nights are getting colder.

~ August 12th ~

The tent has been taken down, rolled up with our other things. We are again sitting at the picnic table, waiting for Tom Jones's truck. I've paid for the groceries from his stores. Everything is straightened up and I managed. But without the corn and apples, the three days at the lighthouse, and this last weekend as Mrs Charles Jones's guests, it would have been a tight squeeze.

Our holiday is over. It's still hours before train time, but the fish have to be loaded into the refrigerator cars before then. I'm short of paper, using bits of newsprint and scaps of sketching paper for these notes. Our visit this last weekend was as unforgettable as the entire holiday. I want to jot down as much as I can before the demands of work and room-hunting obscure it all.

As Jimmy and Lorraine rowed us across the bay and we got closer to Charles Jones's white clapboard house, I could see that it was really quite large and well proportioned, with a screened porch on two sides. What from the distance of our camp had looked like a shed or boathouse turned out to be a half-submerged old boat, one large enough to be taken out fishing in

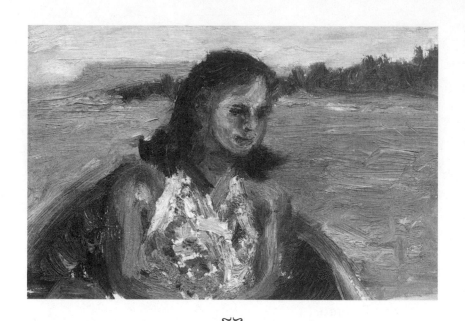

Lorraine in rowboat, Cape Croker,
1943 (oil)

heavy weather. That boat is now used as a dock by a crowd of lively brown children, for playing, for climbing, and for jumping in and out of the water. They looked completely at home, diving in like ducks, splashing one another, shouting with joy.

A sturdy white-haired woman came to meet our boat. Her eyes are bright blue and she has no tan; her skin is young for sixty-odd years, fine and white. She had a lunch ready on a long table in the porch. All of us, including some of the children who played outside, sat on homemade benches. Mrs Charles Jones poured out tea and cut thick slices of homemade bread. There was a bowl of what in Britain is called dripping on the table: fat collected from mutton (or beaver or bear?). The porch filled with more children than the benches would hold, their merry dark eyes studying us shyly.

After they had eaten (there was cold meat and a lot of coleslaw), Mrs Jones clapped her hands and all the children swarmed out, this time towards Hope Bay, the western bay I'd painted from the cliff top. "We have built a cottage there."

She pointed in the direction in which the children had disappeared among the trees. "So we can see Hope Bay day and night, when we are old and have retired there."

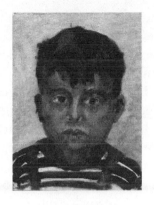

~~
Ojibwa boy,
1943 (oil)

I think there are about fifteen children in all. Lorraine later took us to the cottage these children now occupied. I envied them. They may have had to give up their beds in the main house so that we, the guests of honour, could sleep there. But this cottage, a little like Elsie Raikes's cabin, has such a wonderful view of the open bay, I'd have preferred sleeping there. I coveted it so intensely, it almost took my breath away. I wondered whether it had been for rent, whether Tom Jones would have avoided mentioning that because the old chief is his rival. I had to suppress the idea. It was too painful to think that we might have stayed here all this time.

Lorraine took our overnight bag (my rucksack) to the best room of the main house so Bettina could nap there. We were to sleep there too. There were two large couches in this parlour, one that pulled out to make a wide bed. The room was crowded with furniture, and the walls with photographs of the Charles Jones's daughters, several of them nurses in uniform. Dried flowers gave off a dusty smell. The windows were firmly closed to keep out the heat. Above the couch on which I settled Bettina for her nap, an old-fashioned crank telephone kept ringing in various combinations of short and long rings through most of the day and, as we discovered later, most of the night as well.

There is probably only one party line on this reserve, used by the entire community, holding together far-flung families and friends, coded like Mr Jensen's foghorn and lighthouse beam. The intermittent ringing seldom seemed to be the right code, and no one answered while we slept. But Mrs Charles Jones had happy tidings the next morning. She was baking bread for the visit of one of the chief's sons, who now lives in the United States.

That morning I took Fiona and Bettina over to the cottage on Hope Bay to play with the other children there (and, frankly, to be near that lovely place). Meanwhile, at the main house visitors began to arrive by car and in boats. Near our campsite clouds of dust could be seen moving along the gravel road, then skirting the peninsula at breakneck speed. With a screech of brakes, a truck came to a stop near the chief's house. It was followed by Verna Patronella's blue Ford.

The truck was soon surrounded by Verna's family and many other children, excitedly welcoming a handsome tall man. When we joined the crowd, Verna introduced her brother and his wife, Una, brown-haired, laughing, a native of the western United States. This was now a family gathering. I wondered how we could take our leave without offending anyone. First there was a generous meal: moose pie and more freshly baked bread.

"I have something to tell you," Verna said to me. Perhaps she was aware that I began to feel out of place. "I'll take you back to your camp. We can't leave the sheep for long anyway."

It was late afternoon when she deposited us at our campsite. She hurled two cardboard boxes from the trunk of the Ford: one for our garbage, the other for my paintings. I was touched that she had remembered this at the time of her brother's visit.

"What I meant to tell you," she then said, "is that we need a teacher for our school here. Would you be interested?"

Free firewood, a place to live, and an annual salary of eight hundred dollars. Some provisions. It might be enough. It would be a challenge. But the children? I had no idea what winters would be like here, whether I had the strength to manage on my own, What if the children became ill?

"Teachers here should be Ojibwa. Tom Jones was a teacher, wasn't he? They should tell stories like those you told the other night. In the Ojibwa language."

She laughed. "It will be a long time before that happens. If it ever does."

Am I doing the wrong thing? I wonder. Should I have accepted? But what if teaching became part of the politics played out here? Perhaps they wanted to get a neutral person, neither on the side of the Catholics nor on that of the Orangemen.

I felt deeply sad when I waved goodbye to her and to Lorraine, who had come with us. I wondered whether I'd see them again, ever. They still had this magical bay, almost untouched by elements that have gradually transformed the country.

~ On the train between
Wiarton and Toronto ~

Tom Jones took us to the station early, as he had to load the fish from his own shed onto the refrigerator cars. He did not say anything about the reserve needing a teacher. Probably, he now classes me with the Catholics. I couldn't tell. He'd been so generous, taken us to the camp site, given us credit at his store. I thanked him for all that.

After I'd settled for all our groceries, I found that we had a little money left, enough to have a restaurant meal while waiting for the train. There was time enough. The restaurant was small and did not have much choice, but there was fresh lake trout on the menu. That should be good, here in Wiarton. I ordered some for us all. There were the usual cruet sets on the table, salt and pepper, and a large bottle of tomato ketchup.

Our meal came, generous helpings of salmon, chips, and the ubiquitous coleslaw, but slices of lemon with each helping. Bettina vehemently objected to lemon juice on her tiny helping, so I used her slice of lemon together with mine. During this commotion Fiona had somehow got hold of the ketchup bottle. When I looked at her plate again, it was bright red all over. Nothing could be seen of either salmon or vegetables. I tried to scrape off some of the ketchup, but so much remained that she could not eat what the sauce had covered. Part of this great luxury I'd allowed myself had become inedible. I shared my portion with her.

Now, on the train, I've reread Anna Jameson's thoughts on the way the Ojibwas bring up their children:

> The Indians, apparently, have no idea of correcting or restraining their children: personal chastisement is not heard of. They say that before a child has any understanding there is no use in correcting it; and when old enough to understand no one has a right to correct it. Thus the fixed, inherent sentiment of personal independence grows up with the Indians from earliest infancy. The will of an Indian child is not forced; he has nothing to learn but what he sees done around him and he learns by imitation. I hear no scolding, no tones of command or reproof; but I see no evil results from this mild system, for the general reverence and affection of children for their parents is delightful; where there is no obedience exacted there can be no rebellion; they dream not of either and all live in peace.

Anna Jameson wrote this in 1837. Since then, missionary schools have whittled away at that spirit she saw with such admiration.

I can't get rid of the sadness I now feel. I had thought, when I came to this country and often since, that it has the potential to be the most humane country in the world. I have seen glimpses of such a paradise; I'm leaving one behind right now. One cannot build a good society on injustice. All of this land belonged to people from whom it was gradually taken away. Whether the French or the English had been the first to take it, really seems immaterial.

This feeling of sadness is not unlike that I have about Germany and its treatment of Jews. It's a feeling of shame, as if I had been responsible. I know perfectly well that my inability to condemn Garth's affair with our teenaged Jewish refugee; my insistence that he must marry her and give her, who lost her own family, one secure relationship – all this is rooted in absurd and ineffective guilt feelings. I know I had no power to change things, but these depressing notions persist.

Had I not tried to merely escape? I was a greenhorn when I followed him to Italy and still absurdly ignorant when I married him there. He represented all I wanted – art, freedom, wit, and wisdom – as I saw it then. It took me a long time to discover that this dynamic personality did not represent other values I couldn't give up: decency, the ability to put yourself into someone else's place, an idealism I'd absorbed early in life from reading Schiller, who, with much of the Enlightenment, went into oblivion, overshadowed by his friend Goethe. This realization had been like a dull ache for years. I always assumed that it was I who was at fault, who was naive, who lacked the sophistication of his – to me, aimless and cynical – bohemian world. Until we were separated by the physical barriers of distance and war, until I found others who had the same ideals I had and who actually lived for them, I had not known what was wrong.

~ August 25th ~

We've been at the McCurdys' house for a whole week now, and I still haven't found a place to live, let alone a job. One would think that with helpful appliances like a washing machine, household chores would not take the time they did at camp. But there are six children to wash and cook for, and chores for them are never-ending, though the two McCurdy girls, Janet and Dorothy, are helpful and none of the children are in any way obstreperous.

I don't want to be jobless and homeless when the McCurdys come back.

Upstairs in this large Forest Hill house there are tenants one never sees – quiet professional women who spend most of their day in downtown offices. On Sunday evenings the enormous living room is used by a music-appreciation group who bring their own records. Avis instructed me to make a large plate of sandwiches for them and to keep the family out of the way for this group. We don't spend much time in the living room anyway. There's a shady garden around the house and the victory garden in the ravine. And there are other, less important rooms where the McCurdy children share their activities with mine.

The children are so easygoing that I thought I could take them all, without much trouble, to a unique exhibition of Mexican art at the Toronto art gallery. I don't want to miss that. I asked the girls, Dorothy and Janet, to find some good clothes for themselves and the two boys – clean clothes any-way. The dresses Garth sent are getting too small now, though Fiona still manages to wear hers. For Bettina I found an embroidered dress (dating back to my Polish friend, Anna) that makes her look like a plump little peasant, sunburnt, with a yellow thatch of hair.

Sunday, the opening of the Mexican exhibition drew an un-usually large crowd to the art gallery. The first person I recognized was Frank Hines, whom we haven't seen for months. Bettina welcomed him with every sign of delight, rolling on the floor like a puppy. Her beautiful dress picked up every bit of dust from that well-trodden floor. While I picked up Bettina and tried to clean her dress, the little McCurdy boys, David and Donald, escaped into the crowd. I sent Dorothy after them while Frank used his magical influence over Bettina to make her keep still.

While, still in the entrance hall, we waited for the children to come back, the Cass-Beggses came in with their eldest child, Rosemary. She is a friend of the McCurdy girls. She and Janet went off to find Dorothy and the boys, who meanwhile reap-peared from another direction. Janet eventually came back without Rosemary and reported that Rosemary had shown her some "gruesome" paintings. I decided against extending our visit to see those.

Instead, we all trooped out to the little park behind the Grange, that charming old house, the nucleus of Toronto's art gallery. Frank came with us. He told me that he's giving up his apart-ment; he has applied for a job in New York. His apartment would be ideal for us: it's very central. But they don't take chil-dren there.

Bettina tried to attract Frank's attention by once more rolling on the ground, this time on dirty gravel that wouldn't come off. The more you rubbed, the greater the smudges. Resourceful Janet helped me to turn the little dress back to front so that one wouldn't see the dark spots on the embroidered yoke. It meant pulling the dress over Bettina's head. For a moment her plump little body stood exposed, dressed in bloomers only. She protested loudly. I lost all desire to go back into the art gallery.

~ August 28th ~

Most of our things are still stored in Anna's basement. When I phoned about that, she mentioned that Lecia too is looking for rooms. So I got in touch with Lecia, who offered to come over for an afternoon so I could go apartment hunting. She brought Lenny (a seventh child in this household) and gave me some addresses she'd looked at, not too far from the West End Crèche.

I went to Selective Service first. There were no jobs advertised at Lever Brothers, the plant Elaine had recommended. Right now all job vacancies are at Victory Aircraft. Inspection jobs there are well paid, though shift work is unavoidable. The inspection teams rotate with production. I've worked on blueprints long enough to sign up for inspection at Malton, starting right after Labour Day. Malton is way out west, a train ride from Parkdale or any place close to the West End Crèche. The idea of working on aircraft elated me. But we still have no place to live.

Sweeney, my old friend and helper, has gone. Florence is on holiday until September (I returned the lilo and cot so they could be used then).

I didn't want to spend the first gruelling week (without a paycheque) at the McCurdys', so began to look frantically in the area of northern Parkdale, walking distance from the station where I'd have to take the train to Malton. I went up and down some shabby streets, ringing bells, knocking on doors. Finally, not too far from the station, I saw a sign "Rooms for Rent" in the window of a house that did not exactly fill me with confidence. But – there are two furnished rooms upstairs, without a kitchen.

The woman I spoke to is not the owner. She rents the house and sublets these rooms. She seemed taken by the idea that she could make extra money by minding the children during hours

when they're not at the crèche. She reminds me a little of Catalan girls: she is short, with a large head. Her features are Greek
or Roman. Perhaps that's her origin.

The house is not particularly clean, but the rooms I was
shown are all right – one large front room, where I could have
a hot plate, and a small bedroom. I made a down payment and
breathed a sigh of relief when I was told that the rent could wait
for my first pay cheque. My time is running out: the McCurdys
will be back on Monday.

I hope they won't mind if the large cabin trunk I stored there
when I left Parkdale stays in their basement a little longer. I
won't need our winter things just yet, and there is little space in
those two furnished rooms. I removed a few things from the
trunk and added my new paintings – quite dry now and rather
faint. Most of the colours have lost their freshness. But they are
reminders of scenes that, some day, I might be able to paint
from memory.

~ August 31st ~

People are returning from their holidays. Florence and Bruce
from Muskoka, where the Robinses too have a cottage. It's
where Toronto people go in summer. Avis and Jarvis McCurdy
are back too. They seem to think that the house and the children look fine.

Avis is very busy, getting her four ready for school. As I would
like to do something for them, I asked whether I could paint a
portrait of Jarvis, who might be able to sit for it while preparing lectures or reading assignments. He has a remarkable head,
quite large with almost classical features. He is a minister's son
from Gaspé, in eastern Quebec.

I've bought a few, very few supplies. Most will have to wait
till I get paid. Oh, to be in Paris where artists pay for their supplies only twice a year.

~ September 3rd ~

Yesterday Avis drove us to our new rooms. I was glad she didn't
have time to come inside, for, compared to their pleasant house,
the place looks especially dismal. I walked along Dundas to get

our few things from Anna's basement. I had to make a special trip for Bettina's folding cot, which could not be transported on the streetcar. I dragged it along the road as best I could. It barely fits into the small room where the children are to sleep. A large bed there takes up almost the entire space.

I've met the landlord now, the woman's husband. One should not mind ugliness; people can't help that. But for some reason, this man has a gross appearance, sitting at the kitchen table in his undershirt as Mr McNair did. Yet he is totally unlike Mr McNair, who radiated kindness. Ungainly warts should not disturb one. Is it because one thinks of old witches' tales that they do? Or is it something in those small shifting eyes? He insists on bargaining. If I use a hot plate, I should pay for the power. (How? Is there a meter for that kind of thing?) Even more disturbing is his insistence that I leave the children with his wife all day, not just during night shifts. It would not be worth her while otherwise, taking in kids, he maintains.

For me the West End Crèche is an anchor, a place of friendly security. I chose these rooms because they're close to what I realize I must now give up if I want any kind of accomodation.

~ September 7th ~

I've not had time to record the dilemma of the last few days. Until now, I have not had a minute to spare and no money to telephone old friends like Florence (long-distance from Malton). I don't want to use the landlord's telephone to express my suspicions of him. Of course, there's Sophie Boyd, but I'm on day shift, leaving for work at six in the morning, long before the West End Crèche opens.

The train from Parkdale takes twice as long as driving by car, as most workers there manage to do, in spite of gas rationing. They form car pools. But I don't as yet belong to one.

To start at the beginning: after punching the time clock the first morning, I found that I had not been put on inspection. I was sent to the machine shop where small aircraft parts are stamped with numbers and letters. The people who operate the noisy machines nearby make more money than we do. But at least we are allowed to sit down at long tables to stamp various mysterious pieces of duraluminum that are used, eventually, to form the plane. We use small mallets to hammer in numbers and letters that are incised on the bottom of metal tubes. The same tubes for the same part, always.

Our heads are covered by bandanas, our bodies by grey coveralls, a green stripe on each sleeve. "Victory Aircraft" is printed on the breast pocket. Our lead hand is a very pretty blonde named Lil. Her boyfriend has just been called up for overseas service, and there is general sympathy for Lil, making her work easier. All other lead hands and foremen are men.

I am uneasy about the children; I'm doing the wrong kind of work, paid less than inspection. But I have to hang on somehow until I have my first pay cheque.

On this first shift I have been sitting beside a hard-featured woman who wears a lot of makeup. Stiff peroxide curls bulge from the front of her bandana. Her voice is hoarse; she smokes in every break. The other women speak of her as "that old hussy." But she's the one who told me that Lil's boyfriend has written love poems for her, our lead hand. She was more upset than anyone else by a rumour that Lil had got her privileged position by sleeping with the foreman.

She refuses to accept the story of Lil's lost innocence. She clings to her own romantic version. I finally told her my own troubles, the suspicions I have of my landlords; and that I was sent here by mistake, instead of to inspection. "Go to the personnel office and complain," she croaked. "There's no futue in this dump."

~ September 14th ~

At the end of the first week I followed the "hussy's" advice. I took my courage in both hands and marched up to the personnel office, a glassed-in cage, to ask the personnel officer why I was stamping parts when I had been hired as an inspector. Thick glasses made his pudgy face totally expressionless. He shuffled some papers, mumbled something, then gave me a small card I was to take to the inspection foreman in the fuselage bay.

So from the machine shop and all its clatter, I walked over to the hangars where the plane achieves its final form. In the first

bay they assemble the wings, in the central bay the fuselage.
On Final Assembly the whole plane (body, wings, engine) is put
together. RCAF inspection teams, who in their white coats look
like visiting doctors, walk about with an air of authority in all
the bays. They have the final say.

I learned in the machine shop that those on "production"
have a low opinion of inspectors. If work is completed on
schedule, production crews get a bonus. Finicky inspectors find
fault, nag, hold up production. There is no love lost between

Victory Aircraft inspection crew for fuselage:
Grace second from right, Art (foreman) fourth from right,
Gunda standing behind him slightly to the left

production foremen, who want to forge ahead, and inspection
foremen, who, if they stamp off shoddy work, will be found out
by the RCAF.

The inspection foreman, Art, looks like an apple-cheeked
teenager. He sent me to the very end of the bay where the "formers," the ribs of the plane, are assembled from smaller parts,

to form the skeleton of the Lancaster. These formers look like sculpture by Henry Moore or Barbara Hepworth, except that there are so many of the same shape. At present I am only allowed to inspect the smallest parts that make up the formers., narrow pieces, about a foot long, for the evenness of the rivets and the presence of chrome to preserve them.

There is a chit with each lot. This has to be signed by the lead hand of our small department. Again I sit at a long table, this time with a girl called Grace, who is finicky and opinionated about each small task, determined to use the tiny power she has, determined to please the RCAF inspectors. Grace refuses to wear a bandana because we are not close to any machines. Her thick, curly, dark hair – almost shoulder-length – is her outstanding feature. A country girl from around Orangeville, she has a rather flat face and a figure that looks well in coveralls.

The reason I was given this lowly routine job to start with is that when Art showed me a blueprint and asked a few questions, I'd forgotten that the dotted line on a print always describes the other (not visible) side of a part shown. I'll never forget that now. But it's almost a year since I worked at the Inglis blueprint office.

The assembly bays, because of incessant riveting, are noisy too, but some of the noise is absorbed by their airy space and height. At the very end of Final Assembly are gigantic sliding doors. From time to time they open to let out a completed plane, the result of all this labour and technique. It still has to be tested by RCAF pilots. Not a single foreman here (I'm told) will ever go up in these planes.

In our bay the incomplete fuselage parts are shrouded in silvery webs of scaffolding on which production crews and inspectors climb about. The scaffolding is pushed aside every time a part "moves on" to the next stage.

The rectangular parts we check may look dull, but every hole – every rivet – has its purpose. Wires for the communication system pass through these parts, electric wiring, connections to ailerons and flaps. Unless you know the code of each number and letter, the blueprints don't tell you all this, but knowing where the parts go makes one take a greater interest. To Art's credit, he encourages his inspectors to find out where even the smallest part will go, first on the formers, then on the fuselage, later on Final Assembly.

Most inspectors fear visits from the RCAF, but Grace welcomes them. Her day does not really begin until these men of the Royal Canadian Air Force arrive, their white coats swinging, their steps brisk, their haircuts short. She has confided to me that to "go out" with one of them, a snub-nosed fellow with a boyish grin, would make her wildly happy ("but he is married"). Of course, she is right to romanticize these men, who venture their lives in machines, put together by amateurs who have had to learn too quickly. Only a few foremen and production specialists have had previous experience with aircraft, some at de Havilland's, others building Catalinas in Quebec. Some of the best are French.

As I sit beside Grace, checking rivets, examining blueprints, there is always the nagging worry about the children. Our landlord has had his way: they're not at the crèche but at home. I'm dependent on his good graces because he has to wait for my paycheque next week.

I get home in time to put the children to bed. They've eaten supper, I'm told. But Fiona looks pale and Bettina grubby. The only place for them to play outside is a filthy backyard. I have to wait until we are on night shift before I can see Sophie Boyd. See her I must. The children are still registered at the crèche, and they haven't been taken there. I am now so short of money I can't even telephone or eat proper meals. I have to pay for my train tickets, an absolute necessity.

One evening I met the real owner of the house, a Mrs McDonald, the widow of a CP railway worker. She was once a cook and now owns several houses. She seems friendly, but I am fairly sure that to her money is what matters most.

~ September 17th ~

I could not believe my eyes when I came home today. All we own has been shoved together into the small room where the children sleep. There is not even room to turn around in there. Fiona seems happy to share the big bed with me. The hot plate

169

sits on a washstand squeezed in beside Bettina's cot. The reason? Mrs McDonald herself has moved into the large front room, perhaps to keep an eye on this property. I have no leg to stand on, since I cannot pay until my cheque comes in on Friday, the day after tomorrow.

No wonder Mrs McDonald does not trust the Blacks, but neither of them now trusts me. I was curtly informed that the RCMP had called to find out whether we lived here. I should have told them that last year, when I was thinking of joining Garth in New York, I took all the necessary steps for immigration to the United States. I registered with the RCMP. I had myself fingerprinted and promised to inform them of any change of address. Friends in Carolina had offered to sponsor us. It was Garth who did not come through in the end. I explained that it was a routine check, necessary if I wanted to join my husband in the States. But they now suspect me – my accent, everything (as I suspect them).

~ September 20th ~

Today, when I opened the dresser to take out my only pair of slacks, I found that they were gone. So have two linen pillow cases embroidered with my mother's initials. And my small camera. And my pink sweater. I was incensed (last month, at Cape Croker, I was able to leave everything in our tent and nothing was ever touched). I confided in Mrs McDonald.

"You have to be cairrfool," she said in her broad Scots, when I informed her of my loss. "You can't accuse ainyone of stealing if you don't find the things in their hands. They might accuse *you*."

I am totally dependent on people I don't trust, even for the children's food. Oh, to see Sophie Boyd.

My paycheque has come through at last, after these two terrible weeks. It's been cashed; my rent and board is finally paid (plus electricity for the hot plate). That it is only one room now makes little difference, since the board and care for the children amounts to so much more.

I didn't think that things could get worse before I am on night
shift, free to consult friends during the day. I can't do it in the
evenings, the only time I have with the children. When I came
home after our long day today, I met no one on the stairs. I was
startled when I entered our room and found some of the furniture gone. A smell of smoke came through the open window.

As I went to close it, I saw Bettina's cot down there in the
dirty backyard, its mattress on a bonfire that was still smoul-
dering. The children stood watching it with the couple
downstairs. I ran down, speechless with rage. I was met by
dark looks.

Fiona ran to me, breaking the silence. "Mummy," she cried.
"There were bugs in Bettina's bed."

"Bugs?" I was bewildered. "What kind?"

Now everyone started to talk at once. Mrs McDonald added
her two cents' worth. "Ye must'a known," she said stiffly.

"Known what?"

"Bedbugs. In that mattress. Ye can't get rid of them if ye
don't fumigate."

"Fumigate? Bedbugs? What do they look like?"

No one believed me when I said I had never seen bedbugs. I
now remembered the attic rooms, the itchy bites on the children
I had taken for mosquito bites. Neither Lecia nor Anna had
ever mentioned bugs.

"That mattress was crawling with them," Mrs McDonald
said. "You brought them into the house." (Her house.)

I stared at the crib and mattress with disbelief. Yes, they'd
come from Anna's basement. What if some of the things I
stored with friends brought this pest to them too? Did they
perhaps know and not tell me? Florence, the McCurdys? But
no, the trunk went to their basement before it ever touched
Anna's house. Still, Anna must have known. Was that why Lecia
moved? They never said anything to me. I had no warning.

"What does one do?" I asked. Perhaps, I thought, one could
get rid of this pest with kerosene, as one did with lice. Simple,
as Sweeney had pointed out.

"You have to fumigate the whole house," the landlord said darkly.

"The whole house? Why not just our room?"

"Ye'll never get rid of them unless ye do the whole house," Mrs McDonald said firmly. She knows about things like that.

It was obvious that neither she nor the Blacks believed that anyone could be so protected as not to recognize bedbugs. But where on earth would I have had a chance to see them? German households are fiends for cleanliness, and my English grandmother's spring cleaning included every item in her house, every picture on every wall.

"How much does it cost?"

"Forty dollars, at least."

After room and board for the children, there's barely enough left of my paycheque to cover transportation. I'll have to get a loan somewhere. I have no collateral. How does one do this kind of thing?

I had to keep telling myself that we'd been in worse situations – when I was ill, for instance. I was not sure whether our clothes had perhaps been affected – no one told me – so I ironed everything we own with a very hot iron, as one does to get rid of moths.

Before I go on my first night shift, I'll have to see Sophie Boyd.

I'm not going to approach any of the comfortably positioned professionals, the McCurdys, the Cass-Beggses, even Florence. I thought of Marjorie and the Neighbourhood Workers. That might be the way to go. But I dislike the condescension in the tone of social workers, describing their "clients."

~ September 25th ~

I was not going to leave the children in this terrible house for even one morning. I took them along with me to the West End Crèche as soon as it opened. My reception was a little strained. It's not done, simply not turning up. They have a waiting list. It took a little time before they understood that I had in fact made arrangements to have the children taken to the crèche as usual, and that my landlady had then kept them at home. I should have telephoned. Yes. But it did not take Sophie Boyd long to assess the situation. She understood that I could not have phoned from that house. That my funds barely covered transportation, not even food, and that long-distance calls from Malton would have been complicated.

She listened carefully to what I spilled out. I tried to remain coherent, not to become tearful, describing the terrible weeks with no paycheque, our total dependence during that time on people I suspected of theft and of neglecting the children. Being suddenly confined to one room after having rented two. The children not taken to the crèche as originally planned. And now, this last ignominious discovery. "If I'd only known," I said, "I'd never have brought the children here from our old address."

"Yours isn't the only old house around here where bedbugs have been found. " Miss Boyd said in her calm voice, and, immediately the problem shrank. "It's quite common. You never see them in the daytime. They hide behind wallpaper and wain-scotting. If you see rooms that have recently been painted with high-gloss paint; that's usually a sign that bugs have been found. They don't survive under paint.

"So what you need right away is a loan. The Neighbourhood Workers have a local office near here. I'll phone them." She made some quick calculations on a small desk pad and lifted the receiver. I heard myself described as a steady worker with a a good job. The loan could be repaid in instalments, yes. She vouched for it.

Before I walked over to the office of the Neighbourhood Workers, Sophie Boyd made some thoughtful suggestions: "Find a car pool. It will be cheaper than the train, and it will reduce your time away from the children.

"Malton is in farming country, outside town. There may be a family nearby where the children would find good care. A pity that there'll be no nursery schools outside town. Fiona is doing so well here."

The children were allowed to stay for the day while I made my financial arrangements. The Neighbourhood Workers have a fund for situations like mine. I filled out forms and described what happened. The social worker to whom I spoke suggested that ours was really a case for the Children's Aid. Should the children's father not help? They asked for Garth's address in New York, which I gave reluctantly. I explained that he's a penniless artist, looking for a job.

Back at the West End Crèche, Sophie Boyd let me use the telephone to tell Mrs Black that they could order the fumigators for tomorrow. Tonight the children will still have to sleep in this wretched place. I won't take them to Florence or other friends. I can't even contemplate such a thing. And I don't know where we should go. Staying here is out of the question.

~ September 27th ~

My first night shift at Victory Aircraft. I hadn't slept a wink during the day. I was now determined to ask everyone about car pools and about rooms for rent. I noticed that my hand was trembling when I reached for the razor blade known as a "feeler" that we use to test the tightness of rivets. I felt so jittery, so hungry and empty, so nauseated, that I wondered how I'd last the night.

Grace settled down beside me with a new batch of fuselage parts for us to inspect. "What's the matter?" she asked. My hands were shaking. Worse, tears began to fall on them. I tried to wipe them away quickly, but there were more. I couldn't see anything. I didn't even notice Grace was gone.

I felt a hand on my shoulder. Art was standing behind me. "Come to my office for a bit," he said and walked off. He had not sounded as if he would dismiss me. I wiped my eyes and tried to collect myself before I followed him.

There is more to Art than I first thought. He looks young, he often makes trite remarks. But here he was, listening to me, a comparatively recent employee, a woman with small children, and he was listening with sympathy. I had trouble with my landlords, I told him. I could not trust them with my kids. I had taken those rooms because they were near a good crèche where they'd been before. And now they didn't even go there.

"You want them near that crèche, then?" he asked.

Yes, that's why I'd chosen rooms down there, close to the Parkdale station.

"Most people working here try to live close by, as close as they can," he explained. "I'm from Cooksville myself. It takes only twenty minutes for a car pool to get here. Hardly longer from West Eglinton. The trouble is, you won't find a nursery school around there."

"Decent landlords would be the most important thing." I remembered what Sophie Boyd had said about farms near Malton.

"I know a decent couple," he said. "Used to know them well. Coffey's the name. The area around their house is a bit slummy, but not like downtown. And their own house is very clean. They have two children. It's on Oakwood, way north."

It's where Sweeney's family lives. That was good enough for me.

"They had a bad time during the Depression," Art went on. So had Sweeney's family, I knew.

"The husband is deaf. It's hard for him to find work. He did, recently, in the storerooms of de Havilland's. They bought a house and, like most people, took out a heavy mortgage. They need extra money, and they'd get it if they took boarders. So they asked me recently if I knew anyone at work who wants a room.

"Now, you and the kids would give them a little more than just one boarder. I'm sure that, even if you have one room, they'd let you and the kids share, say, the kitchen. It's a very clean place, and they are very honest people. You can trust them. And it's on the route of a lot of car pools for Malton."

One room, clean, with the run of the house. I at once thought of the Coffey family as something like the Sweeneys.

Art wrote down a telephone number and looked at his watch. "It's not that late," he said. "Just after nine. You can phone them from here. I'll be out on the floor for a while."

In the door of his glassed-in cubicle he turned: "If you've done office work before, would you like to work in here, as secretary?"

Not office work again. But I was so grateful for his tact and his resourcefulness, I nodded my head. I shook it as he went out, then nodded again, the phone in my hand.

I thought back to the time when my fellow workers at John Inglis had found rooms for me. I could see them now, their heads bent over Dennis's paper. Jean, Carol, Sweeney. My friends, my bulwark, my angels. All of them had gone out of my life. I thought of them, and my hand stopped shaking. Art had not asked for compensation, phoning long-distance. I dialled the Coffeys' number.

~ September 29th ~

I left all our things to be fumigated with the rest of the house and took the children up to the Coffeys, in a taxi. I paid the Blacks for everything and left in stony silence.

Our room here is large and bright, and everything in it is pink: walls, bed cover, curtains. There are additional white muslin curtains, but they're not really needed – there is no house very close by. The Sweeneys live two blocks further up on Oakwood.

Mrs Coffey welcomed us into a large, bright, spotless kitchen. She is probably the same age as Art, but while he looks like a schoolboy, she looks as if life has not been kind to her. Her pale eyes behind rimless glasses look kind but tired. Her mouth seems tight-lipped, perhaps because she needs false teeth. Her red hair is tightly twisted into a small chignon at the back of her head, probably because she could never afford to have it permed or properly cut.

Her husband is on permanent night shift. Permanent shifts are much better than changing every two weeks. He walked into the kitchen with a violin case in his hand. Tall and strong-looking, his deafness makes him hesitant when dealing with others, and he appear childlike beside his motherly wife. He plays the violin, she says, because its tones somehow still reach him and perhaps console him.

Their boy, Danny, is about eleven. He was at school when we came. Mrs Coffey told me that he sings in a choir, has, as they say, "an angel's voice." The little girl is barely older than Bettina, plump and solid, red-haired like her mother, who has nicknamed her "McGee" (after a radio program, I think).

~ October 4th ~

I collected the few things we own from downtown. For Bettina the Coffeys have a cot their children have outgrown, and Fiona and I share the big bed in our room. That is, we do when I'm on day shift. At present, I try to catch up on sleep there in the daytime.

Rather than share the kitchen for cooking, Mrs Coffey has given us reasonable terms for board, somewhat like the McNairs. I share an early evening meal with the family before I join my new car pool. I get back from night shift the same time as Mr Coffey. His wife is always up to give us an early breakfast.

I found my car pool through Mr Coffey, who used to take it part of the way to de Havilland's. The driver is a silent man, very sober; he belongs to a strict religious sect. He wears a vi-sored cloth cap, as working people do in England. Here you don't see these caps often. One of his passengers is a man of Spanish origin who, his fedora over his face, rests half-asleep in the back seat. He came to life a little when I mentioned that, before the Civil War, I'd spent a year in Barcelona. He told me that his brother had gone over there with the Mackenzie-Papineau Batallion, to fight for the Republicans.

"They got no thanks for that," he added. "They're now taken for commies. But watch the real commies in our union. Nothing gets done. Nothing must interfere with the war effort."

Now I understand why the Seftons were not very encourag-ing when they heard I worked at Malton. The union there seems to be out of the reach of the Steelworkers. I haven't asked why. And I have no intention of working for it. If only I had Sweeney still to explain all this. But I hear from her family that she's now in California.

The third passenger in our car pool is a large jolly woman whose husband is in some army unit but not overseas.

177

I got a new diary and started writing all this in our room, where the dresser doubles as my desk. The children have the run of the house, and most of the time they play with Brigit, the Coffeys' little girl, in the kitchen. This kitchen is an inviting place; a kettle is always boiling for tea. The radio is on all the time, with news about the war. Towards evening there are comedy shows with canned laughter in which all the children join. There's Fibber McGee and Molly, Jack Benny, Charlie McCarthy – all American as far as I know, and very popular here.

~ October 9th ~

Now that I feel more established, I've contacted old friends again. I finally got around to painting the Cass-Beggs twins in oils. I don't find the new painting better than the pastel study, but once dry, oils need much less care and are easier to frame. I've learnt from my attempts on Masonite at Cape Croker. I either prepare these boards with many coats of gesso or use canvas board again.

I bought a fairly large canvas to start on the portrait of Jarvis McCurdy. That's probably my best effort to date. Jarvis has an imposing head that lends itself to a painting in profile. His daughter Janet has inherited his looks, but she is more mobile. He is a very patient sitter.

Like the Cass-Beggses, he belongs to the high-minded intellectuals who in Britain are called Fabians (whom Millard never quite trusted). Like Marjorie Johnston, the McCurdys are Unitarians and CCFers and belong to the FCSA, the Fellowship for Christian Social Order. This group is at present undergoing a violent upheaval, rent in two by arguments over the kind of Marxism that should be adopted (socialism or communism). This started when Russia had a pact with Germany, but now that Russia is an ally, relations have not improved.

I never encountered Unitarians in Germany but know they still existed in my time. As in the Rudolf Steiner movement, there may be more philosophy than religion in these movements, now all outlawed and overrun by fascism. How was that possible? Perhaps because religions of the mind don't shake you up as fundamental evangelicalism does. Perhaps they don't give you the emotional certainty of Catholics like Sweeney. Instead, such groups developed an extraordinary generosity of spirit: their religion allows tolerance and determines an examplary lifestyle.

In pre-fascist Germany, professors of philosophy were highly regarded. In comparison to their status, the salary and lifestyle of professors here is modest. Jarvis McCurdy tells me that an experienced riveter in a war plant makes as much as an instructor at a Canadian university. "I'd rather do what I'm doing, though," Jarvis said. "It's fascinating."

"Working on aircraft can be fascinating too," I countered.

He did not look up from the text he was preparing for one of his courses, but he replied with words I found unsettling: "They're deadly," he said.

~ October 15th ~

The Cass-Beggses have allowed me to exhibit my work, mostly last year's paintings, in their large living room while they're away at a weekend conference. I've just finished the large one of Jarvis and borrowed back Florence's portrait. I wasn't sure what to do about framing. The Roberts Gallery did a fine job framing the little portrait of Fiona, but I could not afford the cost of more such frames. In the end I decided to exhibit most paintings unframed. If they're sold I can afford the framing.

I don't know what to do about publicity for this small exhibition. Marjorie lives in the same building, so she knows. I contacted friends: Florence, Elaine, Sophie Boyd. They came on Sunday. But I don't yet know many people at work and none came.

To my surprise, Sophie Boyd offered to buy the little paintings I'd done up on the Cape Croker cliffs, though they are only a faint memory of the original attempt. I'm sure she did this to help us. But just these paintings are a reminder of a glorious experience, a real epiphany. In the end I couldn't bring myself to part with them for ten dollars, though we badly need the money.

Two of the visitors, however, were real art collectors. I'd heard about Alice and Bernard Loeb from David and Edith

Smith, who've known them for years. They are also friends of
the McCurdys. Alice is a big, cheerful woman with a booming
voice, an artist in her own right and a member of the Women's
International Association. She offered to buy my portrait of
Lorraine for seven dollars. Again I found I couldn't part with it.
My paintings of Cape Croker, even that of Lorraine (the best),
are really less accomplished than the others, yet they seem to
convey something of the magic of that place. To me, however,
that magic is still so sharp and immediate that I cannot give
them up.

Bernard Loeb is small and lively, with a high colour, his eyes
magnified by the thick lenses of his glasses. He has been an
antique dealer but is now retired. He owns paintings by Fritz
Brandtner. Canadians, he says, don't really understand German
Expressionism. When I was a chlld, the Expressionists' paintings to me seemed ugly and distorted. My instructor was an
Impressionist. Even her harmless pointillism was considered
daring in our small town.

Bernard Loeb likes Jarvis's portrait but is not impressed with
the rest of my paintings. He has just bought a watercolour by
Leonard Brooks, who is new to me.

There's a non-jury exhibition at the Toronto art gallery and
I'd hoped to send Jarvis's portrait there. But Florence is so
thrilled with the idea of her portrait being shown at such a
classy place that in the end I've entered her portrait for it. I
could have shown Elaine's portrait there, but it's only a pastel
and it doesn't really do her justice. You have to be a Renoir
to convey that kind of bloom.

My union friends must think I've deserted them, but my
timetable has been severe. During those wretched weeks downtown I never wanted to leave the children for a minute, and
if I ever have any free time, I have to use it to make money. I
met Elaine briefly, radiant now, married to Larry Sefton. We
both know that Sweeney has gone away because of Bill Sefton,
who's still engaged to that large Protestant girl. We've always
meant to visit Alice Kane again at the Queen Street library.

But we are in a different part of town, miles away, and haven't found a library nearby that has anything like the magic of her children's program.

Since Charlie Millard is now a member of the Ontario legislature, I decided to write to him right after I came back from Cape Croker (I was still at the McCurdys). I tried to describe the plight of the Ojibwas, who still have no vote and whose fish stocks are declining. Recently I received a reply with his signature under an official letterhead, pointing out that Indian Affairs is a federal matter; there's nothing the province can do. He probably sees me as one of those do-gooders, the woolly-minded intelligentsia he distrusts. He may be right, of course, but this negative reply did affect me. He himself often used the term "passing the buck" when responsibility is shifted from one jurisdiction to another. I have had to learn lately that unions have not been kind to other races, American unions in particular. And there's this Mr Walker sitting behind of the Steelworkers. Most unions here have U.S. affiliations.

Perhaps they think that, because I work at Victory Aircraft, I've betrayed the CCF. The way they see it, I should have taken a job where I could be useful to them as an organizer. But I couldn't wait. And I know I'm no good at politics or organizing or office work. I've tried.

~ November ~

Finally, we have a comfortable routine. Mornings are frosty, but the kitchen is always warm. There's always a packed lunch for me to take to work and a thermos of coffee beside the breakfast cereal and toaster. I'm alone on those mornings. Mr Coffey's on permanent night shift.

It's still dark when I stand at the corner waiting for our car. Occasionally, the dawn is brightened by a sprinkling of snow that later disappears.

In the evenings, after day shift, I go on reading, after the children are in bed, by a shaded lamp, as pink as the walls. I am working my way through Dos Passos's *U.S.A.* trilogy and am rereading Upton Sinclair's *Jungle*. I can now vividly imagine what the suffering immigrants went through in the Chicago slums. I find it almost unbearable – our worst experiences seem insignificant beside them. And then, there's something temporary about wartime misery. The war must end. All will change.

Somehow, Mrs Coffey has managed to get Fiona into the local kindergarten, though she's not five yet. She is tall for her age, and her nursery-school activities have made her advanced enough to be with children half a year older. Bettina holds her own with plump little Brigit. Both have a sense of the droll. So has Mrs Coffey, except when she talks of the Depression. Then her stories are as bleak as Sweeney's. The Coffeys, too, boiled soup bones given to them by the butcher "for the dog."

Night shift is easier too, for I can catch up on my sleep fairly well during the daytime. The house is kept quiet because of Mr Coffey's permanent night shift. The children play downstairs, and the radio there has ceased to disturb me. Bettina has an afternoon nap in her cot while Fiona is in afternoon kindergarten. If I wake up then, I soon go to sleep again. We both wake around three, when Bettina stands up in Brigit's old crib, warm with sleep, and in ringing tones announces: "I love everybody in the whole world." She will be three in March.

~ December ~

The machinists' union, to which Victory Aircraft workers belong (if they belong to any union), is associated with the AFL (American Federation of Labor) which originally developed from specialists' guilds (the old crafts guilds). At one time they were quite exclusive, so a much more universal type of union came into being, the CIO, with which the Steelworkers are affiliated. It's an ironic situation that the AFL union at Victory Aircraft is more to the left than CIO unions like the Steelworkers, who make every attempt to improve working conditions. Such efforts are sabotaged by the Machinists of the AFL if the war effort – and with it, help for Russia – is hindered in any way. So where's the difference between far right and far left?

Today we've had a tiny spontaneous strike that was never sanctioned by any union, and of which I am a little ashamed. It was not for better working conditions. On the contrary, it was about clothing meant to create better conditions.

The whole thing started with a well-meant regulation to protect women working on powerful machines. So far, bandanas have been acceptable. Now Personnel have come up with a specially designed hat that has a visor to protect the forehead and eyes. You would think that women would be grateful for such a regulation. Nothing of the kind. It seems that the hat is not flattering enough. You are not allowed to show even a lock of hair (artfully arranged to peep from most bandanas) because locks of hair have been known to be caught in machines. Bandanas showing locks of hair are now outlawed. And hats have to be worn by inspectors too.

Grace was up in arms. Her dark, curly mane of hair is her one good feature. If she has to cover it completely with one of those new hats, will the RCAF still stop at our table for a friendly chat? I couldn't help thinking of the fun Alexander Pope would have had with the incident that followed. Instead of *The Rape of the Lock*, he would have written *The Suppression of the Lock*.

The first thing one noticed was a strange silence, something of which the foremen and lead hands interested in the production bonus for their crew were aware at once. The deafening din of the riveting guns had ceased, then the clatter of other machines. Most of the riveters and machinists are women. One can see how many when all the tools are laid down. At first, only a few began to move towards the personnel office. They were joined by women from each aisle, some still in their bandanas, others, like Grace, wearing their hair defiantly uncovered. By the time they all came together at the bottom of the stairs at the personnel office, they were a crowd. A menacing crowd. I didn't join them but couldn't help wanting to see what would happen. I stood right at the back of the crowd so I wouldn't miss any of the action.

The narrow stairs caused a traffic jam. Up in the glassed-in office the organizer of the International Machinists Union could be seen wringing his hands. I knew what he would say when he finally emerged to speak a few calming words to the crowd of angry women: nothing must stop the war effort.

And that was exactly what he did say. A female personnel officer joined him on the platform above our heads. They looked as if they were preaching from a church pulpit. She tried to make the women feel ashamed that they had stopped work over so trivial an affair. Not for higher pay; not for better working conditions – for looks.

She reminded them that at this moment there were armies exposed to bitter cold, to snow, to lack of food and, especially, lack of ammunition that our planes were to bring them. There were wounded men in the desert, sailors drowning in the icy waters of the Atlantic. "Look at this," she said, holding up a poster showing a head mauled by machines that had pulled in the hair – the unprotected hair of an unfortunate woman machinist.

"What about inspectors," Grace yelled. "They don't go near machines."

"Most inspectors worth their salt go where production works," the chief personnel officer now put in (the very man who'd sent me to the wrong place my first week).

In the end, a compromise was reached. Personnel took it upon themselves to check on women who were in particular danger from machines, to make sure their hair was covered completely. Others who didn't work in such areas were not entirely exempt. They would be checked if they were likely to come in contact with machines at any time. It seemed a ridiculous arrangement, but it might give work to four or five new people in the personnel department.

No wonder the men hooted and whistled at lunch hour when we women entered the cafeteria. I stood in line behind a tiny woman inspector who had just joined our fuselage bay, the first to be given a job on an advanced stage of the formers. "When you think of the issues one *could* strike for," she said. "Think of them: we all work ten hours. And the unions had already gained an eight-hour day. Plus Saturday mornings off."

I nodded. We sat down together and unpacked our sandwich lunches.

"The coffee here could be better," I grumbled. Most of us just get a cup of coffee or a glass of milk to go with the packed lunches brought to the cafeteria in paper bags.

She is French and she knew exactly what I meant. "We could have homemade soup," she suggested. "Instead of this canned stuff."

Her name is Denise. She has transferred here from Quebec, where she worked on the graceful Catalinas, beautiful swanlike seaplanes. Her face is wider than long; she has bright brown eyes and rosy cheeks. Probably in her mid or late twenties, but already showing false teeth when she smiles, which she does often. She's the first person I've seen in this country who, like Scottish miners or Cockney workers, shows signs of malnutrition in her size and bones.

She comes from a large family and is married to a Scot, a Trotskyist. Most people around here, she says, don't know what that means. Trotsky was killed two years ago by someone from the current Soviet regime. I told her that I'd known Trotskyists in Barcelona, where they made a point of living near the most underprivileged people in town. I was not surprised to learn that Denise and her husband live downtown, above a store on a bleak part of Queen Street. It's against their principles to live in a comfortable suburb. I asked what Canadian political party, if any, the Trotskyists supported. The CCF, she said. I wonder whether they are welcome there.

Denise's presence at work is a refreshing change. She is so knowledgeable that the male inspectors have come, reluctantly, to accept her. It's a joy to watch her. She knows exactly where each former goes, what each hole and dent is for, the network of wires and levers for which they are designed.

~ December 11th ~

When Art found out that I had learnt about formers from Denise, he transferred me to that section. As I begin to understand the function of these gigantic shapes that will make up the fuselage, they look less and less like works of art to me. Still, there is something surrealist about them, massed beside the small inspection desk with its stamp pads and blueprints. The silvery web of scaffolding surrounds shapes that become more and more recognizable as they are moved up to Final Assembly.

Lancaster leaving Final Assembly
with entire production
and inspection crews, 1944

The male inspector on formers, whom the production crew like better than anyone else, is Sam, a big, bony, good-natured man. He works on his mink farm during the day, so is usually quite sleepy on night shifts. His mouth full of large teeth, his big lips, give the impression of a horse. His brow recedes beneath a shock of unruly hair. During the last election in June, he ran for the CCF, but in his farming community lost to the Conservatives.

~~

*Fellow inspector,
Victory Aircraft
Final Assembly, 1944
(pencil sketch on reverse
of inspection sheet)*

Sam and Denise, both intelligent and well read, both CCFers, are not on the same wavelength. I was curious to know more about Denise and her husband. So I was pleased when she invited me with the children for a good Quebec supper. Her bookshelves, like mine, are constructed from orange crates or made of bricks and boards, groaning under a load of literally hundreds of volumes. On the whitewashed walls are gigantic prints of paintings by the Mexican muralist Diego Rivera. I'd always thought that Rivera was somehow involved in Trotsky's assassination, but I must be wrong. He is their idol. Angus, Denise's husband, who in spite of his young age is almost bald as well as nearsighted, lent me a book they consider very important: André Malraux's *La Condition humaine*, translated as *Man's Fate*. I haven't yet read Malraux's book on the Spanish Civil War. That pain is still too raw.

~ December 18th ~

Heavy snow. We now live only a couple of blocks from Sweeney's family. When I returned their furniture to them, her brother offered to store my skis in their garage. Today I walked over to their house to retrieve them. There is no recent news from Sweeney in California.

Fiona and Bettina have colds, and that always means a threat of bronchitis, so I can't take them out in this tempting new snow. Fiona had to stay home from kindergarten. While both had an afternoon nap, I managed to take my skis all the way to the Rosedale golf course. The slopes there are just right for me, gentle and undemanding. Everything smelled wonderfully fresh; there was a sharp scent of balsam firs. The Don is a small, brown brook up there, still unfrozen in some places. Dark water was glistening between stalactites of transparent ice and gentle banks of the softest, smoothest snow. There was no one about, just deep silence. It gets dark early now, and I had to go home to read to the children.

I have had a disagreeable letter from Garth. The Children's Aid visited the Black family, where we lived in September, to inspect conditions there. Unless they improve, the Blacks are not allowed to board children. They also wrote to Garth, the children's father, to remind him of his responsibility. Social workers automatically do this, suggesting that he send us an allowance each month. He turned this around and blamed me. They threatened, he wrote, to take the children away from me if I didn't take care of them any better than – yes, what? I wrote back at once to say that we have a satisfactory place to stay and that I have a good job. He maintains that Miss Elgood, his mother's old friend, in Canada has the responsibility for her war guests. Of course, it's an impossible and unexpected burden for her, so I left Barrie. But I was shaken by this letter. Could that Children's Aid threat be real?

Every time the children get sick, I'm in danger of losing my job if I stay home to take care of them. That happened last spring.

~ December 27th ~

The children were still not well enough to travel to Barrie, as we did last Christmas, so we missed the reassuring contact with old friends – Elsie Raikes, the Smiths. Bettina still has bronchitis, and I remember only too well how that turned into pneumonia when she was a baby.

Another letter from Garth arrived at Christmas, with very tragical news. His mother, Dé, who had found it so hard to part with her only grandchild, Fiona, in 1940, has been killed in an accident caused by the blackout. She was cycling home from her Red Cross work in Sutton, Surrey, on a foggy evening and was hit by a car on a dimly lit street.

My mother-in-law was one of those great good women who take the world's problem on their shoulders. She was a suffragette, part of the group around Bertrand Russell, married to an artist much younger than herself. She left him when they both lived near New York, where her two children were born. After spending most of World War 1 in Barrie, helping to establish Ovenden School, she returned to England when she inherited a house in Sutton. Her daughter Fiona died at the age of twelve, at a high Anglican boarding school where her affliction (angina of the throat) was not recognized in time.

Today a small Christmas parcel arrived here, sent by Dé months before her death. She must have spent weeks making a doll for Fiona – a rather flat head and body cut out of unbleached cotton, the face painted with wax crayons, the hair made from strands of light brown wool. She must have knitted all the tiny clothes herself: bonnet, coat, dress, and socks.

Fiona now holds this doll in her arms. She doesn't remember her grandmother: she was only seventeen months old when we left. She'd often been a welcome visitor at Dé's friendly, untidy house with piles of newspapers and magazines in each corner, the rugs and cushions covered by hair from Dé's shaggy little dog. Oh, for such a helpful grandmother, here and now.

Her death is the pain of the known. Like the suicides during the Blitz – by one of Garth's friends, by dear Annie, my grandmother's maid; by Virginia Woolf. The pain of the unknown is like a dull toothache in comparison: the fate of my mother, still living in Germany, and of the family members for whom she remained there. It is always there.

The children are well enough to go out on this sunny day, to
see the Robinses, whom we have not visited for some time.
I brought with me a manuscript I'd started on those long
evenings in Barrie, when I was in charge of boarders at the
Junior House. Usually I was typing on the large kitchen table,
the door open so I could hear what went on upstairs, where
the juniors were going to bed, and a smaller door open to
our own room. The manuscript is about my early childhood
in Germany. I don't know if it's any good, but John R. will
look at it.

We sang Christmas songs, English and German. They even
knew the beautiful, haunting "Es ist ein Ros' entsprungen."
I've never heard that song here. I think it was written by
Martin Luther. We also sang some of the songs we'd sung last
June, during election fever.

The Spanish Civil War loomed again when the Robinses
sang the famous song of the peat-bog soldiers, in German too:

Ewig kann's nicht Winter sein.
Einmal werden froh wir sagen
Heimat, Du bist wieder mein.
Wir sind die Moorsoldaten.
Wir ziehn mit unsren Spaten ins Moor.
(Winter cannot last forever –
And someday we'll gladly say:
Homeland, you are mine again.
We are the peat-bog soldiers.
We march with our spades to the moor.)

It was sung by the International Brigade, but originated in concentration camps, where the peat was cut by forced labour
consisting of socialists, communists, liberals, democrats, and
some members of the confessional church, who didn't endorse
the state church controlled by the Nazis. Many of those released came to Spain and brought this song with them. Where

had I heard it? Perhaps from the remains of the International Brigade, walking sadly through the London streets.

The Robinses also have a collection of Negro spirituals, many of them new to me, and records of the dust-bowl ballads, sung during the Depression. The topsoil of Midwestern farms was blown away by dry, black storms, turning farmers into penniless itinerant labourers. The dust-bowl ballads are songs of the so-called Wobblies, the early American socialists. Where are they now? Was it Roosevelet who saved those enduring the Depression from becoming fascists? Many Canadians admire him, but we hear that not everybody in the U.S.A. does.

1944

Last night was one of those magical nights – like the one I spent over a year ago now with Elaine, Larry, and Clarence Gillis. The McCurdys had asked me to their New Year's Eve party. Of course, I couldn't go until the children were fast asleep. I knew they were in good hands, for the Coffeys were staying home.

The party had gone on for some time when I arrived. Country dancing was in full swing. The large living room had been cleared – chairs were against the wall. Some one was playing "Turkey in the Straw" and I was pushed into the grand chain and tried to remember how to perform do-Si-do, alamain all, and other parts of the dance. The movement, the interchanges, the meeting and parting of friends, in these square dances is exhilarating. I learned ballroom dancing, the tango and foxtrot. You're liable to be stuck with the same partner in those. This meeting and parting of friends, and the contents of a good punch bowl, may have had something to do with the general euphoria. I didn't get home quite as late as last year, but I got home late.

At midnight, when we sang "Auld Lang Syne," I found my-self holding hands with Alice Loeb. She asked me if I had a way home. Streetcars might be hard to find, she said, and offered to drive me.

"Where to?" Bernard asked, tiny behind the wheel.

"North Oakwood," I said.

"Oh, well, in that case, let's drop in on another party on the way. Then," Bernard went on, "you'll see one of the good things for 1944: a doctor living in Forest Hill whose ancestors were plantation slaves in Trinidad."

"It's not Forest Hill. It's up from Bathurst somewhere." Alice boomed. "Forest Hill is hoity-toity," she said, turning to me. "Did you know that the Jews living north of St Clair look down on the Jews south of it?"

"What does that make us?" Bernard giggled. "Jews living in Rosedale?"

"Oh, that." Alice's laugh sounded infectious. "That's only the beginning of the Rosedale ravine. It's south of Bloor. Don't forget that just as with Jews, there's a difference between coloured people with money and those without."

"Those we're going to see are 'with,'" Bernard slowed down to look for a turning north of St Clair. "You'll meet one of the most beautiful women in Toronto. If not the most beautiful. And the most elegant."

"And her husband mixes the best drinks in town," Alice added with satisfaction.

We drove up Bathurst to an area with new, prosperous houses and fewer trees than in Forest Hill. Even under the snow the gardens looked landscaped. Porch lights were on in many buildings, New Year's Eve parties winding down. A pair of visitors were leaving just as we parked in front of a house with its front door open. Parked cars occupied all of the driveway. In the open doorway the hostess stood outlined against still brighter indoor lights.

"Alice," she called out. "Bernard. Come in. Quickly, it's cold."

She hugged herself, a tall slender figure dressed in black. No, not entirely slender. In German she would be described as *vollschlank* – slender yet full at the right places. We followed her into the hall, and the Loebs introduced me.

"This is Marguerite Wyke. Her husband is a doctor, a good one, should you ever need one. He is from Trinidad. She's from New York. The house," Alice said, "looks like New York."

Here too the floor had been cleared for dancing, so one could not really judge the character of the room. Everything looked new and well-kept. Drinks stood about everywhere; a long table was laden with plates of food. Quite a number of people were dancing with abandon, but it was not country dancing; it was very lively, very contemporary. And they looked young, probably West Indian students. The girls looked younger than Marguerite, but none of them were even half as beautiful.

This is what Cleopatra must have looked like, I thought. *No wonder men died for her.* Perhaps it is her hairstyle that makes

Marguerite look more Egyptian than African, long black hair parted at the centre and drawn back to a chignon at the nape of her neck. This neck is long and swanlike, dark gold like the face and elegant hands. Her mouth is not exceptionally full but very mobile, her nose classical Mediterranean. All these harmonious features are dominated by very large, very beautiful eyes.

The light in the eyes was constantly changing, the mouth seldom in repose. The replies she threw back at remarks by the Loebs seemed to have a quirky self-mockery, but could not always be heard above the music. Jazz records were played even when the dancing stopped.

Alice and Bernard settled on a very long, white settee, the kind of settee one sees in furniture stores at out-of-reach prices. Bernard patted the corner near him, inviting me to sit there. Marguerite sank down beside Alice and pointed to the table with the food. "Help yourselves," she urged. "I made the pâté myself."

Quietly, she added to Alice, "I think I'm drunk. Tipsy, anyway. David will mix your drinks."

"What we really need is strong black coffee," Alice bellowed against the noise. "Or we won't get home."

"I'll make that," Marguerite promised. "Later."

She flashed a smile at two plump girls who came off the dance floor and introduced them as Gloria and Fay, Jamaican students at the University of Toronto. "Gloria is studying law. She has a brilliant mind. She never knows whether men invite her to get hold of her notes or because of herself. Fay studies ballet."

If these two girls were descendants of African slaves, they had lost the characteristics of those shipped to the West Indies. Perhaps they'd intermarried with native Caribs until these characteristics disappeared. Their hair, though curly, was quite long, and their build sturdy. They moved with the calm self-assurance I'd envied in upper-class English girls. I imagined they would have to be fairly wealthy to study at a Canadian university. Looking back at the dance floor, I found the white dancers boringly pale beside the elegant bodies, expressive hands, golden skin, and black crowns of the West Indian students.

When we helped ourselves to food, I stood beside a red-haired man introduced by Marguerite as an Irishman who works on the *Tribune*, the commie paper downtown. His wife is a second-generation Jamaican, born in Toronto, smaller and leaner than the others. She has their quick repartee but lacks the other attributes of wealth and ease.

She and Marguerite are from an urban setting, there is a nervous energy about them. "Lucille too was born here," Marguerite said. "She's a writer and a poet. Occasionally writes for the *Tribune* too."

The young woman she spoke of replied in the same musical voice as Marguerite's, though slightly lower.

"Many of those who lived here during the Depression turned communist," Alice explained. "Those sent here by affluent parents are unpolitical. David Wyke is a conservative Catholic. But Marguerite has joined the CCF. Our influence."

I could well believe that David Wyke was reassuring as physician, a rock that inspired total confidence. His square brown face looks like a calm plowed field. He mixed drinks with the same attention to detail he'd pay to medical prescriptions.

These drinks were entirely without colour. I don't know what was in them, but they were so potent that I don't remember how I got home. I'm fairly sure the Loebs didn't have to carry me. And there were no complaints from the Coffeys. I have my own key. I must have come in quietly and got up the stairs and into bed somehow. But then who, Scots or Irish, complains about excesses at Hogmanay?

Curious how intense enjoyment can be with the background of war. It was the same in London. I remember Dorothea, our Jewish protégé, weeping after a movie because she couldn't help enjoying herself, yet she didn't know what had happened to her parents in Vienna.

~ January 14th ~

Deep snow now, but the car always gets through. Some mornings the windshield frosts over and the driver has to halt at the roadside to scrape it. But we'ver never been late.

I wish I had not given in to Art and taken on the secretary's job at his office "for the time being," as he says. I feel I owe it to him (he sent me to the Coffeys, after all). But I long to be "out on the floor," as they say, with Denise. Most of the office work consists in making out chits that have to accompany finished parts from one stage of the fuselage assembly to the next, and eventually to Final Assembly. Art has always been very good at explaining where the parts go. Occasionally he'd take Denise and me over to Final Assembly, to see the complicated system of wires and tubes going through the formers. The blueprints, read properly, indicate whether such systems are electrical, hydraulic, or hand-operated.

~ January 25th ~.

Thank goodness, my stint at the office has come to an end. Art was a little offended that I was so jubilant about it, but his secretary, a very tall, well-dressed girl called Connie, is back and she does not want to be "out on the floor." Art has been grumpy lately. The production foremen have hounded him. They want their bonus. He's too finicky, they say.

"It's worse on Final Assembly," he said. "I would no more want to be inspection foreman there than go up in one of these damned planes." All the same, he let us go, Sam and me, to work in Final Assembly because they need two people over there "to do the donkey work."

It's been my dream to work on Final Assembly. I could hardly believe my luck. "Why not Denise?" I asked Sam.

"She's much too good, that's why." Sam showed all his yellow horses' teeth in a grin. "Don't kid yourself. It's not because we're such good inspectors that Art sends us over there. They want some ordinary joes to stamp off minor installations."

Sam is easy on the production crew: they're always asking for him. "You'll have to do child's work. You'll be the only woman inspector on Final Assembly. On our shift, anyway."

Sam is perceptive. There are women electricians, women riveters, women welders, but on Final Assembly I am indeed the only woman inspector. I may never meet my counterpart, a

197

woman on the opposite shift. We know each other only by the number of our stamp on the board, always on minor installations.

This board – or rather, a large card attached to it – is separate for each plane, like a medical chart for each patient.. All parts installed on Final Assembly are clearly marked there. The whole chart has to be completely stamped off, first by us, then by the RCAF, before the plane to which it belongs is moved to the next "stage." Comments may be made on it, notes attached from foreman to foreman, lead hand to lead hand.

My stamp number is 526. I hardly ever sit at a desk now, though there is a desk for us lowly first-stage inspectors. It's the one furthest from the great hangar doors that open to let out the finished plane (still to be severely checked, on Flight Test, by the RCAF).

Under our desk are a pair of felt slippers, the kind you find in museums, places with sensitive, highly polished floors. I put these on when I have to climb about on the broad wings of the Lancaster. A wonderful feeling, even if I only have to check the rivets around the fuel pump up there. To climb about on the spidery scaffolding, to crawl under the navigator's table inside the fuselage to check electrical connection – all that gives one a sense of great satisfaction.

At our end of Final Assembly the fuselage arrives wingless, without an engine, a poor thing compared to the final stage. By then, wings with ailerons and flaps, propellers, and the great Rolls-Royce engines have been added. Electrical wiring and hydraulic operations have to be in perfect working order.

Sam is now at the middle desk, where the hydraulic equipment is tested over and over again, the great undercarriage going up, going down, moaning and whining as if in protest. Electrical gadgets, too, are installed and checked there.

At the final stage an inspector sits in the pilot's seat and communes with the navigator behind him at the map table and with the man in the rear turret. He can move the tail plane, the ailerons and flaps. Each stage, until the plane reaches this godlike perfection, is checked and stamped off not only by inspectors but also by the RCAF, who have to fly these great machines.

Overlooking the last stage of the plane, in an elevated glass cubicle, is the office of the inspection foreman, a man with enormous responsibilities. Lloyd Sauvé, like Denise, is French and has worked on planes elsewhere. Like her, he is small, grave, dedicated. He has very dark eyes and eyebrows; his hair is white, his moustache grey. He has eleven children. Though he is thoroughly knowledgeable, he is also tactful. He does not interfere with a job well done. We seldom see him at our lower desk.

Our lead hand there is Van, a plump fellow who likes you to believe that he's a womanizer. With him there's a tall French inspector, as skinny as Van is broad, who has a similar repertoire of stories that come to an abrupt halt when I arrive at the desk.

At the middle desk with Sam, there's Ben, the youngest among us and Jewish. He gets on well with Sam. Ben's name is Cantor. His family came from Poland and now live on Brunswick Avenue. He is Orthodox, while the Loebs are Unitarian, and there are many other differences between them. With Alice and Bernard, whose families lived for centuries in Germany or Holland, I have so much in common that only a brief reference to Schiller or Schubert is sufficient to establish the same wavelength. I talk to them with greater ease than to some of my English relations.

On the other hand, Ben in Bedouin dress could be taken for a desert Arab, though he would resent that description. He is probably no more than twenty-four years old. "So, why ain't he in the army," the production lead hand is heard to mutter. Production have it in for Ben because he is so conscientious. He has to be; his job is almost exclusively confined to the hanging of those great wings. In this process, all depends on two great wing bolts. They are checked and rechecked by the RCAF, and of course by inspectors.

Ben is sensitive about the "army" hints. Sam tells me he's been rejected because of something unflattering like flat feet. Lately, his cousin in the air force has been reported missing. He can barely talk about it. No wonder he cares about his job and is what the production foreman and lead hand describe as "finicky." They don't trouble to imagine consequences; they see it as a position of power and they resent this power.

~ January 30th ~

Ben refused to stamp off the wing bolts. He maintained that they should be taken out and inserted properly. The production lead hand thought otherwise. His crew wanted their bonus. The plane was otherwise ready to move up to the next stage. Nothing could move Ben. So the lead hand went to complain to the production foreman, who in turn went to complain to the inspection foreman.

The production lead hand on wing installation is a sturdy, middle-aged man wearing glasses. He is capable, better than most of his crew, but he takes their part when it comes to the bonus. When he stormed off to see his foreman, marching past our desk with another worker, both carrying their heavy wrenches, I heard him mutter something I can't believe or forget: "Damned Jews. If there's something Hitler did right, it's getting rid of them,"

I thought I had not heard right. This sort of remark belonged to pre-war Germany and in my time was seldom stated so openly. It was this sentiment that ended in actions ordinary Germans never envisaged. "Did I hear this," I asked Sam. Roy, the French inspector, nodded. He is a Franco-Ontarian, and Montreal for him is the city of light.

"I hear this same thing in Montreal," he said. As if that made it right.

"Then I don't want to go there," I said miserably.

"Beautiful city," Roy sighed. "Nightlife you wouldn't believe. Night clubs, strip artists, jazz, culture."

The lead hand returned with his own foreman and with Lloyd Sauve, our foreman on night shifts (foremen don't change shifts as we do). Undisturbed by the black looks of the production crew, he carefully examined the wing-bolt installation. I thought that he would in all likelihood not pass it, and that they would then mumble something about "dirty Frogs."

"Ben," he said finally. "This could not be done much better."

"Much better, no," Ben admitted. His jaw worked nervously. "But better, yes. Safer."

"I respect your opinion," Lloyd said. "I know about your cousin. And, God knows, all the others. But they're *shot* down. Not prey to wing failure."

"You'd go up in that plane, then?"

A large group had gathered by now. The plane was ready to be pushed to the next stage, something that was done by hand. By many hands. I loved to watch it when they got behind the tail plane, and some behind those gigantic wheels and the monstrous creation slowly began to move forward.

"RCAF won't pass it," Ben said, white and defiant.

"OK," Lloyd said. "I'll take the blame if they don't. If you don't pass it, Ben, I will."

He took his own seldom-used stamp from his coverall pocket. Usually, it only appears on the very final stage, when all is complete, when the plane is ready to be pushed out of the hangar, when the gigantic doors open to the open tarmac, to Flight Test. The production crew in their dirty white overalls rallied to their appointed places and started to push the plane along. Slowly, the huge shape moved to the next stage (propellers).

"Ugly beast," Sam murmured. "Looks like a gigantic insect, a malicious kind."

I didn't listen to him. I felt elation whenever a plane was moved. The result of all our achievements, of technical progress, but it was still moved communally – by hand, by the force of human muscle.

Ben stood staring at the empty board; the card for this plane, all operations stamped off, had moved on to the next stage, with Lloyd's stamp under "wing bolts." I stood beside him, feeling numb and hurt on his behalf. I didn't know who was right. I just didn't want the lead hand to triumph because ... because of what he'd said.

"I didn't know this could happen here, in this country," I said to Sam when Ben had gone. Turned on his heel and walked off.

"You think this is a perfect country?"

"Yes. No. A country with possibilities."

"What causes anti-Semitism anywhere, I ask you?"

"Envy, greed, ignorance, cynicism, despair. Lack of respect for human beings other than ourselves."

"And you think that doesn't exist here? You think that lead hand is worse than, say, Mackenzie King, who admired Hitler. Or didn't you know? This is not a race of angels."

"I know."

"But you don't want to know. And you want to go on believing that these monsters we create are not destroying human beings."

He had touched a sore point. Many of us believe that these large planes are mainly used to take troops over to Europe. That's what we are (vaguely) told, and that part may be true, but there is a bomb bay beneath the fuselage.

Sam has his own foibles. He is middle-aged, and like some other middle-aged men here, he always maintains he's thirty-nine. That seems to be the cut-off point for middle age. He's ugly yet attractive, and though married, he has a girlfriend somewhere in this plant. He says he doesn't get along with his wife. Funny that other middle-aged men who say they're thirty-nine maintain that too.

Ben, who is only twenty-four and, compared to Sam, is as handsome as they come, is something of a prude. Sam doesn't fool himself. He sees these planes for what they are: deadly machines.

~ February 4th ~

When I'm on night shift, I manage to see more of the children. I don't get so tired that the whole day becomes blurred by lack of sleep. At nights the pace of work is more leisurely – perhaps because the administrative staff are absent. I noticed that certain installations, those inside the fuselage, have a great attraction for inspectors. There's an inviting, if hard, couch beside the navigator's table, where on long flights the flight crew can take turns catching up on sleep (and where wounded airmen can rest?). We too take turns, inspecting inside installations, an unspoken agreement. A short rest, forty winks, makes all the difference during graveyard hours, those hours between three and four in the morning that never seem to end.

Either you spread a blueprint on the navigator's table (as the navigator himself might do) and nod over it while sitting at the table, or you curl up on the couch itself, though that's a little more risky. But in this part of the fuselage there's a truce between inspection and work crews. They don't see us; we don't see them.

The crew of course use the same blueprints we do. Last night, when I crept into the fuselage, a duplicate of the print I brought with me was already spread out on the navigator's table. Two legs in dirty white overalls protruded from under the table, and as I sank down on the couch, an arm appeared to politely move an open tool box a few inches to make room for me. As I compared the blueprint on the table with mine, a head emerged.

I'd noticed this man before. He was a member of the crew responsible for electrical installations, that intricate wiring for which holes had been left on the formers I used to inspect with Denise. I remembered him mainly because on his forehead he has a curious purple mark. He is probably in his mid-thirties; his eyes are light, his hair reddish brown.

Lying under the table, he had not been taking a nap; he had been reading a pocket book. He showed me the title: *Bread and Wine* by Ignazio Silone.

I did not know this work. The only book by Silone I'd ever read was *Fontamara*. I'd been horrified by the description of fascists invading and destroying an Italian village. I'd never seen that kind of beastliness while I lived in Florence (and Garth in Rome), but then, who in Germany saw what went on there? The book *Fontamara* was not available in either country.

"Silone is an anarchist," the young man said. He made this pronouncement in a light, bantering tone, not at all as if he wanted to convince me. I nodded. I could not help staring at the purple mark on his forehead. His greasy hand – the nails black from the oil on his tools – moved there.

"The mark of the Depression," he grinned. "I fell off a freight train out west." Only a few years back, he'd been one of the thousands of unemployed who rode the freights.

"If we were caught, we were thrown off the trains by the train crews. Sometimes we were put in those camps where you were paid twenty-five cents a day on make-work projects." (Like the German *Arbeitsdienst*, I could not help thinking.)

He'd been in bread lines and soup kitchens. When the war started, he could have joined up, though probably he's above the required age. "I'm a pacifist," he explained. "And, of course, an anarchist."

"Then you don't belong to any political party?"

"Well, what party is there that hasn't been wrecked by power when in government?"

"So, you don't vote?"

"Well, I might. For a party not likely to be in power to screw things up. The CCF when they're the underdog, maybe."

I had to laugth. Would the CCF intellectuals, people like Jolliffe, or union men like Millard know (and be embarrassed) that anarchists and Trotskyists support them? But only as long as they have little power. Not a compliment exactly. Anarchists have the conviction that man is basically good and best left without too much government. At least the anarchists in Spain believed this. I'm inclined to agree. But why am I still surprised when I find people doing really good, unselfish things?

~ February 11th ~

There's a new secretary in the foreman's office, and the all-male club at our inspection desk vies with the production crew in their whistles whenever she stalks past. She ignores the whistles, but she's aware of them. She works inside a glass cage, so she doesn't have to wear a bandana. A fine mane of curly, red-golden hair dances around her head and shoulders.

That mane of hair is not really what causes the whistles, though. Above a tightly belted waist the usually shapeless coveralls barely hide two balloons. That's what Roy calls them: "balloons." "She blows them up, you see," he states, as firmly as if he'd examined her brassiere. "They're not her own. They're falsies."

She trips by on her (relatively) high heels, her straight, freckled nose up in the air. But Eileen is not an exhibitionist. I happen to know that Roy is wrong, but what can I say?

Eileen is a member of our car pool when we are on days. Our sober, religious driver places her in the front seat so she won't distract his other passengers. She gets in last and on the way home leaves first, just after we pass Keele Street on Eglinton. At the corner of her street, a crescent with new bungalows curving uphill, there is a curious tall building, a rusty remnant of some industrial enterprise. To the north of this part of Eglinton, plowed fields still stretch to the horizon.

Eileen lives in one of these bungalows. One day in the women's washroom at work, while she was brushing out her rebellious curls, she saw me struggling with bobby pins. She took me in hand and put up the pins in such a way that, under my bandana, my hair would curl while I worked. It did. One thing led to another, so that one afternoon before night shift I took the streetcar to its Eglinton terminal and walked up to her house, where she washed and set my hair.

The Oakwood streetcar turns west on Eglinton near the Coffeys'. It's only a short ride to its terminal below the hill where Eileen lives. She is a truly gifted hairdresser. She set my hair to the tune of "Stormy Weather." She is passionate about such tunes. Her favourite is "Sunlight Serenade," and "Smoke Gets in My Eyes" – if sung by Dinah Shore. Her husband, Norman, likes classical music. According to Eileen, he's a "sober sides," doesn't go out to dances and parties. For that, she has another friend. Like most of us, he does some kind of war work.

Eileen hates housework, or so she says. But while I sat under her dryer, she ran up and down (wearing a most becoming slip) to get a large washing done (all these new bungalows have extensive basements). She then had a shower and for our supper "threw together" (her expression) some toasted cheese sandwiches. Through all this she appeared in various stages of undress, and it was obvious that no part of her body was blown up. But could I tell Roy?

She's on permanent day shift. A neighbour takes care of her little boy, Brian. He came home, already fed, and she put him to bed. Then Norman came home from de Havilland's. I could see his attraction: like his son, he is dark and has the same alluring smile. Reserved and quiet, he makes her feel safe (she says).

While she wrapped my hair around her manicured fingers (she wears silver nail polish), Eileen probed into my love life. "What do you do?" she asked, her mouth around several bobby pins. "About men? With your husband in New York. I wouldn't mind going there if I could."

"I can't," I said. "And I don't know what he's doing."

"I can imagine what he's doing," Eileen mumbled around the pins. "Do the same. Get a boyfriend."

"I thought I'd married for love," I sighed. "But then, maybe I wanted, more than anything, to get away from Germany. Maybe it was a romantic notion. Can you understand what I mean, if I tell you that when I already had one child and another on the way, I fell hard for someone else. One of those impossible, crazy situations. That's all I can tell you about it.

"So now, I can't get enthusiastic about any male."

Eileen nodded, as if she knew what I meant, and turned on the dryer again. "Tough," she mumbled, retrieved the pins from her mouth, and stuck one or two in the net she wound around my hair. "Your husband can't look after you – or won't. And you don't feel like going out with another guy. Keep still."

I laughed. "There are so many women around. They're a dime a dozen."

"Not women like you and me," Eileen said proudly. Perhaps I should feel pleased that she sees me as her equal. She thinks I have style. That probably means that I'm too thin for the current bosomy fashion.

~ March 2nd ~

Mrs Coffey's goodness has caused complications for us all, so that our happy routine didn't last. She took pity on a friend who has nowhere to go, who's been left by her husband and has a thirteen-year-old daughter. Somehow, Mrs Coffey accom-

modated both of them in little Brigit's room, placing a folding
cot there for the daughter, moving Brigit into her parents' room
and Dan to the basement, where there's a recreation room.
The house is bursting at the seams. Through all this turmoil,
deaf Mr Coffey continues, unperturbed, with his violin practice.
Perhaps he can only hear the tune in his mind?

~ March 5th ~

Disaster struck. The thirteen-year-old girl fell ill. She has a high
temperature, and the doctor quickly diagnosed her illness as
scarlet fever. Automatically, all the children in the household
are quarantined, as well as all adults who have not yet had this
contagious disease. That includes myself.

When I was small, scarlet fever was regarded as a childhood
killer. Two of my aunts had turned stone deaf after a bout of it.
My parents took good care that we never came in contact with
that disease. Nowadays, though, there's a vaccine – one the
doctor immediately used on everyone in the household. But in
spite of that, I'm quarantined.

The choice is terrible: either I stay somewhere else and continue at work, leaving the children with the Coffeys (where,
luckily, they get on well), or I stay with them and will then,
most likely, be out of a job, as happened once before. I have
to pay for their keep, though, and to do that I have to continue working.

If I stay elsewhere, I'd be allowed to see the children, but only out of doors, on the Coffeys' porch, say (provided they don't
get the fever). On night shift I could manage this in the afternoon. After day shift it may be harder, though not impossible:
the days are getting longer. Or I could stay with the Coffeys in
their already overcrowded house, help look after the children,
and take a six weeks' leave of absence (unpaid). But how would
I pay Mrs Coffey? It's a vicious circle.

The woman friend who has caused all this trouble feels terribly contrite and has offered to help look after all five children.
The most infectious stage in scarlet fever is the last one, when
the skin is peeling. If I get out now, I can go on working. Where
to go? I thought of the Sweeneys, who live nearby.

Now Eileen has come to the rescue. I can sleep in the spare room at her house, a place already known to me and on our car-pool route. So now, with a heavy heart, I'm rummaging through clothes, restricting what I can take with me to a small suitcase, to travel to Eileen via our night-shift route. Then we'll see.

Fiona and Bettina look well so far. This kind of scarlet fever has been graded down to a less lethal kind, known as scarletina. But Fiona, who loves kindergarten, can't go back to school at present. The children are allowed to play out of doors and in the porch, a blessing because there I can see them (like *Romeo and Juliet*, but less secretly). It's heartbreaking leaving them, but there's simply no other way.

~ March 14th ~

Rain, sleet, and snow. It's difficult to enact the *Romeo and Juliet* scene with my children, especially after day shift, when I have to wait till evening. I tried: they dressed in winter clothes and came out on the porch, but just for a minute while I handed Mrs Coffey my usual cheque. She wouldn't hear of charging me the full amount while I have to stay elsewhere. She looks tired out, and I wonder how long, even whether, she can go on. The friend who caused all this is not a very helpful person; she always talks about her own troubles.

Mrs Coffey tells me that Fiona and Bettina are especially upset after I visit. They miss me more then. I've gone through this harassing experience once before, when Fiona was three and Bettina a baby. During the summer when the school was closed, I had to find a job to tide us over. I found one, housekeeping for an old lady, who allowed me to bring only one child. I boarded Fiona with a kind little nurse who lived near Barrie, and after I visited her, she was always more upset than on other days.

I tried to remember whether I know anyone with medical knowledge in Toronto. The doctor who had diagnosed the children, and vaccinated them, seemed overworked and not inclined to impart any more than the most necessary information. I thought of our New Year's party, now a long way back. At that time Marguerite Wyke had asked me to visit her. I'd even

208

suggested that I would like to paint her portrait. But would she remember? Like Elaine, she'd probably be an elusive subject. And I'd exchanged only a few words with her husband, a physician who looked reliable, someone children would like and trust.

I still have the Wykes' telephone number. Back at Eileen's, in my distress over visiting the children, I found the courage to ring. It was Marguerite, not David, who answered. I said that I now had a new address, briefly mentioned my troubles, and asked whether she would still like to sit for a portrait.

"Do come," she said. "Don't worry. I've had scarlet fever. My artist friends tell me I am a difficult model, but it will be fun to talk."

This northwest part of Toronto where Eileen lives seems miles from my old friends, Florence, the Robinses, the union office. It's even further from downtown than the Coffeys' on Oakwood, and the Oakwood streetcar is slow. Of all the people I've met in Toronto, the Wykes are closest to this address.

The Wykes' house shows an expensive taste – more, a love of luxury. The room where the party had taken place turns out in the daytime to be a bright living room looking out on a garden.

Marguerite made coffee before she consented to sit for me. Her kitchen contains every device invented to make housework easy, even an electric ironer. I remember when a steam iron was a novelty, when you heated flat irons on the kitchen stove. She is older than I am but does not seem to belong to the generation preceding mine.

She settled in an armchair with a cover as white as the settee on which we had sat with the Loebs. She dearly loves the Loebs, she says; also the Robinses. As I put out my paints, I studied her in profile and again full face. She was right: in spite of the impression of symmetrical beauty, the two sides of her face are not the same. Though she looks Egyptian rather than African (she is partly Jewish), she maintains that her husband, who looks darker and hails from Trinidad, has more white ancestors than she has.

Her eyes are very large and liquid but not slanted. Her nose is aquiline, and her mouth has lovely lines. The impression of regular features may derive from the centre parting of her smooth, black hair. Perhaps she straightens her hair, while we try our best to curl ours.

Did Aida look like this, rather than Cleopatra? Did Aida ever exist? Just what is that elusive quality of a very beautiful face? Perhaps only a tiny shadow above or below the eyes, a delicate curve in the bone structure. It's something you can't pin down.

On the table beside us I saw a stack of *New Yorker*s. While I laid on an underpainting, I mentioned that my husband occasionally made small drawings for the *New Yorker*.

"The *New Yorker*?" I felt a click in Marguerite's attention. She asked for Garth's name. She leafed through the magazines, looking for his drawings, but they are tiny vignettes, maybe unsigned.

I understood that, for her, to work for the *New Yorker* at all is admirable. When I mentioned as casually that Garth had made friends with someone called E.B. White – had, in fact, made some illustrations for him – I saw my own status rise with his.

Art and iterature really mean something to this woman. She knows a lot about American literature that's still new to me. On her well-stocked bookshelves are works by Emerson and Hawthorne, by Faulkner, Dos Passos, Steinbeck, Saroyan, Maxwell Anderson, and others not known to me. She says that she herself, rather than her husband, reads these books.

David, she explained, is a devout Catholic. She herself is an agnostic. "He does a lot of work for his church. He's often late," she added and asked me for supper. On Saturday he visits a monastery. He treats the priests and monks free of charge.

When we gave up on the portrait, she offered me the choice of two bathrooms to clean up after painting: one upstairs and one on the ground floor. The house is fairly new, and the bathroom contains every luxury one could wish for in wartime: perfumed soaps, lotions, bath salts, velvety towels, and mats with a deep pile.

The supper was prepared with astonishing speed: a succulent steak (it's three years since I ate steak) and a mixture of wonderful vegetables – hot peppers, aubergines – the kind of thing one used to find in Italy and Spain.

Marguerite has no children and doesn't want any. She can't quite understand why I fret so much, being away from mine. If they are well cared for, it would be the same as having a good nanny. If my mother was English, had she not been brought up by a nanny, rather than by her own mother?

She does understand my concern about relatives, though. Liverpool, near my grandmother, is still bombed. We know next to nothing about Germany, but Grannie assures me that Mother has moved to the country. The news is terribly confusing. It seems that the Russians are beginning to regain the Ukraine and that thousands of German soldiers have died near Stalingrad. The Italians have joined the Allies. But fresh German troops have entered the north of Italy, and there's still fighting around Rome. No one really knows anything for certain.

Marguerite, who reads the *New York Times*, agrees with me that if humanity is to survive, the forces that have overrun Europe must be stopped. Being both Jewish and coloured, she knows about racism. I am the first who can tell her something about pre-thirties Germany, when Marian Anderson made her debut in Berlin.

In the end, I didn't wait for her husband's return. Why had I thought that his medical advice might help? The children are not sick, just missing their mother. And father, if they know him.

~ March 25th ~

Eileen is on the phone a lot of the time, chatting with her best friend, Doreen, and, perhaps, a boyfriend. She's usually in state of undress, which, somehow adds piquancy to these lively conversations. On Sunday I finally managed to get a free line and telephoned the Robinses. I apologized about leaving my manuscript there for so long. It's not even that well typed on my little Remington, the one I bought for four pounds sterling at London's Gloucester Street auction rooms when people left town during the Czech crisis.

I managed some typing while I was on duty as junior matron in Barrie, usually in the evenings when both my children and the Junior House had gone to sleep. Those much-corrected pages can't have been easy to read.

Mrs Robins answered the phone. When she heard about the scarlet fever, she told me that their son, Peter, had also been vaccinated against the disease, and that he had not got it, so the vaccine is effective. She too thinks that the present epidemic is a much lighter variety than the killing disease I remember. She asked me to come for tea. It's an endless streetcar ride down to Bloor, then west past High Park, but it's so enjoyable seeing the Robinses again.

My dog-eared manuscript lay on John Robins's desk. "There's much that's interesting in it," he said. "But don't you want to go ahead and tell a story?"

I was taken aback. "I think the truth is more interesting than anything. I want to tell the truth."

"You can only tell the truth as you see it. It may be from a childhood point of view. Or an artist's. But you have to lead your readers along somehow – that's what storytellers do."

I suddenly realized that you have to be an artist when you write just as much as when you paint. There has to be structure; style; a voice. I have much to learn.

After day shift and a short visit to the children, now the weather's warmer, I also managed to see the Loebs. They have a beautiful house in the Rosedale ravine, just south of Bloor on Castle Frank Crescent. The house is on two levels. You enter it upstairs and descend to a room facing a garden and the lower part of the ravine.

Bernard Loeb showed me the Leonard Brooks painting he bought recently and two paintings by Fritz Brandtner, the German Expressionist who came to Canada a generation ago and became part of the contemporary arts movement in Montreal. In Germany I'd not particularly cared about Expressionism. I loved Käthe Kollwitz and Paula Modersohn, and neither belong to it. But ever since I found Brandtner's linocut

Christmas 1942 at the Toronto art gallery, I've felt great sympathy for this artist.

I feel at home with the Loebs, perhaps because they're more European than others I know in Toronto – more mid-European, I should say, for there's Margot too. Alice Loeb is an artist in her own right, a sculptor, and she does some pottery. She has a very large, comforting presence. I imagine she's a vigorous mainstay for the International Women's Movement in Toronto.

The Loebs promised to come to the non-jury exhibition at the Toronto art gallery, for which I've entered Florence's portrait.

~ April 5th ~

There's much to be said for a jury, however biased. The paintings and sculpture entered in the non-jury exhibition at the Toronto art gallery are of all kinds, and few are real finds: autodidact artists with a fresh approach. Very few even have the immediacy of folk art. Many are clichés, shadows of shadows of improperly understood art movements or imitations of the once vigorous Group of Seven. Bernard Loeb was not tempted to buy a single painting.

I am not particularly proud of showing with this group, but Florence is delighted to see her portrait at so prestigious a gallery. The painting will have a history. She came to the opening, and we somehow came to talk about Fritz Brandtner, now in Montreal. I said how much I'd like to visit Montreal and perhaps see him there.

That's how I found out about Florence's summer plans. She and her friend Ruth have long planned a cycling trip to an area where there are good youth hostels. Between Ottawa and Montreal, she says, there are several, so that one could make the trip, cycling a reasonable twenty-five miles or so daily, in something like five days. There are other hostels in the Laurentians, which, north of Ottawa, are known as the "Gatineaux." At Malton we get an official one-week holiday with pay. Perhaps I can add another week without pay. Six weeks with or without pay would have endangered my job, but perhaps in the summer Garth can take one or both of the children. It's a long way off, but he seems to do better now, and a cycling holiday, if Florence and Ruth won't mind my joining them, would be like old times, cycling from hostel to hostel in the Neckar valley. I keep my fingers crossed. The children will be out of quarantine bv next week. I can't wait for things to get back to normal.

~ April 17th ~

Things didn't get back to normal. Neither of the children contracted scarlet fever. They look healthy and sunburned, playing outside so much. But Mrs Coffey is completely worn out. She simply can't continue the way she has, and that means an end to our staying at that welcoming house.

All through those harassing six weeks, the friend with the sick daughter was close to a nervous breakdown. Now Mrs Coffey might well have a breakdown herself, physical rather than nervous, if she doesn't have a complete rest, without boarders, without extra washing and cleaning and cooking and mending.

We have to move again – our fifth move since we came to Toronto.

~ April 20th ~

My co-inspector, Sam, good-natured as always, came to the rescue. As a farmer, he knows quite a few other farmers, most of them more prosperous than he is. Others just get by, and they have boarders, people who work at Victory Aircraft. They put up notices on a bulletin board just outside the personnel office, where those with car pools pin up requests.

As I expected, most ads seeking boarders are for single males (as in Toronto rooming houses). One ad, instead of a telephone number, gave the name of someone working at the personnel office. I decided to talk to this person and explain our situation.

At the nearby office I asked for Joan Grice. She turns out to be a girl of around eighteen, fresh looking, polite, a recent high school graduate. Joan wears glasses, but they don't detract from her pleasant looks. She suggested I ride home with her to talk to her mother. Their farm is near Cooksville, where one can get a bus to Toronto.

Mrs Coffey encouraged me to see the farm – she would be glad
if I found something suitable. She has got very fond of Bettina
especially, so close in age to her own Brigit. If I'd go this
afternoon, I could come back to town with a late bus from
Cooksville.

The ride to the Grices' farm took as long as our car pool to
Eglinton and Keele. We went on back roads, dropping off passengers on the way. The country around Cooksville is perfectly flat, as it is around Malton. Now, in spring, the roads are
muddy. There were tractors out on the fields, plowing perfectly
straight rows in the dark soil, where puddles here and there
reflected the blue sky. On the roadside there are spring flowers
now, dog's tooth violets, bloodroot, trillium where there's a
maple bush. When we got out of the car, I could hear the honk-
ing of Canada geese flying north in V formation, a sound I
haven't heard since living in Barrie.

The Grices' sturdy, square brick house reminds me of prosperous brick houses in the Barrie area. If, in Barrie, I was overwhelmed by the peaceful life after wartime London, here I was
overwhelmed by the abundance of food, almost indecent in
wartime. The supper table was groaning under its load of homemade pies, butter tarts, pickles, and jellies. There was milk and
cream fresh from the dairy, vegetables from the garden, over-
wintered in a root cellar.

Rationing does not seem to be a problem, except for sugar.
Mrs Grice, who like Joan wears glasses but is twice her daughter's size, made no secret of welcoming the sugar coupons additional boarders would bring. She didn't seem averse to boarding
children and said that what I paid at the Coffeys would do here
too. We could try it for the summer. Their other boarder, young
Cecil, might be called up for military service any time.

There are drawbacks being so far out in the country. For
one thing, school is not very close and does not include kindergarten. Fiona would have to be six to enter school here. The
way into town is slow and complicated. One has to walk a mile
to reach the Cooksville bus, and it doesn't run very often. To

get back to Oakwood I had to take another bus after that one, then a couple of streetcars, to reach the Coffeys'. But that would not be such a great problem later.

~ April 29th ~

Florence and I took the children out to Cooksville on Sunday, so the Grices could get to know them. Florence wanted to find Jalna, the house about which Mazo de la Roche has written so extensively. She says it's near Cooksville, on the lakeshore somewhere. At the bus stop she turned towards the lake, while we climbed into Mr Grice's large car. I hardly recognized him, for he was dressed for Sunday in a suit and I'd only seen him in farm overalls. Why do so many farmers have a high, crowing voice? Is it cattle-calling?

Mrs Grice seems impressed by my children's good manners. Heaven knows, they acquired them simply through the pressures of life. Fiona is going to be five, Bettina is three now, and they are at a pretty age. It's warm now, so both wore summer dresses. Fiona wears her hair in two short pigtails. Mrs Coffey has started to braid it because that keeps it tidy. It is so fine that combing has been an agony always.

The children loved the swing in the garden. This is a very efficient farm; there are no pet animals except for calves raised for cattle shows. The Grices' son has not been called up because he helps his father with the chores. They start very early, with milking. All these farms now have milking machines. Separating is done out in the dairy, before the calves are fed the skim milk. The butterfat goes to a co-operative.

Mrs Grice offered to take us right away, rather than wait for summer. She must really like the children.

~ May 2nd ~

We have moved to the farm. I must say, I never thought I'd miss Eileen as much as I do – her witty asides about men, her reckless yet somehow innocent pursuit of pleasure, her haphazard housework. Her "Sunshine Serenade," "Stormy Weather," and "Smoke Gets in My Eyes" I thought would drive me crazy, but now belong to nostalgia.

The farm routine begins very early, so that there is not the same hushed atmosphere there was when, at the Coffeys', I crept to the kitchen for breakfast and, in winter dark, to our car pool. Here milking takes place so early that all have breakfast at the same time, the men consuming vast quantities of eggs, bacon, sometimes pancakes. Mrs Grice packs a big lunch for Cecil and me. The driver of the car pool stops for three people here, so that he only has to make one other pickup stop, but still, the way to Malton seems slow. Nothing will induce our driver to go more than thirty miles an hour on these back roads. And I don't blame him.

~ May 15th ~

Everything is bursting into spring green at once, overnight. Suddenly, the small transparent copse on the farm turns into a dense bush. Robins here are thrushes and sing more ambitiously than European robins. There are other thrushes too, wood thrushes, very shy, and red-winged blackbirds. But nowhere do you hear the overwhelmingly beautiful song of the European blackbird. Sparrows survived when introduced, but blackbirds never did.

I've looked forward to living in the country. The children are well, and the food is so good – then, why am I not happier? Does physical well-being have to be accompanied by mental dullness?

The talk is mostly about fertilizers, weed killers, the price of stock, the price of grain, the shortage of hay in spring. Nature does not enter into it except as weather. That part of nature still has the upper hand through rain, hail, drought. Last summer, I'm told, a neighbouring farmer walking home behind his cattle was killed by lightning. I was brought up in the country, and life was so full then; so the sense of tedium surprises me. I can understand Joan, who wants to live in town.

~ May 18th ~

Last Thursday I drove to Toronto in my old car pool to see Eileen, so she could cut and curl my hair. Marguerite Wyke, my new friend, has invited me to accompany her to Eaton Auditorium to hear Marian Anderson. I knew vaguely about this singer, who had started her career in the decadent, liberal Berlin of the nineteen twenties when no American concert stage would accept her. So much for racism in Germany then.

The first part of Anderson's songs were a revelation to me. She sang spirituals: "Every Time I Hear the Spirit" and "Go, Tell It on the Mountain." Their power, as sung by her, is the power of the greatest hymns of the Reformation, of Matthias Claudius, of the folk songs I loved. There's a passion in these songs of faith, of the oppressed, that's overwhelming.

But Marian Anderson also sang classical lieder. Brahms's "Sapphische Ode (Rosen brach ich nachts mir am dunklen Hage)" I'd sung myself once. Then some Schubert lieder. But for me the most moving experience was her encore: Marian Anderson sang, in French, the song of the nightingale, "Russiñol," I'd so often heard in Catalonia:

Little nightingale – oh little bird, fly far away
Take a letter to my father on the way
Aya.

After the concert, at another of Marguerite's parties, there again were the attractive West Indian students, including Enid Kelly, David Wyke's newly arrived niece from Trinidad. I had arranged to sleep at Eileen's, so I could take the car pool to work in the morning. But I barely managed to catch the last Oakwood streetcar to the terminal below her hilltop bungalow, the streetcar that had so often taken me back and forth to see the children when they were still at the Coffeys'.

~ May 27th ~

A letter from Garth. He is doing much better these days and has offered to take Fiona for a month this summer. We have to discuss our divorce, a fearfully expensive and endless business. Up to now neither of us has been able to afford it. The only cause for it, here and in New York State, is adultery, and neither of us wants to involve a friend as correspondent.

Florence says I must see her lawyer, and I did. He has warned me not to leave the children with their father, who may keep them and use them as a tool of some kind. Garth is very good with small children, though. Fiona, who was three when she last saw him, has never forgotten, and I don't see how I can deprive her of her father.

In any case, we are only going to discuss the future. Garth suggests meeting in Barrie. He'd like to see his mother's old friend, Mary Elgood, again. Neither he nor I have seen her since the news of Dé's death. Garth did not get along particularly well with Dé and now is filled with all kinds of guilt feelings.

I'd love to see the old Barrie friends again, but having Garth there as well? I just don't know.

Garth would consider meeting in Montreal, a neutral place. It looks as if Florence's holiday plans might work out and include me. Would she mind my meeting Garth in Montreal? No, she says, she doesn't. He may bring some friends, he wrote. New Yorkers seem to prefer Montreal to Toronto.

~ June 7th ~

The Allies have invaded France. Not, as in August 1942, at Dieppe (with disastrous results) but in full force and with success. Their enemy has weakened on three fronts. The Normandy invaders are moving fast, and everyone now thinks this is the beginning of the end. I can't believe it. The time when we felt the enemy to be invincible is still too vivid a memory. When one European country after another fell like ninepins, it looked as if that gigantic military force would never be overcome.

Sam tells me I'm behind the times. The planes we're inspecting are not only troop transports; they now pound German towns. He maintains that these raids are heavier than those we experienced in London and Liverpool. That seems impossible.

"It's a miscalculation, of course," he admits. "Civilians have no power to change a dictator." Of course not. If Hitler's generals can't topple him in the bunker he now inhabits, how can ordinary people? This bombing idea has been hatched in a democracy where leaders can be voted out of office.

"Argue with Churchill," Sam suggested. "Or Eisenhower, or one of those British generals – Harris I think is the name. No one asked me or I would have advised against it. I'm just a little guy."

Sam, Ben, and I have been promoted to the next section on Final Assembly, where most of the electrical parts are added to the plane. Each part, however small, has to be tested to see whether it performs as planned. The production crew for this section are highly skilled. Sam thinks they really know more than we do. One of the most reliable electricians is Chinese. His fingers have a knowledge of their own. He has never made a mistake, as far as anyone on inspection can remember. The parts he installs are so small, you should really have a magnifying glass to check them. One of these, considered a minor installation, is a tiny battery that serves as a connection to blow up the dinghy. There is no marking on it to designate positive or negative elements, or if there is, it's invisible. Both ends look exactly the same. To find out if this battery has been put in the right way, we have to blow up the dinghy each time the installation is checked, blow it up from the pilot's seat. Chan has never made a mistake. The dinghy always fills with air or gas, as it should. It's a long slow process, blowing up the dinghy from its post of command. Many inspectors stamp off that part without checking. Their trust has never been misplaced.

It was towards the end of the graveyard shift when the installation number for the dinghy appeared on our board, ready for checking. The production crew, as usual, were in a hurry to move the plane to the next stage and get their bonus. They wanted Sam to check it; he's easygoing. But he was busy testing the undercarriage, a hydraulic installation further up the line. They didn't want Ben; he's sure to be finicky. So they asked me. I climbed up into the plane. I looked at the part. I'd blown up the dinghy a couple of times; it never failed. The small battery looked exactly as it always did.

I started to move towards the pilot's seat, but Ben was sitting there, testing ailerons. I would either have to leave the small operation to the day shift, thereby infuriating the production

220

crew, or trust Chan and stamp it off. My stamp, number 526, went on the board.

Towards the end of the night shift, the RCAF make their rounds. The crew stood by, ready to push the plane to the next stage as soon as they were given the go-ahead. Grace's heart-throb, the officer with the upturned nose, crawled into the fuse-lage to activate the dinghy. By this time I was crawling around on top of the wings of the plane next in line, testing the rivets on the fuel pump covers. I always enjoy climbing up there, walking on the wings. Those large felt slippers keeping one from falling.

From that height I looked down on the huddle of white RCAF coats. They looked like a team of doctors around a sick patient. The patient, it turned out, was the dinghy. It would not inflate.

My dinghy. My stamp: 526.

RCAF called Lloyd Sauvé, our foreman on nights. Lloyd looked grave. He called me down and took me to his office. I remembered how understanding he had been about Ben not wanting to stamp off those wing bolts. But this was the reverse. I felt sick as I stood by Lloyd's desk.

"The pressure from Production can get you down," he began. "If that's what it was."

"That, as you can tell. And trusting Chan."

"That may be the first time he ever made a mistake. And the first time you did. He's a conscientious worker and you're a conscientious inspector. Neither of you will be fired. But just think for a moment of that dinghy being needed."

I was ready to argue that from what I'd heard the dinghy had never been needed. The Lancasters that were lost were those shot down over enemy territory, not over the sea. But then, in my mind's eye, the shape of a wounded plane crossed the Channel, the North Sea, and didn't quite make it. Now for the dinghy. I looked at Lloyd's grave face, his honest eyes. He is said to be one of the best inspection foremen, and I could see why.

Much later it occurred to me that he and the RCAF could have suspected me of sabotage. As my former landlords had suspect-ed me when the RCMP called. German and Japanese Canadians have been interned, people who were born in this country. I hated Hitler more than the lead hand who had accused Ben, but how were they to know?

But they knew. After this, I began to hate the look of my stamp number. Never, ever, did it appear on anything I had not tested, even if Sam thought I was overdoing it. I was getting more and more like Ben, he said. Production crews were getting impatient. "RCAF won't let even the smallest error through," he maintained. "They're in a hurry for these planes. They're needed badly."

"They're not infallible," I countered, but I wondered whether he was right. Ben and I were holding things up. But we knew we couldn't do anything else.

~ June 18th ~

Our weekend trip to Barrie. I stayed at The Barn with Edith and David, and Garth stayed at Elsie's cabin. Elsie and Miss Elgood had long suspected that all was not well, and now they know: Garth and I plan to divorce.

Sunday afternoon Garth was with Mary Elgood at the school, and David drove us out to Elsie's cabin. What a difference between the Raikeses' wild, rock-strewn Shanty Bay farm and the flat land at Cooksville. Cam, Elsie's brother, farmed, on land his ancestors had been granted a century ago as desirable farmland. He lives in the old farmhouse where she was brought up and has to supplement his farm income as township weed inspector. He has sprayed all the poison ivy around her cabin so thoroughly that I've been able to bring Fiona out there.

We sat at Elsie's picnic table and looked out on the shining lake. Sailboats were leaning into the wind. The scent of red pines was all around us. Elsie's large, black tom cat stalked out of his own little exit in the screen door that slams with the sound of summer.

"You can always come here." Elsie said. "You could have, last summer."

"Had Cam sprayed the poison ivy then? Fiona is so allergic – well, you know that."

"No. He started only this spring."

"The war may be over soon," I meant to explain our plans. "I want things clear-cut, finally. It's better that way.

"If Garth can afford to bring Dorothea over, he should marry her. She's young and beautiful and tougher than I am. She's Jewish and she probably lost her entire family. At least one Jewish person will be made happy."

Elsie didn't reply at once. We'd followed the children down to the lakeshore, where they were now paddling in the clear cold water. Elsie was a high school girl when Dé, Garth's mother, taught at Ovenden during the last war. She too had just separated from a husband in New York.

Elsie didn't try to dissuade me from sending Fiona with Garth. She's a very independent person herself. Her cabin is filled with books on philosophy and religion; she plays the piano; she is still the school nurse at Ovenden.

She thinks it sensible that I should continue working in Toronto, possibly as a social worker. One of her fellow students at Ovenden now works at a Toronto settlement house. "Settlements were started by volunteers, without much training," she explained. "You could teach art to children at the University Settlement. Or Central Neighbourhood House. You won't make as much money as you do now, though."

Teachers and social workers are not well paid. When we left Ovenden, Mary Elgood asked me to continue teaching art at Ovenden on Saturdays, but the bus fare from Toronto would have swallowed almost all the school could pay. And now war work includes (once free) Saturday mornings.

On this lakeshore, visitors have enjoyed swimming and sailing every summer. Elsie's cabin consists of only one large room, a tiny curtained-off kitchen, and a tiny curtained-off bedroom. Yet dozens of people have come and gone, camped here, sat around outdoor fires on summer evenings.

On Cam's farm, teenagers from downtown Toronto worked for the summer, boys whom no one else could handle. It was Elsie who accommodated them and whom they came to trust.

I love this place. Perhaps I could bring our tent here.

Fiona's little suitcase is packed. She is excited about taking the train from Barrie to travel to New York with her father.

At Elsie's cabin the train roars by very close. The tracks go through the Raikes farmland; they separate the land around her cabin from the family farm across the highway. There is a sharp curve, and the train always hoots there, sounding exactly like air-raid sirens. But I don't have nightmares any more. I now listen for dogs howling in response, owls hooting back.

It will be hot in New York. I offered to send the tent so Garth can camp out of doors somewhere. It's his mother's tent, after all.

Frank Hines came out to the cabin in the evening. He admires Garth, whom he now sees as a New Yorker. Frank is all set to go there himself, once he finds a job as foreign correspondent for some paper. He hopes an Australian paper will hire him.

Bettina, who loves Frank, started prancing around to please him. Garth was amazed at the difference in her. She was an ugly duckling, a black-haired baby, when he last saw her. Now she is whitish blond and tanned by the sun, a cuddly three-year-old. When she was tiny, one of her eyes seemed larger than the other, and Garth had even suggested an operation. There is no sign of that now. Her eyes are deep blue and mischievous, her brows darker than her blond hair. Frank still thinks she looks like a Renoir model with her short nose and full lips.

Bettina doesn't want to go with Garth; she doesn't know him and prefers Frank. One child is really quite enough, anyway. The Grices are so fond of Bettina, it will be no trouble leaving her there if I have to meet Garth in Montreal later this summer. Frank, who has to go to New York for an interview later, promised to bring Fiona back with him.

Sitting around the picnic table, we look like a group of good friends. The two men fair, sandy-haired, Garth a little broader and taller, his features more acquiline than Frank's, his hairline receding. The two lively, fair children. Elsie, tanned, quiet-spoken, her large, dark eyes holding together this fragile group. She is as old as this century. She's seen great changes.

~ July 2nd ~

If Frank has not yet gone to New York, the reason is Marguerite. We'd met him accidentally at the Marian Anderson concert, and Marguerite asked him, as my friend, to the party at her house after the concert. He fell madly in love.

Marguerite impersonates the city of his dreams, New York. Everything about her – her wit, her elegance, her taste, the luxury she enjoys as her setting – all contribute to his passion. Marguerite is used to attracting men, young and old. Should it annoy me that Frank has always maintained I'm too tall to have him as an escort? Marguerite is taller than I am, but it makes absolutely no difference to his infatuation.

Things money can buy have much to do with Marguerite's special beauty. Her clothes are made for her by a designer-dressmaker. She can afford the most delicious kind of food. She has a cleaning woman to keep her house in tip-top shape. But she also has real taste in the arts, and she actually reads the books on her shelves. She enjoys her power over men, and Frank is neither too young nor too small to be a good lover (is my guess – I have no direct experience). So for the moment, Frank remains in Toronto. I just hope he can tear himself away as promised, at the end of the month, to bring Fiona back from New York.

~ July 8th ~

Florence's holiday plans are well laid. I hope to add four extra days to my official week to fit her agenda. She has written to youth hostels in Ottawa and along the route to Montreal. They charge twenty-five cents a night. She has figured out what we need as provisions and what we can carry on our bikes. She and Ruth have their own bicycles, and she has borrowed one for me. Our bicycles travel free on the train to Ottawa. The province of Quebec is just across the river from there.

I have sent our tent to Garth. He and Fiona need it more than I do at the moment.

~ July 12th, Ottawa Youth Hostel ~

With our bikes in the baggage car, we travelled in comparative comfort (return fare, thirteen dollars). Florence has thought of everything, and our purchases are carefully distributed in our rucksacks: dried fruit, packaged soups, rice, noodles, things that can be cooked quickly. We each carry a cup and plate. The hostels are supposed to have crockery, pots and pans, blankets. Each of us also carries a light sheet–sleeping bag. Fresh fruit and vegetables we'll buy on the way. We'll cook morning and night when at a hostel and make sandwiches for a long break around noon, the hottest time of day. Wherever possible, we'll do our cycling early or late in the day.

Ottawa is almost as far north as Algonquin Park. I was surprised, therefore, by the intense heat that beat down on us as we pushed our bikes out of the station. A cool underground passage leads privileged travellers to the Château Laurier, one of the CP châteaux, but of course we could not afford to go there.

Blinded by the sun, we started cycling westward. Almost at once, my bicycle tire got stuck in a streetcar track. Luckily, there was no streetcar bearing down on us. We took refuge on a square with a large war memorial and studied our city map. To the north of us towered the Parliament Buildings, separated from the Château by locks on the Rideau Canal, the original raison d'être of this town.

The heat is overwhelming. We are sitting around, wearing the scantiest underwear, in the attic of a fairly modern house, the Ottawa Youth Hostel. The house may be ordinary, but the hostel parents are far from ordinary. Sylvia, our hostess, is one of the Woodsworths, a cousin, I think, of the young man I met in Barrie. Politically, she's more to the left than the CCF, started by her family. She is married to a librarian.

We had a cold supper, for who wants to cook in this heat? I've taken the opportunity presenting itself, two models clad in less than bathing suits, to make a few pen-and-ink sketches of

Ruth and Florence, stretched out on hard hostel bunks. We won't need blankets tonight.

~ July 13th ~

Florence took us on a tour of the Parliament Buildings today. The only remnant of the original edifice is the Parliamentary Library, a circular building – quite beautiful. Its gingerbread Gothic style seems exactly right. It was saved, I think, by steel doors between it and the other buildings, consumed by fire in 1916. For a whole century, fires were the curse of this lumbering town, once named Bytown after the builder of the Rideau Canal. In those days and all through the nineteenth century it was also known as "Slabtown." Piles of lumber on both sides of the Ottawa River, frame houses, a river choked by sawdust, great rafts floating downriver towards Quebec City – those are the images early artists had of this town. There are still a few log booms on the river, but nothing like the quantity that at times choked this enormous waterway.

The great impediment to shipping, the Chaudière Falls between Ottawa and Hull, was useful for industry. There, rafts had to be taken apart and the logs tumbled singly down the steep rapids. Then, when the great pines had been demolished and pulpwood was used to make paper, the power of the falls was harnessed by Eddy's paper mills. They still occupy several islands around the once spectacular rapids. Before the power was harnessed for a dam, these falls, known as "Asticou" in the Algonquin language, could be heard for miles in every direction.

Florence and Ruth
at Ottawa Youth Hostel
(pen-and-ink sketch)
~~

In this civil-service town Eddy's are the only large industry. According to Florence, this industry provided a fortune for a fat prime minister, who during the Depression, instead of sharing his millions, went to England to buy a peerage. When the wind blows from the north, people in Ottawa still complain about the smell of sulphur from these paper mills.

Ottawa could be a very beautiful town, with its three rivers and a canal, but so far only private mansions have been built along the waterways. This afternoon we cycled to a parklike area with great shade trees, where most of the foreign diplomats live. We looked across the majestic river towards Gatineau Point with its shining church steeple and old clapboard houses. Every spring, when the snow melts on the upper Ottawa, this point of land is flooded.

Florence, who studied geology, told us that the Ottawa, like its tributary, the Gatineau River, originates way up in the Precambrian Shield, their sources not very far apart. A network of these rivers constitutes an enormous area, partly in Ontario, partly in Quebec, still ruthlessly deforested by lumber companies. Across the river to the northeast, we could see another paper mill, its several stacks occasionally blowing sulphur fumes into this part of town, known as Rockcliffe Village. There we rested our bikes at a lookout point not far from an old canoe club, enjoying the refreshing breeze from the river and the aspect of canoes and sailboats out on the wide stretch of water.

The river is enormous, as wide as the St Lawrence in places. Famous European rivers, the Rhine, the Seine, the Thames, would look puny beside this great waterway, yet I don't see the excurstion steamers, houseboats, and other river traffic one sees in Europe.

Tomorrow we'll cycle up to the vicinity of the current prime minister's summer retreat in Quebec, known as Kingsmere. Hard to believe that it was his sister, Mrs Lay, who in Barrie provided Bettina's large crib.

~ Kingsmere, Quebec ~

The road to this charming clapboard house near Kingsmere Lake is uphill all the way. The twelve miles seemed endless in this heat. First, the long hot ride through the industrial part of Hull, then up Boulevard St Joseph. This street, north of town, becomes Highway 11.

Habits die hard. Cycling from hostel to hostel in Europe, we'd never bothered wearing hats, let alone sunglasses. Ruth wears both, and Florence protects her eyes wearing an eyeshade as well as dark glasses. I had not thought of bringing such things and now wished I had. The sun is fierce, blinding; your eyes hurt from the dust on the back roads. One suddenly becomes aware that, even this far north of Toronto, we are still on the same meridian as Milan.

We came to a village named Chelsea, here in Quebec, far from the artists' Chelsea I've known in London. In fact, they say this village is named after a place in Vermont by settlers from New England.

As I'm the only one who speaks French, I was asked to do our shopping in a little store there. But when I spoke French, I was answered in English. We stocked up on supplies and, with relief, finally found a shaded road to Kingsmere from Chelsea.

Mackenzie's summer retreat is just south of this lake, where we are now spending the afternoon. Florence looks gorgeous in her two-piece white bathing suit – a daring style compared to Ruth's modest, dark red one-piece and my blue and white striped one with its ballerina skirt. Ruth has a Spanish surname but is the fairest among us three.

Too bad we can't get into the grounds of the prime minister's farm. I'd have liked to see the ruins he has rebuilt there, some from the burned Parliament Buildings and some from a senator's old residence. I can't quite believe what they say: that when we were bombed in London, this prime minister telephoned, not to offer assistance, but to ask for pieces of ruined London buildings.

There are quite a few summer cottages here, only twelve miles from Ottawa. These hills are known for good skiing in winter.

Even now, it's a little cooler here, and an afternoon of lazing about, swimming, and sunbathing leaves us feeling wonderfully refreshed. I wouldn't have minded extending our stay here, but Florence has booked us at a Luskville youth hostel for tomorrow, and one at Sainte-Cécile-de-Masham the next day. We then return to Ottawa, and from there cycle to Montreal via three more hostels: Lochaber, Stoneyfield, and Saint-André Est (all in Quebec).

~ Lusk Farm, Luskville, Quebec ~

We got here all in one piece, but don't ask me how we did it. The road from Kingsmere down the escarpment to Luskville is the steepest I ever cycled on, and I've cycled in the Odenwald and in Provence. It's a badly maintained lane full of potholes, perhaps a logging road at one time, a trail taken by early Irish settlers who moved down to the fertile plains from the rocky Gatineau hills when a raging fire destroyed the great pine forests along the Ottawa River. They did it in slow, cumbersome ox carts; we at breakneck speed.

The Luskville hostel is a prosperous farm, the family descended from original settlers. The hostel mother, Mrs Lusk, is a vigorous woman with brilliant blue eyes and white hair. She may have been red-haired at one time like her two bachelor sons. They didn't say much when they stomped in, leaving their boots politely at the door. It seemed to me that they appraised our anatomies somewhat like farmers might judge cattle at a fair. Perhaps the hostel register had informed them of Ruth's unmarried status. She is also the most buxom, most wholesome-looking, among us. But her profession is far removed from that of a perfect farmer's wife: she is a career editor at a well-known publishing house.

The Lusk brothers were busy cutting and baling hay, much later here than in Europe, where, if one cuts in June, one can usually gather a second crop. Perhaps we should have taken the hints in the hostel handbook and offered our help. But now that they use new machines and tractors for the job, there's none of that manual gathering I remember from my childhood, when a ride home in the hay wagon was a special treat. And right now we were also exhausted from our reckless ride down that mountain road.

After an early supper, we walked down to the tiny community hall, where there was some kind of council meeting. I managed a sketch of that little building, seen from the direction of the river, so that it appeared dwarfed by the steep escarpment of the Gatineau hills. Florence, who studied geology, said that at one time the riverbed was so wide that the escarpment was its banks. As the northern glacier melted, the Ottawa valley was, for some time, part of the Champlain Sea. All this flat land was under water.

Around the community hall a group of dusty, well-used cars were parked, like chicks around a mother hen – model T Fords, most of them. The setting sun bathed the escarpment rocks in a glowing light, hard to capture in paint.

~ Sainte-Cécile-de-Masham ~

At last we are in a French community. We reached it via a long, dusty road, so steep that we had to push our bikes part of the way. We came to a flat stone ledge beneath some large pine trees, a lookout with a wonderful view over the broad sweep of the Ottawa valley. It was so still here that the tapping of a woodpecker quite far away sounded startling. There was not a soul to be seen.

In no time Florence had shed her clothes and was sunbathing on the flat rocky ledge. I got out my sketching stuff – one never gets enough chances to make life studies – and began to draw, while Ruth kept a lookout in case the Lusk brothers came this way. Their farm goes way up into these hills, where there are caves, even a lake, named after them. But no, they were still busy haying, way down in the fields below the escarpment.

The name of the Masham hostel parents is Brazeau. Their house is typical of the older buildings in this village. It is shingled with small cedar "shakes" and surrounded by what is called a *galerie* (a wraparound porch). Behind the house is the Lapêche River. It flows into the Gatineau at Wakefield and at one time may have been used for log transport. It descends peacefully from the heights we crossed on our bikes and has few rapids. What a joy to see the silvery steeple of the Masham church in the distance.

Now there are deep shadows everywhere. The sky has taken on an indescribable hue of transparent amber, streaked with pale green and carmine. Spruce, pines, hemlock, balsam outlined against this sky look inky black.

Here too there is the scent of hay, the sound of crickets. There is also the sound of laughter from the river and from the *galerie*. This hostel is more crowded than those we've visited so far. The dormitories and the hostel kitchen are packed with students, some French, some English. Down by the Lapêche a few voices rise, clear and true, in that most beautiful of folk songs: "A la claire fontaine."

On our way here we cycled through another village on the same river, Saint François. From that direction we now hear quick steps to the tune of another song, "Auprès de ma blonde," and the rhythm of "qu'il fait bon, fait bon, fait bon."

This approaching drum-like beat mingles with the slow sweetness of "Ça fait longtemps que je t'aime – jamais je ne t'oublirai." The approaching group enter the hostel. They are hikers, later than the recommended arrival time. But they're not turned away.

Tomorrow morning we'll get up early, as most hostellers do. We'll follow the Lapêche River as far as Wakefield, where Florence wants to show us a covered bridge, typical of Quebec covered bridges.

~ Ottawa Youth Hostel, Sunday ~

It took us three days to reach the village of Sainte-Cécile-de-Masham. It took less than a morning to get back here. Wakefield is four miles from Sainte-Cécile; then there are twenty miles to Hull. But oh, glory, it's all downhill, all the way from Wakefield, with its covered bridge. What's more, the road south from Wakefield is paved. We sailed along on smooth asphalt, a real treat after the dusty gravel roads.

Wakefield is one of the nicest places I've seen in Canada. The houses are simpler and smaller than the prosperous Barrie brick houses, with their Gothic fretwork. Some houses in Wakefield also have elaborate fretwork, but it goes well with these frame buildings. Some are summer cottages. Many have the pleasant proportions of a Scottish-Irish building style common around the turn of the century, usually with a fan light over the front door and a half storey above. Some, Florence said, are original log houses later covered with siding.

The Victorian Gothic of some of these residences borders on the fantastic: there are turrets at the corners, a widow's walk on

Log boom,
Gatineau River,
Wakefield, Quebec

∽

top of the house. The exuberant fretsaw decorations seem to express the exuberance of that strong rushing river with its many rapids. One sees hardly any canoes. Instead, there are log booms chained together, guided downstream by tugboats. At the next dam these booms have to be taken apart, to rush down swift chutes, to be again regrouped into booms by employees of the pulp and paper companies in Gatineau and Hull. On that wonderful paved road we reached Chelsea, where there is such a dam, in record time.

As we crossed the Interprovincial Bridge between Ottawa and Hull, church bells rang on every side of the river. It was only eleven o'clock on a Sunday morning! We celebrated our effort-less return journey with the only restaurant meal we allowed ourselves on this trip – pancakes, maple syrup, and sausages – so filling we couldn't eat another meal that day. I'd seen maple syrup making in Barrie, but this is really the heart of syrup-making country. Sugar maples don't exist in Europe. I remem-ber that in Tuscany, where a couple of expensive delicatessen stores cater to British tastes, Garth became nostalgic for this treat of his Barrie childhood. He simply couldn't resist buying a small tin of fearfully expensive maple syrup sold by, I think, Fortnum & Mason, so he could add quantitites of liquid gold to his own recipe for crepes.

Back at the hostel, we glanced briefly at a local paper. The 'world news.' Florence looked at the entertainment page. "Shall we be wicked and see a Sunday movie?" she asked. "You can't see a movie anywhere in Ontario on Sundays. So here, everyone crosses the river to Hull cinemas."

I was surprised. We had been told that we should avoid scanty clothing – very short shorts, for instance. We might be held up by the Quebec police.

Sober Ontarians would most likely have approved of the movie we saw in Hull, after recrossing the Interprovincial Bridge. It starred a young actress everyone likes, June Allyson, in a film entitled *Music for Millions*. In this, she has the popular role of a soldier's wife who plays the cello (and who, to complicate matters, is also pregnant). An additional plum was the child actress Margaret O'Brien, the Shirley Temple of recent days. There's nothing in this film that could not be seen on Sundays, and we were vaguely disappointed.

~ Lochaber Hostel, Monday evening ~

This youth hostel is a farmhouse in an area settled by Scottish immigrants in the early nineteenth century – both sides of the Ottawa River were. From Ottawa we'd cycled to Cumberland, south of the river, then took a ferry across to Masson on the north side. It was pleasantly cool, crossing the water. At Masson the Lièvre River provides power for the MacLaren mills. Standing on the bridge crossing it, Florence recited "Morning on the Lièvre" by Archibald Lampman, an Ottawa poet who'd often canoed on this turbulent waterway. Right here from this bridge, in July, the broad river looked dry and rock-strewn.

East of Masson the road goes through Lochaber Township before reaching Thurso. The smell of sulphur announces the paper mill there long before you reach the town. Here we are

Stoneyfield,
1944
(area now flooded
by Carillon dam;
pen-and-ink
sketch)

roughly opposite the flat country southeast of Ottawa traversed by the South Nation River, the logging road of the Scots from Glengarry. There is a Nation River on this north side as well. The word "Nation" does not refer to the Scots or to the French (*la nation*) but to the Indians whom they replaced.

Here the Ottawa River has an almost oriental quality: reedy marches stretch to small islands. Rowboats, probably fishing, drift lazily between willows, like boats in Chinese paintings. I remember first setting eyes on the shores of the St Lawrence when our Cunard liner, in November 1940, entered its vast expanse. Then, too, I thought that this was like entering some great river in the Far East.

I made a sketch of this shore while Florence and Ruth had their noon-hour swim.

~ Stoneyfield, Quebec ~

This village is well named; fields along the shore are rockier here than in Lochaber, where the Laurentians seem miles to the north. Here they are close again and the landscape is more dramatic.

From Lochaber we cycled along the north shore, through Papineauville with its exquisite frame houses, the seigneury of the Quebec patriot Louis-Joseph Papineau, who in 1837 incited

Quebec Patriotes to rebel. He fled to the United States, as did the Ontario rebel, William Lyon Mackenzie. Mackenzie was a reformer, but Papineau remained a seigneur, a patriot but not a radical. He built a Victorian-style mansion in the grounds of what is now the exclusive Seigneury Club of Montebello. To get a glimpse of Papineau's mansion (and a rest from cycling), we took the ferry south from Montebello. From a distance, on the river, we saw the mansion, but the Seigneury Club itself, the

*Stoneyfield, 1944 (area now flooded by
Carillon dam; pen–and–ink sketch)*

largest log building in Canada, remained hidden within its extensive grounds.

It was a long day. We continued cycling on the south side of the river until we came to the bridge at Hawksbury and crossed over to Grenville. There a canal was built early in the nineteenth century to bypass the longest Ottawa rapids. A lovely town with fine stone houses and shade trees, a good place to have a picnic.

The fieldstone houses along this north shore have a distinctive Scottish building style, all the way to St Andrews, now Saint-André Est. One of the finest buildings at Carillon has been turned into a museum, the right setting for pioneer furniture and household items: cradles, butter churns, dough boxes, most of them from this area, Argenteuil County.

It was refreshing to enter this cool building. By now, my nose is peeling; my hair feels as dry as straw; my eyes are red from the dust on the roads. I haven't yet bought an eyeshade or sunglasses because I don't know how much money I'll need in Montreal, where the hostel is in the YMCA and more expensive.

We were tired out when we reached this Stoneyfield hostel. Luckily, the next leg of our trip, to Saint-André Est, is shorter than that covered today. The good thing about the Stoneyfield hostel is its swimming beach, stony but clear. On one of the rocks sat a tanned girl. I was again reminded of those Tahitian beauties painted by Gauguin. I thought of Lorraine last summer. This girl is older than Lorraine, in her early twenties probably, and like Florence, she is wearing a white two-piece bathing suit that sets off a kind of a tan none of us have achieved so far. Her dark, pleasantly curly hair is cut short, her very feminine figure plump in the right places, otherwise small-waisted and fine-boned.

In a youth hostel you make friends very quickly. You share cooking equipment, sometimes food. The name of this beautiful girl is Edith Frenkell. She is Jewish and lives in Montreal. Her bike broke down irreparably and she hopes to thumb a ride back to town tomorrow. Hitchhiking has become acceptable during this war, but it's not without its problems for attractive girls.

After an evening of shared food and talk, we offered to put Edith's bike on the Montreal train at the nearest station, so she can get an early start. She, in turn, invited all of us to her apartment on Durocher, an invitation we gladly accepted. Florence has not had a reply from the Montreal Y.

I don't look forward to Montreal as much as the others. They know I have to meet Garth there and somehow arrange for a divorce that I can't afford. He doesn't want to assume the role of "guilty party"; that might saddle him with responsibilities he doesn't really want.

As far as I know, he is bringing two witnesses – all expenses paid – to Montreal, a desirable *but de voyage* for New Yorkers

because of its nightclubs and jazz connections. Or so Garth
maintains. If he succeeds in getting his friends to lie about the
situation (my being the guilty party – should I care?), OK, so
he may have financial advantages. Florence thinks I make
it too easy for him, but he has promised – if I agree to the divorce – to send a monthly allowance for the children. Even
the smallest sum would help. I'm sure to earn less once the war
is over.

~ Saint-André Est, Quebec ~

Edith, dressed in the briefest of cycling outfits – a matching top
and short skirt in tiny black and white checks – didn't have
to wait long at the roadside this morning. There aren't many
cars on the road, but she was picked up almost at once. Ruth
wondered whether hitchhiking might not be risky for someone
as young and attractive as Edith. So we telephoned her from
this hostel tonight. She arrived home in good shape, slightly before noon.

Meanwhile we'd plodded to the station with her bike. It's in
such poor shape that it seemed hardly worth while even regis-
tering it as freight, the slowest and cheapest way to Montreal.

The road to Saint-André Est is one of the most beautiful on
this trip, past many fine old stone houses of a classical design,
surrounded by shade trees and luscious gardens. Argenteuil
County has spectacular scenery. This youth hostel is on a large
dairy farm halfway up the hills that rise towards Lake of Two
Mountains, the confluence of the Ottawa and St Lawrence.

One of the neat white-painted stables has been turned into
the hostel dormitory, so one is independent of the main house.
The byres and barns are also painted white, Quebec-style. There
are wagon sheds with cars, buggies, cutters, and large sleighs.
In a separate dairy building, the milk from the Holstein cows is
separated and the butterfat sent to a co-operative.

Here, as in Sainte-Cécile-de-Masham, there are many students.
One of them, Michelle, has given us her Montreal address.
Florence would like to meet her mother, who was active in the
early Antigonish co-op (probably the very co-op that includes
Clarence Gillis).

Our next stretch, tomorrow, will be the longest on this trip: forty miles.

~ Montreal, Edith's apartment on Durocher Avenue ~

We made it. But there were a couple of times on this long haul through industrial suburbs, rows of nondescript houses neither village nor city, when we nearly gave up. The warehouses, garages, and bleak corner stores that we assumed were at last part of Montreal gave way to further stretches of open road. We crossed a bridge and thought we were now on Montreal Island, but Florence's map put us right: this was Laval-sur-le-Lac. Hot and dusty, totally exhausted, we took time off and swam at a beach crowded with vacationing families. Again, we telephoned Edith.

She gave us clear directions to find her apartment house. It meant another stretch through industrial suburbs and a haul across Montreal's central mountain. Durocher is not far from McGill University, on a road that goes uphill from Sherbrooke towards Mount Royal. From this moderately high apartment building there is a fine view of the town and the St Lawrence, but on our arrival we were too tired to appreciate any of this.

It's wonderful what a shower can do for you, especially if you've done without one for a week. Then, suddenly, we needed food. Edith cooked a steak, something beyond our budget. And she prepared vegetables in unusual ways. Where, I wondered, had she got hold of aubergines? Ah, she said, that's Montreal for you.

This is really a bachelor apartment: a living room, kitchen, and bathroom. There is a pullout couch in the living

~~

Ruth and Edith meeting in the United States after Edith's marriage

room, which Ruth and I are to share. Edith's parents are vacationing in the Laurentians, so Edith is taking Florence over to their townhouse to sleep, once we've eaten here.

~ Montreal, next day ~

Tried to telephone Fritz Brandtner. No reply. Most likely he is out of town for the summer. Florence and Ruth want to visit the French girl, Michelle, in Outremont, a French residential district just across the mountain. Edith, meanwhile, is quite sympathetic towards my meeting with Garth. She's in love with a married man, so she sees Garth with greater understanding than my two companions. We could meet here at her apartment, she says. But we decided that a restaurant on Sherbrooke might be better. Garth and his friends will be in Montreal for only one night. He has, magnanimously, invited us all to a nightclub where a male escort (according to Edith) is advisable. There are no nightclubs in Toronto (or if there are, Bruce would not approve of them), so Florence is anxious to experience one. Ruth imagines nightclubs to be like the dance hall at Sunnyside where Bert Niosi plays his famous clarinet, but Edith says they're much more like New York.

I walked down Durocher to the restaurant on Sherbrooke with a mixture of trepidation and defiance. My hair was like straw, my nose peeling, I wore a seersucker two-piece suit I hate. But it doesn't need ironing, so it's been the most practical garment to pack in a rucksack.

Garth's two friends turned out to be exceptionally nice people: a husband and wife and, like Edith, probably communists. They came, not so much for a holiday in Montreal, but because they genuinely like Garth. They think his work as an illustrator original, perhaps even slightly kinky (much as I had thought when seeing his drawings for the first time). I don't think they quite understood the situation when it was explained by Garth: they would have to declare on oath that they had found me in flagrante, i.e., committing adultery.

Each one in turn took me aside and asked me, in all earnestness, whether they were in any way doing me any harm. I assured them, with a sigh, that it was the only way. I couldn't afford an Ontario divorce, said to be an endless undertaking. And Ontario accepts New York above other states where divorce is made easy.

I gave them an address. Edith didn't want her own apartment mentioned, but is keeping an eye on another one in her building where the owners are away for the summer. It's not likely that judges in New York would come here to check. I asked them to sign Garth's statement or whatever else had to be done. They still remained hesitant.

These two at once established a political accord with Edith. They were as used to nightclubs as she was, so they sat at a table talking to her while Garth, Florence, Ruth, and I sat at a table, closer to the jazz band. The players, mostly coloured, were quite excellent, the saxophones especially. Garth appreciates jazz and was really impressed.

He asked Edith to dance. We looked on, the New York friends at our table now, still hesitant about their role. But I hadn't changed my mind. They will leave in the morning, and it will all be over, decided, done with.

Edith had plans for the next day. We were to accompany her to a political meeting in the Jacques Cartier quarter of Montreal, one of the poorest. The "Padlock Law" is in force under this Duplessis regime; that is, the police can close and padlock any house or hall they think poses a political threat. She wanted us to experience what it's like when the speaker is Joe Salsberg from Toronto, a well-known communist.

~ Montreal, two days later ~

Garth and his friends departed yesterday morning. Edith has been a good guide to Montreal, showing us the old town, the Château de Ramezay, the markets, the harbour. In the evening she dragged us along by streetcar to the political meeting in a shabby hall, perhaps a union hall or community centre. The hall was packed. There were police sitting and standing at the back. But they were stumped by a speech that was given in neither French nor English. They could not understand a word, for Salsberg, the visiting speaker, talked in Yiddish. He was not arrested; the Padlock Law was not applied this time. Perhaps Salsberg's non-Quebec residence protected him.

A strange contrast: jazz musicians from New York in nightclubs never padlocked (they bring in money), but speeches about freedom of thought checked by mean laws. The contrast between rich and poor is very marked in this town.

~ On the train from Montreal to Toronto ~

On the day before we took the train home, we went by bus to Sainte-Adèle in the Laurentians, where Edith's parents are staying. It's a steady climb; we were glad we didn't use our bikes. The charming old village is turning into a tourist resort, with all that implies. There are many impressive holiday houses here as well, summer cottages (chalets). The Laurentians are higher here, more spectacular than the Gatineaux, but still not mountains like the Alps. Somehow I prefer the intimate beauty of the Gatineau hills. If I could choose where I wanted to live, that's where I would go.

We spent most of our money in Montreal, so we couldn't afford bunks on the train. We slept on the seats of the night train to Toronto, our bikes safely stacked in the freight car. Have we seen the real Quebec? No, probably not. We got a glimpse of old Montreal, but should really see Quebec City, the Gaspé Peninsula, the Saguenay so loved by my fellow inspector, Denise.

~~
Joan Grice and
her brother
with Bettina, 1944

~ August 4th ~

Back on the farm. Bettina looks cheerful and tanned. The Grices really love her. Frank Hines, back from New York, took Fiona to Barrie to stay with her little friend Marta Smith. But it was hard for her; she cried bitterly leaving her father and not finding her mother at this end of the journey. According to Garth, they had a good time together in spite of the heat and the fact that he didn't bother getting the tent I'd sent out of U.S. customs (because customs charged too much, he said; but he managed to pay for a trip for three people).

Much as the Grices love Bettina, they now think that two children are too much. Fiona should really go to school, and that, here, is a fair distance. She'd been happy in kindergarten, but when I phoned Mrs Coffey, the poor woman still sounded too exhausted to take more boarders. I should look for a place close to schools, up near Eglinton perhaps, where transport to Malton is easy.

Bettina looks healthy, but she drives everyone crazy, eating incredibly slowly. She sits over her meal for hours, long after everyone has finished. While I was away, someone else had to sit with her. Now I do. Is this some kind of eating disorder? But she looks so well. Her weight is perfect.

I try to think back to my early childhood. Did this ever happen in our family? No, on the contrary, we were blamed for fast, competitive eating, even when the times of starvation and food shortages were over.

I went to see Florence's lawyer, Andrew Brewin, for whom she'd worked during the CCF campaign. He is quite adamant that I must keep the children with me during divorce proceeding; it is my only chance to keep them if the divorce is heavily weighed against me. The fact that Garth has, so far, not supported us may mean that he will have to pay little later on, in spite of his promise.

"It's not a hostile divorce," I tried to explain. "It's simply an agreement we came to." That too is a problem; it's called collusion and not allowed either.

~ August 7th ~

Back at work I notice how worried inspectors and crews now are about their future. When the war is over, factories like these will close. The women won't keep their jobs once men with military service come home to take over.

I ran into Eileen in the washroom. I was really glad to see her. She took one look at my straw-dry hair and vowed to restore it to "something human." I went back with her in our old car pool, which hasn't changed much. While the conditioner she'd poured over my head was taking its effect, I told her of our woes – the children, divorce, our whole untenable situation.

"Go see the Scobies, across the road," Eileen suggested. "Their bungalow is just beside the Browns, the couple who mind my Brian. Their house has one more room than ours, and they've been talking about taking on boarders to pay off their mortgage.

"School's not far, and there's a kindergarten. Their little girl must be about your Fiona's age, so they would both go there."

The bungalow on the south side of the road looks exactly like Eileen's, except that the positions of kitchen and bedrooms are reversed. Eileen's breakfast nook looks north across plowed fields, while the Scobies' picture window has a magnificent view over all of west Toronto, right down to Lake Ontario.

Like Eileen's house, the Scobies have a finished basement where, in addition to laundry equipment, there is a recreation room, pleasantly littered with children's toys. A girl named Linda, a sturdy child with a freckled nose and curly dark hair, was playing there. Her brother, Johnnie, is a year older and will be at school all day.

Eileen was right. The Scobies had thought of renting out their own bedroom "for the duration." They'd sleep in a large curtained-off alcove beside the dining room, a large room but seldom used, since the breakfast nook off the kitchen is handier for meals. The board for the children and myself would be considerably more than what they'd charge a single person – enough to pay off their heavy mortgage if the war lasts another year. It would be a little more than I paid at the Grices' and the Coffeys', but I had a raise and can afford it if I'm careful. The children would have the run of the house and share a fairly large bedroom with me.

Fred Scobie is, I think, an accountant. He and his wife have certain features in common: they are both dark-haired, pale, with slightly receding chins. Fred's eyes are hidden by glasses, while hers are her best feature. She says she reads a lot of women's magazines, and from them and the radio, she gets ideas about rearing children and a wholesome diet. On the table in the breakfast nook there are little bowls of celery and carrot sticks for the children's snacks, not crackers or chocolate cookies or any of the rich food we had at the Grices'.

The Scobies think Brian, Eileen's little boy, whom they often see at their neighbours, is spoilt and rambunctuous, "a real handful." Before they take us, they'd like to see my little girls. I promised to bring them over this weekend.

This arrangement would be better than Cooksville. The drive to work takes no longer. The Oakwood streetcar terminal is walking distance, just down the hill. I can reach my old friends from here. There are other children, and Fiona's school is more accessible.

~ August 21st ~

The day I took the children to see the Scobies there were rumours that an assassination attempt on Hitler had failed. Details are vague. Some reports maintain that the coup was carefully planned by a group of aristocrats; others say by military people who wanted the war to end. It would have succeeded if it had not been for that curious second sense that has saved Hitler before from attempts on his life. He left the meeting before the bomb exploded – something like that.

I wondered whether my former boss at Deinhard's, Freiherr von Vitzthum, was involved in this attempt. He had been able to leave the country as a traveller for his firm, the rival of Henkel (Ribbentrop's in-laws). Even while Ribbentrop was ambassador in Britain, Vitzthum had remained popular there. He was scathing – and, alas, careless – in his remarks about the Nazis.

The last time I saw him was in the spring just before Fiona was born. I was heavily pregnant and had been told to do a lot of walking. So Vitz and I walked up and down in Green Park, discussing the situation in Germany. I noticed that he had developed the habit of looking around as if there might be a spy behind any of the trees. *Sotto voce* he described his worries.

"What happens back there is terrible," he said. "First those camps were mainly for communists, socialists, religious protest-ers, gypsies even. Now, since the Kristallnacht it's mainly Jews, almost only Jews. I keep my eyes open. I travel."

"Vitz, we had two Jewish girls at school and both passed senior matric with us in 1933. And my mother had a Jewish doctor, who delivered my youngest brother."

"Do you know where they are now?"

"Well, I was away for years, in England, in Spain, in Italy, where I got married. During the time I worked for Deinhard's with you I heard that the girls had got away to England or to America. I don't know about the doctor, I'm afraid. We'd moved away from Darmstadt, you see."

If Vitzthum was involved in the attempt on Hitler, he's doomed. There are rumours that those touched by even a shad-ow of suspicion will endure fiendish punishments, medieval kinds of torture. Hundreds have been rounded up. I don't know how the BBC get their information, but their bulletins are quite detailed.

~ September 5th ~

For their first day at kindergarten, Martha Scobie went with the two little girls, Linda and Fiona, holding one by each hand. A good beginning. Fiona likes her new friend, and Bettina has become quite attached to Johnnie, who is not too bad a tease of little girls. He's in first grade and marched off to school on his own.

I stayed with Bettina while she finished her slow breakfast. Then, when Martha came back, I crept back to bed (we are on night shift) before the radio brought its daily consoling string of soap operas. Neither at the Coffeys' nor at Eileen's did I ever hear anything like it: a steady murmur of voices, cajoling, im-ploring. I never understand what is said. But each program can be identified by its musical introduction After much repetition, even a Tchaikovsky theme sounds tediously sentimental. These radio melodramas go on and on, and by the sound of the voices are full of pathos, of dramatic events, of family intrigues. I have yet to find out why they relate to washing soap. It must have something to do with washing always being done by lonely housewives.

After Martha has hung out her own washing, using the soaps dramatically advertised – Ivory, Oxydol, Sunlight – she has a cup of coffee in the breakfast nook and switches on her daily dose of melodrama, stories that go on and on through years and years of intimate life: *Big Sister, Young Doctor Malone, Laura, Stella Dallas*. Housewives probably identify with these strong female characters, who sometimes take a whole week of radio time to get through twenty minutes in their lives.

Certain introductory melodies would make me aware that noon was not far away. The children would come home from school. I don't get up for lunch, I try to sleep – at least pretend to sleep – when Bettina is put into her crib for her afternoon nap. When she gets up, I do too. We enjoy the warm September sun out on the terrace, a blue haze veiling the outlines of the city far below.

In the evening, on weekends, or after day shift, the Scobies, like the Coffeys, listen to Jack Benny and Charlie McCarthy. Sunday evening programs are designed to make people forget their wartime worries. The Scobies have a player piano. On it Martha likes to play her favourite tune from the movie *Casablanca*; "As Time Goes By." She plays this tune with her feet alone, her hands sedately folded in her lap. Her all-time favourite tune is "Always," but she has not yet found a Pianola roll for this sentimental wartime song. But they play a record of this tune, and sometimes Fred leads her around the dining room in a slow, solemn dance.

I've made a few sketches of the view here, mostly in pastel. Also (after work) some drawings of the crew pushing a half-finished plane to the next stage, and of Ben holding the level needed to test the position of the wings. I'd like to enlarge that sketch into a proper painting if he'll agree and if I find a good place to paint a portrait – perhaps at the McCurdys'.

"Always," I found out, is really an excellent tune for a slow
waltz. Sam and Ben have taken me to the dance hall at Sunnyside (the one Ruth had mentioned) to hear "the best clarinet
in town," that of Bert Niosi. I know the clarinet in classical
compositions, but Niosi uses it as jazz players in Montreal use
the saxophone (did they have clarinets too? I can't remember).

They were surprised that I dance as well as I do. Sam confided to me that when I first came on inspection, they had spec-
ulated about my character. "We took you for an adventuress,"
he grinned.

"What exactly do you mean?" I asked, wondering whether I
should be annoyed.

"Well, a good-looking woman, divorced or about to be.
Separated, anyway. On her own."

"Divorce costs the earth. And it never occurred to me to cash
in on my looks. I don't think they're quite up to that."

"Oh yes. You look nice in a clinging dress like this one."

So that was it. In coveralls you are neutral. I really had
to laugh.

"Oh, we know now that you're definitely not – I mean, an
adventuress. None of us think so now."

True. Somehow, I feel safe with those two, with Lloyd, even
with Roy, the nightclub aficionado.

~ October 10th ~

Frank has finally departed for New York, leaving Marguerite
in Toronto. At one of the Wykes' parties he found out she
has a sister who actually still lives in New Jersey. The brilliant West Indian students, two of them studying law – Gloria
and Eugenia Charles – don't impress Frank as much as they
impress me. There's a big fellow from Barbados whose name
I can't remember, who has his eye on Marguerite and despis-
es Frank.

"If I don't sleep with him, he'll maintain that he's been discrim-
inated against" was one of Marguerite's typical asides. "He'll
probably write a book about it. He has literary aspirations."

This fellow isn't one of the affluent students from the West Indies. Nor does he belong to another group dear to Marguerite's heart: those of Jamaican origin born here, whose life has been much harder than that of the students. This young man is in fact married to a Toronto-born girl of Jamaican descent, a nurse who supports him. Lucille Gilmour, the poet who works for the *Tribune* – another Toronto-born Jamaican – is Marguerite's special friend, though they have very different political opinions.

~ November 12th ~

The war overshadows everything we think and do. The radio news is more positive, but there is still a fierce struggle. Soldiers have returned in a shaken state; whole European cities have crumbled under bombs. Almost every family has some connection with a loss, near or distant. My first cousin Paul, the second son of my mother's sister Nora, fell – as they say – quite early on, the same year my brother crashed into the North Sea. During the Blitz technicians who examined planes that crashed on British soil concluded that in Germany the rush to get out planes led to poor maintenance. Because of unexpectedly strong British resistance, the limited air power of the German navy had to be drawn into the battle.

The losses on the Atlantic have been terrible. On the very route we took across the sea, recently returned soldiers saw a circle of skeletons, still in life jackets, still holding hands, bobbing up and down in the icy water. No one could tell whether they were Allied or enemy skeletons. Death had made them equal. They'd been left, the way seventeen men from our torpedoed convoy had been left behind in the iceberg-haunted northern sea. The liner that took part of the British treasury, military personnel, women, and children to safety could not afford to stop.

The shadow of the war had reached us long before the war itself did. On a still, hot London night shortly after Fiona was born – I was still weak and over-sensitive – I got up to feed the baby just before dawn. It was early summer 1939, two months before the war broke out.

I'd lost too much blood and felt light-headed. I couldn't go back to sleep, so I climbed up to the flat roof of our tall Kensington house. The sun was not yet in the sky, but a grey light had stolen into the clouds. These clouds hung heavy, low, lead-coloured over a sleeping town. They seemed to descend, to envelop us, to become dark, totally black, overwhelming, terrible. Ghost-like shadows seemed to travel among them; there were voices moaning and mourning; I could distinctly hear them, feel the threat of those gigantic shadows. The shadows of the coming war, the ghosts of those who would die.

The shadows I foresaw still envelop us. They are still indistinct, because we don't yet know what has happened in the darkest parts of Europe. Even among us, so far away from the scenes of devastation, there are differences of opinion about the war. Sam and Ben have arguments. Ben thinks, as I do, that one has to do everything in one's power to defeat the forces of the fascists. Sam hates any kind of war. He admires the Quakers, who refuse to fight; the German Mennonites, the most peace-loving farmers on this continent.

"Talking about Quakers," Ben said, "did you know that a wealthy American Quaker went to Germany before the war with enough money to pay for the exodus of 40,000 Jews? The Nazis took the money and were prepared to let that number go. The problem was, no country would take them.

"Do you know how many were eventually able to get away?" No, we didn't know.

"A little over half that number: 25,000."

Poor Ben. He is right to remind us. That number does not include the many who left when there was still time, refugees I met in Spain and, a lesser number, in England.

~ December 10th ~

We've had a curious, grey, cold, but so far snowless winter. Fiona has swollen tonsils; she and Bettina have had infections of that kind on and off this season. Marguerite had given me David Wyke's office number, and I called there, hoping he could give me some advice. He drove up to our address as soon as he could make it, examined both children, gave me a prescription,

250

and strongly advised a tonsillectomy for both children. There is a difference of opinion about removing tonsils. They may take infections away from other sensitive areas – bronchial tubes, kidneys. After a series of kidney infections I had when still in Barrie, I finally decided to have my tonsils removed while still there. The result: I've had no further infections. That's my experience.

Garth thinks tonsils should stay to take the brunt of worse infections, but he's not here. It's easy to have a theory when you

Fiona with Eaton's
Santa Claus, 1944

Bettina with Eaton's
Santa Claus, 1944

don't struggle with day-to-day problems and it doesn't cost you anything. But there's a point when one has to make a choice. I agreed to a tonsillectomy for both children in the spring.

~ December 16th ~

The children are better, but not well enough to make plans for Christmas. We'll just stay here and take it easy, spend some time with Florence and other friends.

Last night, fairly late, when both children were fast asleep, I decided to follow Maguerite's invitation to a pre-Christmas party. I've come to love the liveliness and beauty of the West Indian students and people like Lucille.

I came back early in the morning. I still can't believe that I walked all the way here. I seemed to float three feet above the ground. I knew it was bitter cold, but I didn't feel a thing. David Wyke had mixed his usual potent drinks. He pressed more than one of these on me, and I actually joined in the dancing.

The party petered out at last, too late for the Eglinton bus (and the dear Loebs were not there to take me home this time). Nothing daunted, I walked – seemingly high above Eglinton – to the corner where the bus connects with the Oakwood street-car. At two a.m. – or was it even later? – there was no streetcar. Effortlessly, I continued walking – or rather, floating high above the tracks, past residential sections and plowed fields. Everything seemed wonderfully clear, as clear as the sky with its millions of stars. Everything seemed right and in its place. Effortlessly I climbed the hill to the Scobies' house. A light had been left on above the front door. I always carry a key, for when I come home from night shift, no one is up yet.

The kitchen was warm and quiet. I took off my coat, hung it in the hall, switched off the porch light. I sat down on a kitchen chair to take off my overshoes. They don't go up very high, and my winter coat is no longer than my dress. There was a curious sensation around my ankles. When I peeled off my best stockings, I found that both my legs, from ankle to thigh, were covered with red blisters. This was my first experience with frostbite. It was not a serious burn, but when the feeling came back, it was bad enough. I crept into our room, using my flashlight as I always do so the children won't wake up. I don't know how I managed to take off my clothes. I remember nothing at all. I woke up to a cold, sunny Sunday morning or, rather, noon. The children had long left the room to play down in the basement with their friends. A light snow began to fall, but didn't stay.

I reread a letter from Grannie in England. Rationing is much worse there than here. I'd sent her a small parcel with ham and salmon. It didn't arrive. On the Continent there's absolute chaos. The Allies have reached Belgium, the Canadians Holland. They are about to cross the Rhine.

1945

Snow started falling the day before yesterday and has not stopped for three days. No one went out over the weekend. Some old people had heart attacks trying to shovel snow from their driveways, yards, and front doors. Doctors and nurses have used skis to get to Toronto hospitals. Snowplows have fallen behind because the masses of snow are more than they can handle. They've tried to free the streetcar tracks to keep the main routes open; but in an hour they were covered again. There is a veil over everything as the wind shifts and lifts and rearranges the drifts, covering well-known landmarks so that they become unrecognizable. Lights are on everywhere, even during the day.

When it started, no one worried much. Bert, our driver, telephoned to say that it might take longer to get out to Malton, so he would leave early. When I waded down to the corner of Eglinton to meet our car pool, snow got into the tops of my overshoes, and my coverall pant cuffs were wet with snow when I got into the car. They dried quickly at work, where it is warm and one moves around. It snowed all night.

If traffic had moved slowly on the way to work, at five-thirty a m., when we left Malton, it was almost at a standstill. Snowdrifts had been removed from the main roads, but the wind had created new ones, straight across. Snow fences along the open stretches were almost entirely covered. People without snow tires were sliding about like crazy. And everyone yelled at them for obstructing traffic.

Bert, of course, does not curse as explicitly as those in the back seat of his car. He uses euphemisms – "Jeepers, creepers," "What the dickens," "What the deuce" – while grinding his teeth and clenching his fist on the driving wheel. A car slid across our path and remained sideways, so that we, with Bert putting on the brakes, also ended up sideways. We got out and shoved. Bert broadcast handfuls of sand from the ever-ready emergency bag he keeps in the trunk. Behind us and facing us, the dim headlights looked like tired eyes from under snowy hoods. Here and there, where there was a hopeless jam, small red flares had been put up.

At long last, shivering with cold, we were off again. Meanwhile, the windows had fogged over. Bert sat hunched over his wheel, staring through a tiny clear space in front of him. And, being Bert, murmuring a prayer. It took hours, but eventually we got through to our corner. I didn't recognize its landmarks.

At the corner of Eglinton and our small crescent there's a strangely derelict rusty building, too tall to be covered by snow. It was still there, but nothing else seemed the same. Lanes had disappeared; fences were invisible, posts and gates buried. There was no guiding line up to the Scobies' house, like the ropes that prairie farmers leave between barn and house to find their way in a blizzard.

The way up to the house isn't really long. I usually run down to the car in less than a minute. But now the road was invisible, the snow piled five feet high in places. The street lights at the corner were blurred by more snow falling. I started walking and sank in at every step, sometimes up to my waist. I flailed my arms in front of me to create a dent into which I could throw my weight.

My breath made a hissing noise in the silence. It would have been nice to just lie down in the snow. It did not seem cold and I was so tired. I was exhausted. Just when that crazy idea got hold of me, I saw the Scobies' porch light. It was not close yet, but at least I knew where I was. I made a superhuman effort and finally pushed through the gate. My hands shook as I tried to put the key into the front door. When the door finally opened, I fell into the house.

I don't know how long I sat in the kitchen, just getting enough strength to take off my coat and overshoes. A curious noise attracted my attention – a sharp heaving and hissing sound – radiator pipes perhaps. A rasping noise, almost a rattle. It took some time before I realized it was my own breathing, that strange sound. It gradually diminished. My heart pounded less painfully. Even when I finally reached my bed, my heart still pounded like an ancient grandfather clock.

I slept a very long time. I was used to the children getting up. I didn't hear them or, later, any soap operas. Fred Scobie hadn't gone to work. It took him all day to shovel the walk from the front door to the gate. Out there he had found my woollen hat, my lunch bag, and one glove. Martha Scobie, when she got up, found puddles on the kitchen floor, snow from my clothes. By the time I joined the family there, the floor had been neatly wiped. The children were playing down in the basement.

Schools, hospitals – everything is closed. Trains and bus schedules have gone haywire. But in a couple of days, all will be back to normal.

Not so in Europe. There weather like this will be disastrous for the long lines of refugees that now cross France and Germany. Waggons packed with those fleeing from the east encounter ragged released prisoners, returning to find nothing. There are fire raids, still, over whole towns, while those who caused the carnage hide in deep underground bunkers or sneak across borders into Switzerland or Spain.

~ February 10th ~

We now have a family allowance for each child in Canada. It was introduced by the Liberals to win Quebec, they say. It amounts to six dollars per child. That will at least pay for shoes and dental checkups. Perhaps I can save towards the children's tonsillectomy in the spring.

Andy Brewin, the lawyer, tells me that support for the children is likely to be measured by this Canadian family allowance (which he himself sees as quite inadequate). Can the New York courts possibly be so ignorant as to assume that twelve dollars a month will support two children in even the most benign conditions (a middle-class home, a mother with soldier's allowance, etc). They seem to think that doubling this amount to twenty-four dollars a month is a generous allowance, the one Garth will have to pay, though enforcing this in another country still remains difficult. It will never even pay the rent. But at least Garth is willing to have the children this summer so that I can take a short course in social work. Then he may find out that twenty-four dollars will not even cover the expenses of a week.

Florence has friends in the YM/YWCA who told her about these courses. There will be grants for social workers to help soldiers returning to their families. Veterans too will be given grants for special training at universities. Eventually, immigrants from Europe – now called "displaced persons" – will arrive, and their needs will also have to be met by social workers.

The Allies have crossed the Rhine.

I went down to the West End Crèche to ask Sophie Boyd's advice. She maintains that the need for social workers will be so great that even with a short summer course I'll have a chance of employment. She recommended choosing group work over casework. Settlement houses in Toronto have after-school groups of children, and my having taught art should be useful there. Some centres also assist groups of older immigrants – Italians, for instance – who have not learned English. My languages may come in useful.

"And," she said, "if you do well in the summer courses, a settlement, though they'll not pay as much as you earn now, may give you free time to continue your courses through the winter. Apply at the Y."

I went to see one of the YWCA administrators, who explained about grants. It means taking a job with the Y later on. Then, another afternoon, I went to the School for Social Work. All my life I've wanted to go to university. It's always been out of my reach. Now it looks like a real possibility (if all goes well, if Garth will take the children, if I've saved enough to survive for two months without working, if, if, if ...). No one knows how many months aircraft production at Victory Aircraft will continue.

~ March 6th ~

I arranged for the children's tonsillectomy (while I can still afford it). Two of my friends have lost a child under a general anaesthetic, so I am very nervous, not absolutely sure I'm doing the right thing. But a local anaesthetic, the kind I had a few years ago to have my tonsils out, is so harassing I really did not want the children to go through that kind of ordeal.

David Wyke assures me that there are now reliable tests that can be given to children before an anaesthetic to see if they can take it. He suggests I take the children to a downtown clinic where he'd be assisted by a a professional anaesthetist with whom he's worked many times and whom he considers totally trustworthy. Fiona and Bettina are now well enough to go downtown by streetcar. David offered to drive us home after the operation.

He is calm and reassuring. The children like and trust him. But when they followed him from the waiting room in the clinic, where I was asked to wait, to the building's interior, they suddenly looked to me like lambs going to slaughter. I could barely suppress crying out, to get them back. I sat hunched over in agony until a nurse came out to tell me that all was over and that the children were well. She asked me to pay my fee so that the specialist could get his share. I hadn't brought money; I don't even have a cheque book. David had not warned me of this; he'd told me the exact amount the operation would cost, and I knew I'd have that with our next paycheques. I felt extremely embarrassed. It suddenly occurred to me that perhaps he was doing this operation together with someone else so that he would be sure to get paid. He has never charged me for calls, though I've always asked him to do so. I'd begun to see us in more or less the same category as the Catholic brothers to whom he donates his services.

Perhaps I've been on the wrong track when I've seen people who helped us as "angels." Perhaps we are more of a nuisance than I realize (so enamoured with my children that I am convinced everyone wants to help them). But David helps others too, those in religious institutions and the needy for whom they care. There is something so warm and kind about him that the Scobies, who at first were surprised that our doctor was West Indian, now envy me. His reassuring presence, his expensive car, his clothes made from good English material impressed them.

After the operation, when the big car arrived at the Scobies' house, Martha had enough ice cream ready to feed the two little girls for several days. She swears by this remedy, and it did seem to work when the children began to feel the first pains. She maintains that this post-tonsillectomy food once worked well for the Scobie children, who are, of course, quite ready to share the treat.

They still whimper today, and Bettina has brought up the large helping of ice cream she swallowed. I'm spending most of the day reading to them. There are the books about *Babar the Elephant* and Fiona's favourite, *Madeline in Paris*. Ever since Alice Kane read this story to the children, she has known it by heart.

I am filled with gratitude, looking at the two, both together in the big bed I normally share with Fiona. They look safe and sound, beginning to look rosy. The afternoon sun illuminates the many rose tints of this room and gilds the melting snow outside. How peaceful, compared to most of the world right now.

Tomorrow night we get our paycheques. The first thing I must do on Saturday is to take sixty dollars over to David Wyke to settle our account. From then on, everything I can put aside will be for the summer courses.

~ April 12th ~

President Roosevelt has died. It's tragic that he should not see the end of the war, so near now. Canadians love and admire this American president more than many Americans do. Here artists, musicians, and writers wish they had the kind of New Deal he introduced in America during the Depression. That period, with its suffering and unrest, could have led to fascism, as it had in Germany. In this country both Liberal and Conservative prime ministers crushed any attempt at protest. It says much for the patience of Canadians that they survived without violent confrontations. In the west the CCF came into being – a movement the opposite of fascism.

~ April 24th ~

The Russians have entered Berlin. There is unbelievable turmoil all over central Europe. After the Allies had crossed the Rhine in March, they came to one wretched camp after another, deserted concentration camps and those for prisoners of war. They found survivors from the French Resistance (a few), from the east (fewer), and from Jewish families (hardly any). Many of the inmates of these camps were too weak to join the long lines of displaced people on the crowded highways. They have been taken to hospitals, and some of the Resistance fighters and prisoners of war are now recovering at the sanatorium Vincent Massey has set up in Britain for the purpose.

The further east the Allies move, the larger and more brutal the camps. People who survived are skeletons in rags. Many many more died there than we were led to believe. Horror stories arrive daily, and for the moment they overshadow other accounts of towns in ruins, levelled to the ground, destroyed by our own bombers, the very Lancasters we built with such care. Why did they never bomb those camps? In war there is no one who is not guilty. It will take a long time to sort out how things came to such a pass.

There are wild rumours about the Nazi leaders. Several, it seems, tried to arrive independently at a truce with the Allies. They were refused, and were regarded as traitors by their own ranks. There are even wilder rumours that Hitler has committed suicide in his Berlin bunker. That he had really been killed last summer after all, and all this time has been replaced by a substitute. That he escaped long ago to South America, there to continue a secret Third Reich. That he committed suicide with a large following. No one knows for sure. The whole eastern part of Germany is occupied by Russians troops thirsting to avenge their own suffering. Until the Allies get to Berlin, it will be difficult to find out what really happened.

It has been impossible to find out anything about individual citizens. I have no idea where my mother is, whether she survived, and what happened to my sister and young brothers.

~ May 8th ~

THE WAR IS OVER. THE WAR IS OVER. THE WAR IN EUROPE IS AT AN END.

Germany has surrendered unconditionally. Turmoil and confusion continue. The roads are packed with refugees from the east, including some of those from abandoned prison camps. For these displaced people, the Allies have created new camps in western Germany. Roads, railway systems, postal service, all means of communication are so damaged that it's still impossible to find out whether my mother, my sister Gisela, my brothers Heinz and Erik are alive or where they might be.

Grannie, in England, has tried her best to keep in touch via the Red Cross in Switzerland. During the early war years that was still possible, though it took a long time. News of her grandson Detlev's death took over a year to reach her and then me. My English cousin Paul – like Detlev – died the first year of the war. His older brother Harry, closer to me in age and my special friend, is now missing in Burma, where the war with Japan continues. For the time being, armament production also continues.

I've told the Scobies that I'll not stay with them after June. Like the Coffeys before them, they seem relieved to have the house to themselves again. Garth is renting a farmhouse in northern New York State for the summer, and the children will be able to stay there with him while I study. The divorce lawyer still warns me that this is a risky thing to do; fathers have been known to kidnap children even after all was settled. But I have no other way of continuing our life.

To return to Europe would be madness. If Mother didn't stay with Grannie and her sisters (a few months before the war she visited us all, just after Fiona, her first grandchild, was born), it was because they could not afford to look after her, while in Germany after my father's death she had a small pension (and younger children to care for). It would be worse for Grannie if all three of us returned to England, where rationing is far from over. In a country bled white by war I'd be less sure of a livelihood by my own earnings.

Here I may earn less as a social worker than I do now on inspection. (With steady increases, I now make nearly two thousand dollars a year). But if I find social work at a settlement house with a children's program, there may be a chance that the children could spend after-school hours there as well. Fiona will go to school all day from September on. The wartime nursery schools, so slow in starting, have been so successful that they may continue for the time being. If we live near such a nursery school, Bettina would profit from that too. Lucille Gilmour's friend Hazel works in one of the combination kindergarten–nursery schools in the east of town. Perhaps I should look for rooms in that area.

~ June 4th ~

Fiona is six years old. We're still with the Scobies, who gave a little birthday party for her. Their daughter, Linda, is almost exactly Fiona's age, and they have been good friends. Bettina, for whom we couldn't find a nursery school nearby, has been harder to look after. She was often the only one at home, so Martha had to stay in for her. She's stubborn and outspoken, and perhaps the Grices and Coffeys spoilt her a little. Perhaps I do too, when I'm tired.

I had an interview with Professor Jaffary at the Toronto School of Social Work. I hadn't been aware that this institution is for post-graduate courses, that those who go there already have a BA. However, the special courses that are to be given this summer will accept some who have not completed their undergraduate studies; their experience as social workers at the YM/YWCA would count.

I have no proof of my senior matriculation in Germany, but I can let credits accumulate until I can get some kind of certificate. Dr Jaffary said that standards for senior matric in Germany are high, equal to the first year of university here. If I manage to continue taking courses during the winter, I might accumulate credits for a BA in the next few years.

There is a shortage of staff for courses in community organization and group work at this college. Here the emphasis has been mainly on casework up to now. But for this summer they've been lucky to get an eminent group-work specialist from Cleveland, and Dr Jaffary strongly recommended that I take both group work and community organization. He thinks there will be a great demand for social workers after the war, so great that even with a summer course I should find employment at a settlement house or Y. And he maintains that these institutions are supportive if one wants to continue one's studies.

He gave me a staggering reading list – about forty books on psychology and education. To my joy, I find that I am familiar with some of them; they were on the library shelves of the Barcelona Vocational Institute, where I worked in 1935.

~ June 18th ~

The YWCA has granted me the scholarship for which I applied. It will cover the cost of the courses and some board. In return I will have to work for the YWCA when I've completed the course.

There's a students' co-operative on Prince Arthur, only a block away from the School of Social Work. I'd known about it through friends in Barrie. Board there is cheap because chores like cleaning are shared. Unlike some fraternitites, these co-ops accept students of every nationality and colour. To my delight, I found that some of the bright West Indian students I met at Marguerite's are living there, Gloria and Fay among them.

At Victory Aircraft the atmosphere is strained. The first reaction to the end of the war in Europe was jubilation, especially by women whose husbands would be home soon. But it turns out that military forces will continue to occupy Europe, while others now move to the Pacific.

Many women, especially the machinists, welders, and riveters, those that work long hours and still have to care for their families, suffer (like men) from battle fatigue. They want to get out of their coveralls and wear dresses, be at home. But women have learned to be independent. Giving up their well-paid jobs will not be easy. And the men at Victory Aircraft are now uncertain about future jobs, which will most likely go to returned military men.

Men will, on the whole, again have priority when it comes to work. Ben thinks that is as it should be: it was like that during the Depression. If there are not enough jobs to go around, men should get them first. They are the providers. Six years of war have not shaken his conviction. Sam, on the other hand, doesn't mind at all returning to his mink farm. Not that he ever really gave it up. He did all the chores on the farm whenever he was not on shift work. It's a pity he didn't get accepted in politics He really has a good mind, a sort of odd wisdom. I'll miss those two.

The McCurdys have allowed me space in their recreation room to paint Ben's portrait. We've had two sessions. I made quick sketches at work of the background at Victory Aircraft – the half-finished planes, the silvery skeletons of ladders and scaffolding. I've also sketched in the level Ben so often held while checking the wings of the aircraft. Now that we are about to leave these surroundings, such shapes have regained a strangely surrealist aspect.

While I was painting Ben's portrait, we were able to listen to the radio. He is terribly affected by the revelation of the death camps. His own family, who now live safely on Brunswick Avenue in Toronto, originally came from Poland. The horrors one now hears about are worse than anyone could imagine. All the same, Ben maintains, the Allies must have known.

I told him that until I went to England, and later to Spain, I had *not* known. Vitzthum, with whom I'd worked at Deinhard's, told me about Dachau and Buchenwald on a visit to London. As traveller for Deinhard's (wines and sparkling wines), he was in contact with buyers outside Germany. But even at that time the camps were mainly known as holding political opponents of the Nazis.

Ben thinks there is something lurking in the German psyche that makes it possible for them to see others as non-human. It's no use arguing with him that racism exists all over the world. The Iroquois saw Algonquins as primitives, and no term was barbarous enough to describe the Iroquois in French-Canadian history books. Ben's own people think themselves vastly superior to others very much like them (Semitic people like themselves – Arabs, for instance). It's often ignorance but not always.

At the second sitting he brought me a magazine that contained part of a serialized novel entitled *Between Earth and*

High Heaven. He was very impressed by this story about a
girl from a well-known Montreal family (of the Canadian elite
– believe it or not, there is such a thing) who falls in love with
a Jewish intellectual. I asked him if he believed in marriage
between different religions and races. He shook his head; he
would never marry any other than a Jewish girl. He would
know she was brought up to be pure and innocent (no use
telling him that this sounds Arab or at least Islamic). Did he
know, I asked him, that the Nazis said the same about German
Jewish girls? That they saw Jewish families as depraved (since
many of them were liberals), living it up in Berlin nightclubs.
The *Stuermer* spread rumours about Jews, men who were lech-
ers, women who were promiscuous. It's an old formula.

What about Japanese citizens in Canada? I asked Ben. Born
in Canada, law-abiding citizens – why were they put away into
camps? He had no answer.

~ June 23rd ~

Europe – or rather, Germany – is divided into occupied territo-
ries, British in the north, Americans in the centre-west, French
in the south, Russians in the east. The city of Berlin, for the
time being, is shared by all these forces. I keep hoping to hear
about Mother, but at present most means of communication
have been disrupted. There's no postal service in central Europe,
and many railway lines have to be repaired before normal traffic is restored.

To celebrate the victory in Europe, Sam has taken me to the
Woodbine races, the Queen's Plate. They're important here,
as important as Ascot races in Britain. When I was a student-
teacher at an Ascot boarding school for girls (way back in
1934), I used to watch the preparations for those famous races.
They were always attended by royalty. We'd all watch for the
Prince of Wales, adored by all school girls (who's since given
up his claim to the throne). Huge floppy hats were worn by
most women that year. The inner circle of the race course was
occupied by brightly coloured gypsy caravans. The gypsies were
always ready to tell your fortune, if you crossed their hands

264

with silver. For me they predicted a fair husband and four to six children.

I'd always assumed that Canada's soul was in ice hockey rather than in horse racing. It's the most beautiful and certainly the fastest game. How many winter evenings at the Scobies' were spent listening to broadcasts about famous teams (though I never remembered their names)! We'd watch players race around brightly lit rinks all over the city. We'd applaud Johnnie when his school team played another. The banging of hockey sticks against the boards, the hissing of skates on the ice – those are the happiest sounds of winter. They defeat winter.

Horse racing is beautiful too. Sam recommended some horses that might win, and I bet a few dollars on those. I lost as many dollars as I won, so I came away no richer. The dream of those who bet (many did, at Victory Aircraft) was that you'd come away rich. It seldom happens.

~ June 29th ~

We were to meet Garth in Barrie again, so he could take the children to New York by train. So we are back on Lake Simcoe. And how I wish we had our big tent. There is no bedroom at Elsie's cabin other than the little curtained-off cubicle in which she sleeps herself. The children are accommodated, one on a lilo, the other on the living-room couch. I sleep on the porch, where there is another couch. The mosquitoes are a nuisance, but it's wonderfully fresh out there. I gaze out at the starry night, at the lights on the other side of Kempenfelt Bay. Much of the life at Walden takes place on this porch. We eat our breakfast porridge on the picnic table there, and after swimming, we hang our bathing suits on the porch railings.

School is over for the summer, and Mary Elgood hopes to go back to her old home in the English Cotswolds. She hasn't seen it at all during the war. Garth is staying at Ovenden with her, his mother's old friend, before taking the children south.

Ovenden is still my permanent address, and yesterday a telegram arrived there for me from Grannie. She has been told that my mother is living but nothing more. It was a deep shock

265

for Grannie that her favourite grandson, Harry, my first cousin, was killed in crossfire between British forces somewhere in Burma, where the war still goes on.

~ July ~

Before we went to Barrie I'd moved my few belongings into the students' co-op on Prince Arthur. As soon as Garth left with the children, I took the bus back to Toronto, much as I would have liked to extend my stay at Elsie's.

I want to start on the demanding reading list for our courses. I share a large room, wood-panelled, art nouveau like the rest of this old-fashioned building, with two other students. One is Chinese, the head student at the co-op. The other is David Wyke's niece Enid, from Trinidad, whom I'd met at Marguerite's.

Enid is a hefty, broad-framed girl with long, thick hair who looks younger than her twenty-five years. Like David, she is a devout Catholic. Every morning at six o'clock sharp, her shrill alarm wakes us all, and through sleep-heavy eyes we glance at her wide rear. She's on her knees, praying. After a late night studying, I find it impossible to wake up properly. With a groan I drop off to sleep again and then have to rush to get to the first lecture on time.

~ July 9th ~

Dr Newstetter, the Cleveland professor and authority on community organization, has made the rounds of Toronto settlements to find the right atmosphere for the fieldwork his students will be required to do. He has trodden on some Toronto toes when he rejected most of them as "too old-fashioned and patronizing in their attitude." All eighteeen group-work students will do their fieldwork at the YMHA, the Jewish Y, on Brunswick Avenue.

He warned us not to expect up-to-date facilities. We'd find an old building, shabby rooms, limited outdoor space. But we would profit from an imaginative program in the arts, in drama, music, dance; and more input from the community than anywhere else. We'll be taught by specialists from the Toronto art gallery's Children's Art Centre, started by Arthur Lismer. Each student is to work all through the summer with the same small group, to get to know its members. At the end of the course, there'll be a festival of the arts.

The theoretical part of our courses seems easier to me than the practical part. I like writing essays. I am fascinated by the books we're told to read. I'm the only one who's done factory work during the war, the only one who has children and can therefore speak from experience; but that doesn't seem to improve my fieldwork. The older students are mostly Y staff. One, my special friend, is newly married to a psychiatrist who's been in one of the Canadian camps for Jewish internees from Britain. She too is Jewish but is taking casework, so I don't see her during my hours at the YMHA. Curiously enough, the only students taking our courses who seem to have problems are two younger ones who have just completed their BA; yet they have all the proper requisites in psychology and sociology.

It's very hot now, a humid, sticky heat. At the co-op I usually wear shorts or, when going to classes, a brown and white striped seersucker sundress. The old building is shaded by trees, and with its dark beams and stained glass in the downstairs hall, it's cooler than new houses.

There's a lounge and glassed-in porch downstairs, and there I read and read. The noise around me doesn't disturb me; I'm used to noise at Victory Aircraft. The din of riveting may have made me slightly deaf. That is getting better. But now, reading a book a day, my eyes are giving out. I may need reading glasses, another expense. Luckily, we can live very cheaply here; we do our own cooking.

Our fieldwork is quite demanding. Most of the groups with whom we work at the YM/YWHA (the Young Men's and Young Women's Hebrew Association) are children, and that suits me fine. I want to work with children later on, if possible. Immersed in noise and dust, our hands covered with clay, paint, and paste, we make papier mâché animals and masks. We make posters. I have to report on my special group to our supervisor at the Y, Bud Bell. She is not the director of the Y, but she seems to be the most vital presence there. She is big and wholesome, and her laugh comes straight from the solar plexus. Her name "Bud" is derived from the word Buddha. Nothing seems to shake her.

It seems that most of the Y workers with whom we come in contact are far left politically – in other words, communists. If they don't find it disturbing that half my origin is German, it must be because those who left the Reich – some deported, others fighting for the International Brigade in Spain – were for the most part (if non-Jewish) communists or socialists. They may have noticed on my CV that I lived in Spain in 1935. So perhaps they assumed that I'd be politically further to the left than the other students.

These social workers at the YM/YWHA are touching in their conviction that Russian pogroms are a thing of the past. That all will be well once communism reigns in Europe. And particularly, Jewish people harbour this dream, it seems. If only they knew.

Whatever their political convictions, the work of this staff is superb. The specialists enrolled to teach us are the best in the field. Barbara Pentland, one of the few women composers in Canada, gave a talk on music for small children. The teacher from the Children's Art Centre is an artist in her own right. Their enthusiasm has infected us all, so the heat, the dust in the small yard, the cramped quarters at the Y appear negligible.

~ July 15th ~

Bud Bell read my first report and began to chuckle. "So you still think that Jewish children are more intelligent than others?" she remarked. "Prejudice in reverse. The three you work with aren't too bright, you know. They've been underprivileged in every way."

It dawned on me that all Jews I've known so far – my classmates, the Loebs, refugees in Barcelona – were middle-class, and most of them intellectuals. Now I am discovering the Jews "south of St Clair" Ben described, those of the Kensington Market, Bathurst, Brunswick Avenue.

Whatever my prejudices in reverse, I remain persona grata with the Y staff (to my surprise, for I'm not their best student). Bud asked me to accompany her to the YMHA camp in Haliburton for a long weekend. It's very much like any other summer camp: songs around the campfire, organized games, canoeing, and lots of swimming. I brought my watercolours. Even in a rowboat I managed some quick sketches, dipping my brush into the water of the lake.

The girl who rowed me was called Zelda. She has astonishingly blue eyes and brown curly hair. She didn't mind doing all the rowing while I sketched. These quick, spontaneous watercolours turned out better than anything I've attempted in oils. Later I gave these sketches to Bud, then wished I hadn't.

Zelda invited me to her apartment on Huron Street, only a block from Prince Arthur. There is something about this small apartment that reminds me of Edith's in Montreal. The details in this bright, modern place are overshadowed by the personality of a big heavy fellow called Nathan Cohen, who's just arrived from the Maritimes. He reminds me of pictures of Oscar Wilde, and he is as witty and knowledgeable. Perhaps Wilde even used the monotonous drawl Nathan has adopted; one doesn't know. He's passionately interested in the theatre and one of the few people in Canada who really know something about the ballet. He was impressed by my having seen Diaghilev's London production of the *Three-Cornered Hat* (its set designed by Picasso).

We find we have a friend in common. Nathan Cohen has worked with Lucille Gilmour at the *Tribune* and thinks of her as one of the finest Canadian poets. He saw me home to the co-op and we met again the next day. We walked up and down Spadina, talking about everything in the world. He doesn't like Bernard Shaw but admires O'Casey. He has very definite opinions and I don't share all of them. But his ideas are so stimulating, I can't help liking him.

~ July 24th ~

Nathan Cohen does not seem to be a happy person. He told me that he is "in the hands of a psychiatrist." Why?

He says he sees the sickness of mind in others but is blinder to his own. He thinks that I too suffer from some kind of sickness of the soul, and no wonder. "But who doesn't, in this world? Those who see clearly are the ones who become neurotic."

I think that the "sickness of the soul" I carry around with me is the "sickness of man" seen by William Blake. Right now I feel guilty about almost everything. I am numb because of the horrors discovered in Europe. Heavy with guilt about my German origin. Equally guilty about the suffering inflicted on towns annihilated by our Lancaster bombers.

Nathan tries to make me see clearly, as if that would help. "Don't forget that some of the craziest, the most stupid things people do are done out of a sense of guilt. "

How right he is. I have to think of *Nathan the Wise*, the Enlightenment poet Lessing's famous eighteenth-century play (suppressed by the Nazis).

"During a war, when you feel one side must win, you have to do something. Is there nothing that is not destructive?"

"Nothing. Destruction, creation, destruction. It's mankind's game."

~ July 30th ~

Paul Robeson has come to Toronto for a recital. He's been playing *Othello* in New York and is still wearing a short beard for that role. He was not allowed to make any speeches at his recital. The authorities are critical of his politics.

But he didn't have to make speeches to convince us. At his concert he sang songs of the Spanish Civil War. Inevitably, tears streamed down my face when he sang "Los cuastro generales" (Madrid, your tears of sorrow). He sang in Spanish and in English, and he sang "Un Canadien errant" in French. His voice is immensely warm and powerful. I found the spirituals he sang even more moving than those sung by Marian Anderson.

After the concert, there was a party for Robeson at a house on Spadina that belongs to Hazel and Bill Forbes, friends of Lucille Gilmour's. Portia White, a shy young woman soprano from the African settlement in Nova Scotia, sang a few songs for Robeson, to which he listened with great sympathy. One day, later in her career, she may remember this special occcasion.

Bill Forbes, like Lucille and Nathan Cohen, works at the *Tribune*, and their house has some of the characteristics I found in Denise's apartment or Zelda's. The house may be old and shabby, but the furniture is modern and any art on display is contemporary, often daring.

I don't suppose I'll see Robeson again, but there are, luckily, some wonderful records of this unique voice. Someday I may be able to afford them. He again sang songs of the Spanish Civil War. My tears flowed and Nathan handed me a large handkerchief to stem their flow.

~ August 7th ~

We woke up this morning to find that an atomic bomb has been exploded over Japan. It destroyed a place called Hiroshima. Oh, FDR – you died too early. Would you have let them do this?

The war in Europe is over. Sooner or later, Japan is going to be defeated, with all the forces of the Allies ranged against them. So why this inhuman act? Will the United States develop into another Germany? Didn't Europe teach them that civilian suffering, however great, doesn't reach the decision-makers?

~ August 10th ~

There's not a single student in our course and at the co-op who isn't shocked by the atomic explosion. And now another bomb has been exploded, this time over Nagasaki.

~ August 12th ~

Amidst all this excitement, I have to make personal decisions about our future. I went to interviews with two YWCA boards, one in St Catharines, the other in Kitchener-Waterloo. In both cases my work would be with adults or teenagers, and I am much better working with children. I went by bus to both towns, Kitchener being perhaps the more interesting. The country around both is flat, like that around Cooksville.

Well, perhaps some work at a Toronto Y may still come up. The trouble with the two jobs is that they mean evening hours instead of regular daytime work while the children can be at school or nursery school. I'd hoped that I could find work in a settlement like the YMHA, where children are cared for after school. In fact, I applied there, but Bud told me that almost every student in the course did. I have little chance there.

Through my Barrie friends, I heard of a Toronto settlement looking for staff. Central Neighbourhood House on Sherbourne Street is not far from the church to which Sweeney took me for Christmas midnight mass. Not far, either, from the Neighbourhood Workers, where I could have applied if I had specialized in casework. If I can work with children after school in crafts or

Italian women at Central Neighbourhood House, Toronto, 1945 (pen-and-ink sketch)

music programs, or with Italian immigrant clubs, or even in the small nursery school at Central Neighbourhood House, that would be much better for my own children.

"Take it. Go there," Nathan said. "Pay back the Y grant!"

"Can one do that? Would it not be – unethical?"

He just looked at me. He could look right through me.

Because, of course, I want to stay in Toronto. I've discovered that I love this town.

Bud Bell, in our final long interview at the end of the summer, suggested the same. She told me that I work better with children than with adults or teenagers. There will be many immigrants coming to town in the next few years, whom I might help, since I know several European languages. But perhaps I am still too much of an immigrant to help them. I'm not a case-worker, anyway.

So I went for an interview at Central Neighbourhood House. My fellow student Dorothy, a music specialist, also hopes to work there. This settlement has the reputation of having a conservative board but an enterprising new program director, known to my Barrie friends. A former Ovenden student has worked at this centre for some years and has just retired. The director, Honora Lucas, is a pleasant-looking person in her early thirties. She seems to have an open mind, an interest in new programs. My salary there (and wherever I applied) would be four hundred dollars a year less than what I earned at Victory Aircraft. Yet there are so many advantages, particularly for the children. Working at Central Neighbourhood House seems to be the best choice I can make at present.

So I had to heap another guilt on my already guilt-laden shoulders: I had to tell the Y that I couldn't take a job with them. That through the course they'd helped me with, I'd found out where my talents lie, namely, with children's programs. It means paying back a grant of $150. I don't know how I found the nerve to take out a loan from the Household Finance Company. I was surprised to be granted such a loan without difficulties, simply on the strength of a steady job. It has to be repaid in instalments of $13 each month, another financial burden added to the coming year.

Now all I have to do is find a room somewhere, unfurnished if possible. Fiona will be at school in September. I hope I can find a nursery school for Bettina.

~ August 16th ~

FINALLY, FINALLY, THE WAR IS ENTIRELY OVER, EAST AND WEST.

On VE day, when the war in Europe came to an end, Toronto went wild. But the celebration of VJ day had to be seen to be believed. Fireworks everywhere. One could hear jubilant voices and noises through every open window, on loudspeakers, and indoors on the radio.

Our celebration at the Wykes included Enid, the law students Gloria and Eugenia Charles, Lucille, and a dozen others. After the party we walked arm in arm all the way down Bathurst Street, taking up the entire width of the road. We walked from north of Eglinton down to Bloor Street. Singing.

The next Sunday, to further celebrate, Nathan, Lucille, and I took the streetcar out to the east of Toronto, a part of town I don't know at all. There is a fine beach there, giving the area its

~~

Victory decorations on Yonge Street
in August 1945

name. Lake Ontario is cold, but a beach nearby is always inviting. To see if there were rooms for rent, I walked up a residental street, Scarborough Road. When reading the paper, I didn't have a clue about the location of this street, but I'd seen rooms advertised there. Here it was! The sign was still out; the rooms were still free.

The streetcar ride downtown is fairly long, it took us nearly half an hour. But from the West End Crèche the distance to Sherbourne Street was almost the same. And this area is more open. Most houses have gardens.

The two rooms for rent are attic rooms. The landlady looks very young. She, her husband, and a new baby occupy the ground floor. Another couple rent the middle floor. A door then closes off a further staircase leading to the attic. There the front room looks out on the street, the back room on a vacant lot with quite beautiful trees. Between the two rooms is a little hall where one could put a small electric cooker, one of those that don't need heavy wiring. The rent is twenty dollars a month. I made a down payment at once. After three years, I'll have a room of my own again!

~~

Front Street decorated
to celebrate the end of the war

The landlady – her name is Joan – told us that there is a school with a kindergarten close to the corner where I have to take the streetcar to go downtown. "I think it's the kindergarten where Hazel works," Lucille said.

Back at the co-op I phoned Hazel Forbes. Yes, she works at that school. Her little girl, Bonnie, roughly Bettina's age, will be there too. It seems too good to be true.

To add to all this good fortune, Bud Bell, who's going to New York at the end of this month, has offered to bring back the children on her return trip. Garth has agreed to send the children with her. (I'd like to see the person able to oppose Bud!) I don't have worry on that account now.

There is a heavy letter from Grannie, and as I open it, my hands tremble. There is another letter inside, and I at once recognize the handwriting – my mother's inimitable, almost illegible, yet somehow beautiful hand, one we've known all through childhood.

I read the letter over and over again. Communications are still haywire. Mother doesn't know where any of her children are except for myself, the one furthest away. My sister, because of the food shortage in Mother's area, had gone to stay with friends in Mecklenburg, where she'd trained in household science. The hope had been that she and her two-year-old girl would get enough to eat on a huge farm growing its own produce. Then the Russians occupied Mecklenburg, and now no one knows what happened to Gisela. Her husband, a metallurgist, was taken by the Americans. But there'd been an agreement that all prisoners taken in the eastern part of Germany were to be turned over to the Russians. Mother thinks he has been exchanged, and no one knows where he is now.

My youngest brother, the one who has always been closest to Mother, was not quite twelve when the war broke out. During the last terrible war year he had to join the Home Defence, consisting of old men and the very young. As far as Mother knows, he was taken prisoner by the Americans, but she's not heard from him at all. The confusion in Germany is unimaginable: post office, telegraph, trains are barely functioning.

~~

Bettina
in our Scarborough
Road attic,
1945

My second brother, Heinz, who was in the navy, Mother assumes to have been somewhere in Norway at the end of

Fiona, Bettina,
and Gunda
at Lake Simcoe,
1945

the war. A captain, he may have turned in his boat to the British navy. No doubt he's a prisoner somewhere in Britain. Grannie may hear from him before Mother does.

Her own letter was taken to Grannie in Cheshire personally by a British officer. The post office is still in turmoil. So far, we, who live so far away, are the only ones of whose whereabouts and safety she is assured.

Things have turned out well for our little family. The children have safely arrived in Bud's company. Fiona goes to school all day. Bettina is registered at the nursery school where Hazel works. I have started my new job.

Long ago, before World War I, my mother, Maud Lee Williams, had planned to go to Canada as a teacher. Instead, she married my handsome father. We three have now closed the cycle, completed her old plans. She too had meant to go to Toronto.

Epilogue

Examining this diary from the distance of time, I find it says much about the position of women in that era; especially their low self-esteem, which persisted through the post-war years. I also discovered that several people who greatly helped us during those years were not mentioned in these pages, since there were days and weeks when the pressure of events meant that the journal was discontinued. One of these, who remained my friend throughout those years and for many years to follow, was Jean McAdam. Like us, she had come to Ovenden School from England and was teaching there when we arrived. In 1942 she married Sam McAdam. She lived on Woodlawn Avenue in Toronto (where my first watercolour of the Toronto skyline was painted) while her husband was overseas with the army. Like Elsie Raikes, she attended my wedding to Bill Lambton in 1949, and in 1952 she became the godmother of our first son, Ian. Whenever possible, our family also visited Elsie Raikes, usually on Labour Day weekend, until her death in 1979.

Several others mentioned in these pages, whose help had been invaluable, did not live as long. Sophie Boyd, whose counsel had sustained me through many a crisis, later headed the Toronto School for Social Work. She was killed in a car accident while still in mid-career. Joan Hall, Barker Fairley's daughter and perhaps Toronto's finest nursery-school expert, died of an illness long before her father began his most remarkable paintings. Nathan Cohen became a well-known critic in the 1950s; he too died much too young.

Fiona and Bettina went to school near the Goodwood farm, where we lived until 1956, when our second son, Renny Lambton, was born. Both excelled at school and later at university, Fiona at Toronto and Edinburgh, Scotland (where she married), Bettina at Queen's University inKingston. Later, at McGill University in Montreal, she married Bruce Shore. Until

Garth's death some years ago, they continued to visit their father in Mexico. Through his three subsequent marriages (the first being to Dorothea), Fiona in particular remained his closest friend and achieved indirect fame through the drawings he made of her as "Fern" for E.B. White's book *Charlotte's Web*.

David and Edith Smith moved to Saskatchewan in 1946, where David took over the Department of Adult Education. He later worked for UNESCO in Thailand. It is his earlier work in Simcoe County that is described best in his book *First Person*

Fiona at a farm in northern New York State, at the time Garth drew her as Fern in Charlotte's Web

～

Plural, published in 1994 by Black Rose. In his introduction to this book Ted Jackson describes David Smith as one of the brightest lights in Canadian adult education. He died in 2000 at the age of ninety-four, not greatly impressed by what he saw of the twenty-first century.

In 1957 we visited their and our old friends, Alice and Bernard Loeb, at their cottage on Snake Island on Lake Simcoe. Alice was by then greatly disillusioned with the progress of the women's organizations she had so valiantly supported. However, I found that she was a fine artist: she started a clay sculpture of our five-year-old son, Ian, which I took home and finished. When we returned from several years, first, in northern Ontario and then in Scotland, we found that both the Loebs had died.

Marguerite and David Wyke in 1946 moved to Trinidad, where David was put in charge of public health. Their niece Enid married Ulrich Loewenthal, the fellow student at the Prince Arthur co-op with whom she used to wash the dishes. Florence and Bruce Morris eventually separated; Florence became a librarian and married the graphic artist George Johnston. They live in Portland, Oregon, where I visited them in 1982.

Sculpture by
Alice Loeb
of Ian Lambton,
five years old

In October 1945 my mother still did not know whether any of her children were still alive, except for us in Canada. The first person who returned to Mother's house was my sister Gisela. The Russians had taken over the landed estates in Mecklenburg where she had gone with her little girl to find enough food for them both. She and other women with small children hid in outbuildings and made themselves as inconspicuous as possible. What saved them from death or rape were their children; Russian soldiers loved children. They liked to listen to mothers singing lullabies to their babies in the evenings. In the end my sister managed to get out of those buildings in a load of hay. With great good luck, she was able to get on one of the trains going to Berlin, still a shared zone.

Sealed trains from the British zone began to arrive in Berlin with food for the occupiers. When these trains returned to the west, they were empty but unscheduled. Hundreds of people lined up in the bombed stations to try and find a place in them. Early each morning Gisela and her little girl joined this line. No one knew the exact departure time of these transport trains. At last, she and her child found a place in a crowded carriage. Their long, dark, grim journey in that sealed train continued in western Germany, when they travelled from the British to the American zone, where Mother's village was located. By October 1945 the war in Europe had been over for nearly six months, but the overcrowded trains still had to manoeuvre on damaged tracks. Every wooden seat in the carriage was filled. Gisela and her child had to sit in the luggage net, their legs hanging over the edge. Her legs swelled to elephant size as their circulation slowed. After uncounted hours, night turning into day and again into night, they finally reached Mother's house in the Bergstrasse.

Gisela's husband, meanwhile, was taken to Russia, where metallurgists with his experience were in demand. He was offered a position in the Crimea if he would co-operate in the field of atomic science. Some German scientists who once worked for the Nazis in fact became Russian atomic scientists. But my brother-in-law was of Flemish stock, a stubborn person, brought up with strict religious principles. He refused to work for Russian atomic science, so he was sent to Siberia.

Meanwhile, Grannie in England had heard from my brother Heinz, who was in a British camp for prisoners of war. He was kept there for two years, and Grannie was eventually able to visit him. There was little food in England, but the prisoners did not starve. There was even less food in Germany, where they returned in 1947.

By that time my youngest brother, Erik, had also come home. When an American sergeant with a megaphone announced the Allied victory, asking all Germans to surrender, he rose, arms raised above his head, from a shell hole to his full height. The sergeant was startled when he was addressed in fluent English. The Americans were nice to this youngster, whom, because of his name, Davidson, they called "Scottie." But then he was transferred to a camp in France for German prisoners of war, where, since the war was over, the Geneva Conventions were not enforced. The shock to the Allies when they found starved survivors in concentration camps was great. It influenced the decision by an American general that prisoners should be deprived of food. They had been forced into service by sheer terror and they heralded the Americans as saviours. It was incomprehensible to them that they were now victims of a system they had welcomed. Some were old and ill and did not survive.

Erik did; he returned even before my mother, with the help of the RAF, was able to finally visit Grannie in England.

She was probably the first person who was able to come to England from Germany, perhaps because she'd taken back her British citizenship. I still have a photo taken for her passport at that time. Looking at the hollow-cheeked face in that photograph, I understand the official's remark when she explained the purpose of her visit: she wanted to see her mother. "*You,*" he is said to have exclaimed, "have a mother? She must be a *very* old lady."

True, Grannie was then ninety-one years old (she died in 1950, aged ninety-five). But the face in the photograph did not look much younger.

Mother recovered her health and spirits and visited us in Canada, where, five years later and remarried, I presented her with her first grandson. With him I visited her in Germany in 1954. The town where I had gone to school had been carpet bombed. I (who had worked on Lancaster bombers!) did not recognize a single building there.

My sister's husband was still in Siberia. In 1955 I wrote to Lester Pearson at the United Nations, asking whether German prisoners still in Russia had a chance of being returned. I'll never forget the reply of that kind and thoughtful politician: if still alive, the prisoners would return within the next year. They did. Gisela's husband was one of the survivors who, after eleven years, came home in 1956.

Like my mother, I had left the country where I was born. Like her, I found what I thought was a better new world. The world she had chosen, a world of music and culture not available to her in provincial Cheshire, later crumbled around her, destroying the ideals she and others held.

I too chose a new world where everything seemed possible. I know that liberty and humanity are always and everywhere in a precarious state. Sometimes I visit Lester Pearson's modest burial place in Wakefield, not far from our Quebec farm. Looking across the beautiful valley, I think of this unpretentious Canadian who represented a kind of low-key goodness and, when it was needed, the strength of a lion – all that's best in Canada.

These pages are meant to pay tribute to all those who, during the stressful war years, helped my small family to survive. They gave me the courage to continue what became a full and remarkably healthy life, close to a large family of children and grandchildren and, in particular, close to nature and its changing and ever-rewarding seasons.

Alcove, Quebec, September 2002

Acknowlegments

In the early 1980s, Candis Graham, a member of my class at the University of Ottawa, read my old wartime diary and suggested I submit part of it to the feminist journal *Fireweed*. This magazine published some pages (on my encounter with the Japanese girl) in 1984. Ruth Latta, who also read the diary, included a part on working at John Inglis in her anthology *The Memory of All That: Canadian Women Remember World War II* (General Store Publishing 1993). In 2000 Joe Blade of Broken Jaw Press in Fredericton, New Brunswick, chose the description of Cape Croker (the lighthouse and storm) for his *Great Lakes Project*. All left the copyright to me and gave me the encouragement to, eventually, submit the manuscript to McGill-Queen's University Press. My sincere thanks go to the editors of this press, Joan Harcourt, Joan McGilvray, and Elizabeth Hulse, production manager Susanne McAdam, and the designer Christine Mantzavrakos, who helped to give the publication its final form; and to my family, who had to endure my agonizing over forgotten photographs and drawings for the illustrations. All of them helped to create what I see as a permanent tribute to those who during three war years helped a small family not only to survive but to settle permanently in a country and a town they came to love.

Illustration Credits

Except as identified below, illustrations are from the author's collection.

Art Gallery of Ontario (Fritz Brandtner linocut)

City of Toronto Archives: TTC fonds, series 71, items 14352 (King and Strachan), 14831 (Yonge and Davisville), 15046 (Toronto skyline), 15229 (Front Street decorations), 15232 (Yonge Street decorations)

Esate of Paraskeva Clark, National Archives of Canada: PA-195500 (Paraskeva Clark)

National Archives of Canada: C-098730 (C.H. Millard and Andrew Brewin), PA-120742 (Agnes Macphail and Eamon Park)

University of Toronto Archives: A78-0041/018(35) (John D. Robins)